DATE DUE

FEB 2 5 2000		
FEB 1 6 2000		
OCT 0 7 2010	NOV 1 8 2010	
APR 2 1 2014	APR 0 9 2014	

CARR McLEAN, TORONTO FORM #38-297

Little Italies in North America

162703886

edited by
Robert F. Harney and
J. Vincenza Scarpaci

1981

The Multicultural History Society of Ontario

Toronto

ISBN 0-919045-02-2

© 1981 by the Multicultural History Society of Ontario.
All rights reserved.
Published 1981
Printed in Canada

The Multicultural History Society of Ontario
43 Queen's Park Crescent East
Toronto, Ontario M5S 2C3

Contents

THE PROVINCES OF ITALY

Introduction

Robert F. Harney and J. Vincenza Scarpaci

Historians have become accustomed to thinking of North American cities as remarkably heterogeneous places. Even smaller cities are honeycombed with spatially distinct communities and culturally separate networks. Ethnic neighbourhoods are among the most obvious of these sub-communities. Little Italies, Chinatowns, ghettos—first of East European Jews, then of southern Black migrants—barrios, immediately come to mind when one thinks of the great cities. Of these enclaves set apart by their ethnicity, Little Italies are probably the most ubiquitous. Discernible clusters of Italian settlement seem to appear in every town with heavy industry, construction, sewer, road or canal work, or major railroad or seaport connections.

Being such salient features of our cities, one would assume Little Italies, had been thoroughly documented, and their formation, history, life patterns—and increasingly their demise—explained. This is not the case. Scant attention has been given to drawing a historical and sociological profile of the Little Italy in North America. No comparative studies of Little Italies exist, and the sources upon which such study could be based—a combination of associational papers, parish records, the memory culture of those who grew up in the neighbourhoods and the ethnic press—are rarely, and never systematically, preserved. As a consequence, what we think we know of the ethnic enclave depends far too much on sources external to it, such as city records, the census and the English-speaking press.

Local studies of Little Italies do exist. Most are unpublished; many are marred by excessive filio-pietist or antiquarian concerns, or skewed by the research perspective out of which they emerge. Traditionally, serious study of Little Italies has been undertaken by three groups: urban sociologists, social historians, and visiting intellectuals or officials from Italy.

"Every large city on the continent has its fourfold problem of the slum, the saloon, the *foreign colonies* and the districts of vice," wrote a social evangelist at the turn of the century. Italian neighbourhoods have only rarely, as in Caroline Ware's *Greenwich Village* (1935), escaped guilt by association with urban pathologies. From the earliest scholarly depictions of the ethnic enclave such as the Little Sicily in Harvey Zorbaugh's *Gold Coast and the Slum* (1929), through William Whyte's use of Boston's Italian North End in *Street Corner Society* (1938)[1] to describe "the social structure of the slum" to Herbert Gans' *The Urban Villagers* (1962) about Boston's Sicilian West End, sociologists have studied Little Italies less to understand their ethnoculture and society than to make a point about the nature and problems of North American cities. More recently, research emphasis has been on rates of social, occupational and geographical mobility, on the "cost of community," and on the white ethnic's racial and political attitudes. But this focus adds little to our ethnographic and historical understanding of the immigrant neighbourhood and its residents.

The social gospeller's or immigrant restrictionist's litany of occasions of sin has been transmogrified into the social scientist's study of urban problems, and for many years, the only defence of the Little Italies against inclusion on the list of shame came from Italian-American filio-pietists. Like most crusaders, these last, often amateur local historians or ethnic notables in search of an instant pedigree, answered bigotry with bigotry, smear with unfounded assertion. To that most damaging of all North American charges—being new to the land—they responded with long and inventive accounts of the antiquity of the Italian presence in America. Such emphasis drew attention away from the Italian-American masses and their world to a stage set of friars, discoverers, revolutionary heroes and globe-trotting artists of Italian descent. Rarely did the writers feel able to defend Italianity in America by offering a detailed and honest account of a half-century's life in Little Italies.

As a major part of the urban landscape of industrializing America, the Little Italy should have been an appropriate topic of research as postwar American social historians rediscovered the common man's story. The reasons that it apparently was not, hint at, without fully defining, systemic problems in the recruitment and training of professional historians in the United States and Canada. Located somewhere between European studies and the new urban history, research on emigration from Italy and the immigrant settlement areas required knowledge of the Italian language and the use of sources such as oral testimony and ephemeral ethnic publications with which most professional historians were uncomfortable. So for the graduate student in history, the field promised only hard work, inadequate research supervision, and low status in the profession. It seemed to many to be far wiser to gain respectability by studying Dante or Leopardi or by escaping into non-ethnic American history. For some time, the history of the so-called new immigrants and their settlements in America remained as unwelcome as they themselves had been in the country's consciousness. Moreover, surrogates for the study of the immigrant's ethnoculture appeared in the form of social mobility and voter behaviour studies, sub-disciplines of social history that in their dependence on official sources and their emphasis on the relationship of Italians to an American norm betrayed an assimilationist perspective.

By the mid-1960s, however, small numbers of scholars had become active in the study of Little Italies, and serious ethnocultural research had begun on the large Italian neighbourhoods, expecially in New York, Chicago and Philadelphia. Most of this work remained unpublished. The only book-length study of Italians in an urban setting by a historian to appear in those years was Humbert Nelli's *Italians in Chicago* (1970). Significantly enough, that volume was subtitled *A Study in Ethnic Mobility* and its author saw the immigrant colony and its institutions fulfilling "their functions, not of prolonging old world traits and patterns but of providing important first steps in assimilation." More recently Little Italies have received attention in John Briggs' *An Italian Passage*, Joseph Barton's *Peasants and Strangers: Italians, Rumanians and Slovaks in an American City* (1975), and Virginia Yans McLaughlin's *Family and Community: Italian Immigrants in Buffalo*. It is fair to say, though, that each of these works is more concerned with the relationship of Italian immigrants to modernization, to their industrial and entrepreneurial adaptation in North America, than with the culture and society of the ethnic enclaves studied.

Since Little Italies were an observable phenomenon in North America from the 1880s on, questions about their origins, internal form and culture should have been raised earlier, not just in North America but in Italy. We have seen the reasons why American social scientists, historians and the educated children of the Little Italies have been slow to focus their work on the Italianity, the separate history of the enclave. It is not so immediately obvious why officials, travelling intellectuals and, more recently, scholars from Italy who have shown interest in the overseas Italians have contributed so little to our knowledge of the *colonie*. Perhaps nothing more exactly sums up the attitude to Little Italies and epitomizes the marginality of being immigrant, than the fact that while the immigrant enclave was being treated as an aberrant and temporary problem for American cities by North American scholars, Italian intellectuals dismissed them as an embarrassing misrepresentation of Italian civilization.

From the earliest days, a barrier of culture and class, the arrogance of the metropolitan toward the creole, has kept visiting Italian intellectuals and consular officials from comprehending and appreciating the historical evolution of Italian settlements in North America. For such observers, the term *piccola italia* itself described not just the colony's *ambiente* but also involved resonances of other diminutives and pejoratives such as *Italietta* and *bas Italia*. In short, the expression smacked of all those aspects of immigrant pre-selection which made the neighbourhood untypical or a caricature of Italy itself—in other words, Little Italy stood for the preponderance of rural, southern and under-educated poor among the immigrants to America. Moreover, the Italian-American efforts to cling to remnants of the popular culture left behind made for anachronism. So the neighbourhood and its ways made natural targets for the facile humour which often masked the ethnic embarrass-ment of Italian officials and junketing intellectuals. It was not a propi-tious conjuncture for serious study of Little Italies as a phenomenon.

For example, one of the most intelligent Italian observers of America at the turn of the century was Luigi Villari. A consular officer, political analyst, and scion of a great scholarly family, Villari, nonethe-less, could not resist dismissing the emerging Italian-American society as a vulgarized fossil of Italy's high culture. "We have therefore," he wrote, "an amorphous and incomplete society, lacking many of the elements that constitute a normal social organism. This is an army without officers, commanded by corporals and sergeants." Put rather more wist-fully and sympathetically, the same judgment on the culture and society of Little Italies has characterized the metropolitan Italian view, from Amy Bernardy's account of Boston's North End in the 1900s in her *America Vissuta* to Anne Maria Martellone's description of the same Little Italy in *Una Little Italy nell'Atene d'America: La communità ital-iana de Boston dal 1880 al 1920*, in 1973.

The result of this double disapprobation—suspicion and hostility from acculturating America, disdain and ridicule from metropolitan Ital-ians—was *atimia*, an attitude of ethnic self-disesteem, among those who should have asserted the importance of recording and preserving the his-tory of Little Italies. Education was used to increase distance from the greenhorns and peasants of the community. The problem is epitomized in the writings of Constantine Panunzio, admittedly further removed from Italianity by his Protestant rearing. He described Boston's Little Italy as a place where "the misfits of Italian society were the *prominenti*," a place of "a thousand trifling provincial and local animosities ... a conglomeration of folks which would have been as much an anomaly in Italy as it was in America."

If it is true that the Little Italies of North America would have been as much cultural anomalies in Italy as they were in English-speaking cities, and that their social structure was distinct from that of both Italy and the host society, then surely the ethnographer and the historian should undertake the sort of detailed study of these unique communities, neither American nor Italian, that will make possible comparisons of their formation, history, institutions, quotidian society and economy and their ethnoculture.

The socio-economics and distinct culture of ghettos—Jewish and Black—as well as Chinatowns have been the focus of such structural investigation with a consequent advance in understanding and scholar-ship. Perhaps this is because such enclaves seemed more permanent and more consistently the source of the ethnoculture for those groups than did Little Italies for North American Italians. Yet, in many instances, Little Italies have shaped local experience for nearly a century. A number of us,—historians and sociologists,—studying the Italian Ameri-can experience felt a need to re-emphasize and analyse again the role of the settlement area in the life of the ethnic group. The result was a call for a conference on the subject.

The essays in this volume were originally prepared for a conference that took place in the spring of 1979 under the auspices of the University of Toronto's Ethnic and Immigration Studies Program and the Multicultural History Society of Ontario. The American Little Italies discussed were those of Chicago, New York, Philadelphia, Baltimore, the canal town of Oswego in upstate New York, Tampa, New Orleans and St. Louis. For Canada, Little Italies in Toronto, Montreal and Thunder Bay were described. The cities were chosen to show some of the variety of settlement in the United States and Canada as well as to contrast the Italian-Canadian and Italian-American experiences. We were interested in seeing if we could limn more precisely the ways in which such variables as the size of each Italian colony, the predominant *paesi* of origin of the settlers in each, and the magnitude and nature—in terms of occupational possibilities and the presence of other ethnic groups—and the attitude toward immigrants of the host city or regional ecosystem, affected immigrant settlements and the subsequent Italian ethnoculture.

The description that we sought of each ethnic neighbourhood had to include an explanation of the development and location of the Italian community, to show how the target city or area drew an appropriate type of immigrant from Italy or from other parts of Italian North America, and to characterize both the real and stereotypical occupational structure of the ethno-community. The profile also required analysis of the extent and the intensity of the *ambiente*—the palpably Italian geographical and psychic core of the colony which was made up of, first mutual aid societies, fraternal organizations, political or *paese* clubs, and Italian-speaking union locals; and secondly, of parishes or Protestant missions with their dependent entities such as parochial schools, sodalities, sports teams, or credit unions, as well as their related enterprises from caterers to undertakers and florists. Around this nucleus in each community clustered those businesses such as travel agencies, immigrant banks, grocers and food importers, ethnic newspapers and *tipografie*, restaurants and boarding houses, which provided the ethnic density and material culture of the neighbourhoods studied. The essays also set out to record differences in the relative position and presence of such elements in the ethnic configuration. It is clear from this initial reconnoitring that only further research of Italian settlements and the host society's attitudes, and comparison of the differing North American careers of people from the same hometowns who settled in different Little Italies, or of the differing fortunes of people from different *paesi* in the same Little Italy will fully explain these contrasts.

There are, of course, many other Little Italies, large ones such as those in Cleveland, Boston, Pittsburgh, Hamilton and the West Coast cities, which should be studied as well. In that sense, the essays that follow are merely prototype entries in a compendium and atlas of the Italian settlements in North America that should be undertaken. Such a volume could view the immigrant experience both in its holistic, *Italia oltremare*, perspective, and in its practical aspect of finding a livelihood and forming a supporting community in the modern city. By reasserting the history of Little Italies that way, by finding sources and methodologies to make their inhabitants as articulate, alive and various as they were, we might escape the shadow of filio-pietism. In this way, we might help to return the focus of ethnic studies to what Fredrik Barth described as the "stuff" of ethnicity, to the study of community and its ethnoculture, and away from the historicism that concentrates on boundaries, acculturation and mobility studies.

Note

1. It was published by Laterza in Bari, Italy, in 1968 with the more straight-forward title, *Little Italy: Uno Slum Italo-Americano.*

The Mulberry District of New York City: The Years before World War One

George E. Pozzetta

New York City has long held a special place in the history of Italians in America. Why this has been so is not difficult to understand. New York not only occupied a pre-eminent position among the nation's urban centres, but it also attracted the greatest concentration of Italian settlement in the United States. In 1910 the United States census counted 544,449 persons of Italian birth or parentage, a total that far outnumbered any rival city. This population was impressive for its size and for its diversity and restless vitality. What happened in New York influenced much of the economic and cultural climate in the rest of Italian America.

The importance of New York to the wider Italian American experience, however, did not rest entirely on its permanent residents. The city became the nation's major entry and transshipment point for the great Italian migration of the late nineteenth and early twentieth century. Facilities at Castle Garden and Ellis Island annually processed the overwhelming majority of arriving Italians, and the docks, railway stations and streets of New York provided access routes leading outward to virtually every corner of the North American continent. Statistics for 1899-1900 revealed that the port of New York received no less than 97.4 per cent of all Italians coming to the United States and 54.5 per cent of arrivals at other locations listed New York as their destination.[1] The perceptive social critic Luigi Villari undoubtedly had some of these factors in mind when he labelled the city "il centro commerciale e morale dell'italianita d'America."[2]

By 1910 Metropolitan New York possessed in excess of seventy

THE HEART OF THE MULBERRY DISTRICT

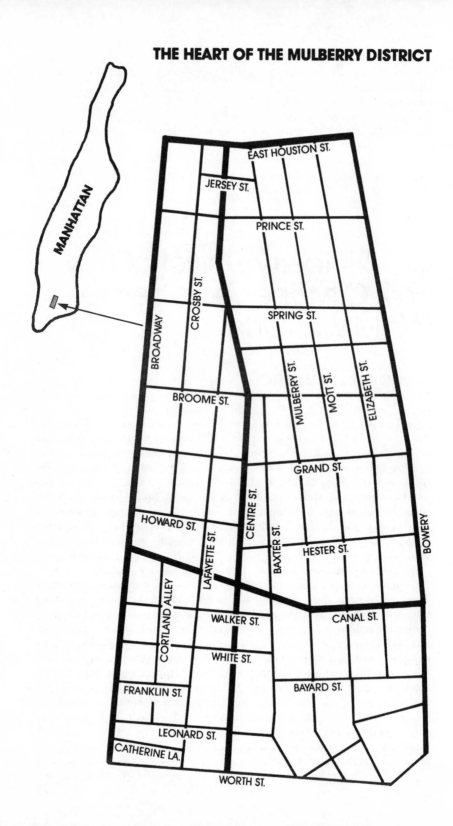

recognizable centres of Italian settlement. The following essay will attempt to provide an overview of the oldest and most notable concentration in the city during the pre-World War One era. This area consisted of a roughly rectangular section of lower Manhattan which possessed as its most readily identifiable feature the Mulberry Bend (a tenement area near the long, gentle curve at the lower end of Mulberry Street). As this settlement expanded under the influence of successive waves of Italian immigration, it earned for itself several different appellations: "New Italy," "The Bend" "Bowery Colony," and so on. For the purposes of uniformity, this essay will use the term "Mulberry district" throughout.

In its maturity, the district was bounded on the west by Broadway, on the east by Bowery, on the north by Houston Street, and on the south by Worth Street (Chatham Square). The principal streets of this district—and perhaps the best-known streets in all Italian America— were Baxter, Mulberry, Mott and Elizabeth. These thoroughfares traversed through the city's Sixth and Fourteenth wards and encompassed two of New York's most infamous slums, Mulberry Bend and the Five Points area. This section served as the great downtown receiving neighbourhood for the bulk of early Italian movement into the city, and it acted as an area of first settlement for many Italian immigrants until well into the twentieth century.

Evidence exists of an Italian presence in New York dating back to the 1600s, but it was not until the early part of the nineteenth century that appreciable numbers of Italians settled in the city. Those early pioneers who made their way to Gotham fell into several broad categories. The most publicized of them were political exiles who fled the revolutionary upheavals which periodically disrupted the peninsula before unification. Many of these refugees were educated liberals who possessed professional skills, though they were not always able to use them in America. Small clusters of these individuals dotted the city, with one concentration of about fifty residing on Staten Island. The most famous exile was, of course, Giuseppe Garibaldi, who worked at making candles on Bleecker Street. Unlike Garibaldi, more than a few of these individuals chose not to return to their homeland and remained in the city as teachers, journalists, lawyers and small businessmen.[3]

Included also among these early immigrants were professionals and artists who came with the intention of permanent settlement. The majority of these people possessed certain widely marketable skills desired by the American public. Italian musicians, opera performers, singers, portrait and landscape painters, sculptors, glassworkers and engravers, to name just a few, appeared in the city's newspapers and directories well before the Civil War. More important to the future development of Italian New York, however, were the labourers, tailors, barbers, fruit vendors, confectioners, saloon keepers, vendors of plaster statuary, and other petty merchants who trickled into the city during these early decades.[4] Composed primarily of Ligurians, but containing many Piemontesi, Toscani, Veneziani and Emiliani as well, these pioneers supplied much of the leadership and direction, for good or bad, that was manifested among Italians in New York until well into the twentieth century.

One Piemontese, Antonio Cuneo, was representative of this breed. Emigrating to New York in 1855, he started his new life by selling fruit and roasted nuts from pushcarts in the Mulberry district, ranging as far north as Bleecker Street. By 1859 he owned two small groceries, which launched him into a thriving business in banking. In 1881 he abandoned his grocery trade and opened a large bank at 28 Mulberry Street, which soon earned him a reputation for sound business judgment and honesty, commodities that appear to have been in short supply in this locality. Cuneo ultimately made a fortune in real estate, specializing in transactions which capitalized on the Italian desire for home and property ownership. Two brothers remained in the grocery business (owning several large stores which bordered the Mulberry district) and two others specialized in the fruit trade. Both of the latter become large fruit distributors who lived far away from the immigrant quarters and catered to the needs of the American public.[5]

By 1850 Italians resided in all but one of Manhattan's twenty-two wards, but the single section of significant concentration was the Five Points area of the Sixth Ward.[6] A few blocks north of City Hall, the Five Points received its name from the star-shaped square formed by Mulberry, Orange (Baxter), Anthony (Worth), Cross (Park) and Little Water (built over). The area had been a notorious slum area for several decades before the Italian arrival. Composed of crumbling wooden tenements, stables and warehouses, Five Points had been built directly over a filled-in basin known in earlier days as the "Collect." For years it had been "a dumping ground for garbage, dead animals, and all sorts of trash." Noxious, unhealthy gases seeped through the pavement throughout the century. By 1830 the area enjoyed a reputation as the city's most sordid centre of vice and crime. One commentator labelled it simply as "synonymous of whatever is degraded and degrading, loathsome and criminal." After 1835 it was inhabited principally by Irish and German immigrants who were generally regarded as being of the "lowest and most disreputable class." Recurring epidemics of typhoid, typhus and various other fevers added to the region's undesirability.[7] Such were the surroundings that greeted the first Italian pioneers.

Charles Loring Brace was among the first writers to note the presence of Italians in this area. As often happened, his attentions focused on the most visible of the newcomers—organ grinders, bootblacks, street sweepers, sellers of plaster statuary, and ragpickers—and initial impressions were shaped in large part by these individuals. Brace claimed that Italians were clannish and exceptionally dirty, but he recognized fundamental differences between these residents and their longer-settled neighbours. "They cannot be reproached with intoxication, prostitution, quarreling, stealing," he pointed out, but even Brace missed the fundamental dynamics taking place among these first arrivals.[8] The Italian population at this mid-century junction was one that little resembled what was to come in later migrations.

Of the 968 persons of Italian birth residing in New York in 1855, approximately 40 per cent of those employed were professionals. Musicians and "artists" accounted for the greatest number; for the most part these individuals were able to merge easily into the wider community. The remaining categories, in order of descending rank, consisted of domestic servants; clerks; barbers; carpenters; labourers; masons, bricklayers, plasterers; tailors; merchants; and ragpickers, scavengers and organ grinders.[9] These were the occupations that predominated among the Italians residing in the Sixth Ward. Heavily northern Italian in composition, these immigrants sought permanent settlement and an opportunity to practise their particular *mestieri*. They sent out the first important chain migration networks that brought Italian movement to the city. Such locations as Gattinara, Novara, Cuneo, Azeglio, Piscina (Piedmont), Firenze, Lucca (Tuscany), Olevano Romano (Lazio); Parma, Piacenza (Emilia), Pavia (Lombardy); and Santo Stefano d'Aveto (Liguria) became the principal feeder sources which supplied immigrants to the streets of lower Manhattan.

These hardy pioneers sought out the Five Points for specific reasons. The area offered the cheapest housing and most convenient access to the downtown business districts. The docks, warehouses, factories and business streets of the city's industrial-commercial core were only a short distance away. Moreover, easy approaches linked the district with the Battery landing areas located a mile or so to the south. By the late 1850s Italian merchants, artisans and common labourers had already created the basis of an institutional life within the city's central district. Clustered initially near Baxter and Mulberry streets, there soon appeared Italian saloons, groceries, boarding houses, import stores featuring *paste d'Italia*, and a variety of trade shops throughout the district.[11] The city sported one successful Italian-language newspaper (*L'Eco d'Italia*) founded by G. F. Secchi di Casali, a native of Piacenza, a large variety of mutual aid societies and, after 1866, a distinctively Italian Catholic parish.[12] Italian New York was already set apart from its sister settlements in America in that appreciable numbers of southern Italians had arrived in the city. Though outnumbered by their northern Italian neighbours, and often scorned by them as well, these early arrivals included a random sprinkling of barbers, fruitmen, street musicians, common labourers, and political exiles who trickled in from places such as Palermo, Laurenzana, Viggiano and Naples. Even in its most homogeneous phase, therefore, Italian New York was a multilayered community. It was to become even more variegated as the century progressed.

Indicative of the men who were able to make the transition from this generally prosperous and accepted settlement to meet the demands of the great southern migration was Luigi Vittorio Fugazy. Born in Santo Stefano d'Aveto on April 30, 1839, he had taken part in the wars of independence as a captain with Garibaldi. He claimed to have served for a time as a soldier and later as chief of secret police for Victor Emmanuel before coming to America in 1869. He initially opened a small Italian bank at 147 Bleecker Street (a location that already bore witness to the inexorable northward drift of Italian settlement) and quickly began doing business among his *paesani*. A branch at 206 Spring Street to the south was not long in coming.[13] By the late 1870s advertisements for his various enterprises began appearing in a wide variety of New York City papers. He operated one of the city's largest transatlantic passage and emigration offices specializing in prepaid tickets. His business activities included listings as notary public (always listed in bold type, perhaps to distinguish himself from the hundreds of newcomers who became *notai improvvisati*), insurance agent for the Home Insurance Agency, money-changer, banker and labour agent.

Fugazy reflected a pattern of development which mandated that the most successful of the new *prominenti* were those who could supply a variety of services to the newly arrived. They acted as intermediaries on many levels—legal, political, social and financial—each of which often reinforced the other. "Pappa" Fugazy turned his attentions to each of these, though he appears to have been particularly active in the formation and leadership of mutual aid societies. He claimed by 1900 the actual presidency of at least 50 societies and a guiding role in some 145 more.[14] The respect paid to him in America was perhaps influenced by his exploits in Italy, but the primary shaping force undoubtedly came from his ability to provide services to his clients in the city. Such was the base upon which the new *signori* was typically built.

Nor were these the only routes to upward mobility and financial success available to early pioneers. The Tuscan Carlo Barsotti began business with a single lodging house located at 4 Centre Street. During the 1870s he acquired several additional boarding houses scattered throughout the Mulberry district. These tenement units provided the basis for a career in labour-contracting and banking which placed Barsotti among the most powerful (and controversial) men in the city. The rapidity with which Barsotti turned over property and business operations provides a sense of the fluidity and opportunities for profit which existed in the district. In 1880 he began printing a weekly newspaper, *Il Progresso Italo-Americano* (which became a daily in 1881), with offices at 12 Chambers Street. The paper soon became the largest circulating Italian-language paper in the city and nation. By 1880, Barsotti's business empire included four lodging houses, each located on different streets of the Fourteenth Ward. One year later, directories listed his lodging house at 300 Bowery Street as a "hotel," and the three additional lodging houses still under his name had all changed locations. By 1885 Barsotti listed a large banking house along with his other business ventures. Five years later, he owned lodging houses located at 37, 212, 300 and 358 Bowery, 9 Mulberry, 180 Park Row, and 93 Sixth Avenue as well as two banks situated on Centre Street and one at 37 Mulberry Street.[15]

Like Fugazy, Barsotti extended his business operations to provide for the full needs of the mass migration that began to flow into the district by the 1870s. In addition to his publishing, lodging house ownerships and banking, he served as agent for the General Trans-Atlantic Company, the Red Star Line, the Anchor Line, the Fabre Line, and Italian agent for the West Shore Line, "one of the richest and greatest railroad companies in the United States." Barsotti also advertised that he would transmit money, change money, buy and sell gold and silver, provide post office services, write letters, and more.[16] Yet, Barsotti's career illustrated that money and power did not automatically confer the old respect due the *signore*. Relationships were in flux, and during Barsotti's many years of operation he was attacked by an unlikely array of opponents, including fellow *prominenti*, socialists and anarchists, the American press, various reform organizations, and ordinary immigrants. The only source of consistent praise was the Italian government, which bestowed upon him the title Cavaliere.[17]

Italians initially joined company in the district with a cosmopolitan population mix. To the southeast, primarily along Mott and Pell streets to Chatham Square, were clusters of Chinese, forming the basis of the city's first Chinatown. The section beginning at Canal Street and running to Bayard Street was inhabited by Jews and a sprinkling of Germans. Outnumbering all others, however, were Irish residents who occupied the streets to the north and west, and generated the most friction as Italians exerted pressures in the area. As one commentator noted, "The advance of the newcomers is resisted on every side," and most often the resulting confrontations involved the Irish. Meeting in tenements, churches and job sites, Italians and Irish compiled a record of antagonism that extended well into the new century.[18] Fights, scuffles and gang confrontations were very much part of the district until the Italian presence succeeded in dominating the section and moving the zone of immediate conflict to other localities.

During the 1850s and 1860s the district was visited by an institution which was to have important consequences for the future of Italians in the city. The traffic in children employed under contract as street musicians, boot-blacks and beggars by padroni became a prominent feature of lower Manhattan. The number of these children who arrived in the city is impossible to assess with any accuracy. Many of them appear to have been recruited from the provinces of Campania and Basilicata.[19] The exploitations characteristic of the system soon provoked the outrage of the city's population. Charles Brace caught the essence of the experience from his personal observations of the Five Points. "The children I saw every day on the streets," he wrote:

> following organs, blackening boots, selling flowers, sweeping walks, or carrying ponderous harps for old ruffians ... The lad would frequently be sent forth by his *padrone*, late at night, to excite the compassion of our citizens, and play the harp. I used to meet these boys sometimes on winter-nights half-frozen and stiff with cold.[20]

A vigorous campaign against the padroni, waged in part by di Casali and his newspaper and the Children's Aid Society's Italian School, succeeded ultimately in eradicating the system. Former street children were soon reported engaged as printers, waiters, carvers, jewellers, shoemakers and carpenters. Augustine E. Cerqua, a founder of the Italian School, noted

> two who keep and own a neat confectionery and ice-cream saloon in Grand Street; a shoemaker in business for himself; another ... a foreman in the very machine-shop in which he

served as an apprentice; one a patented machinist in a steam chocolate manufactory; and ... [a] foreman in a wholesale confectionery.[21]

The negative images surrounding the term "padroni" and the Italian population in general, however, lingered far beyond these years and served to colour the reception afforded to later immigrants and their labour bosses.

The decade of the 1870s witnessed fundamental transformations in the district's Italian composition. During this time period large numbers of southern Italian male sojourners began arriving in the city seeking transient, short-term economic goals. Campania, Basilicata and Calabria were the major sources of this movement of unskilled labourers.[22] The month of December 1872 appears to have been a pivotal juncture in this migration. More than two thousand *meridionali* passed through Castle Garden and entered the city in that month. Described as being "wretchedly poor and unskilled," many of these migrants had apparently been hoodwinked into believing that they had booked passage to Buenos Aires. Others had plans to arrive in New York from the start as they "arrived with letters for friends and relatives in New York." The great majority were absolutely destitute and without prospects for work; more than four hundred had to be taken to Ward's Island, the city's pauper institution. Several reports indicated that many had sold homes and farms to make the trip and that at least a thousand more were soon to follow.[23] Thus were contact points linking the district with the Italian south further extended.

A. E. Cerqua visited the docks and interviewed one boatload of these new arrivals. This group consisted of 108 men, one woman, and two children, with the males distributed into the following categories: 71 from Basilicata (mostly bricklayers and labourers); 31 from Potenza (bricklayers and labourers); 3 from Calabria (labourers); and 3 from Salerno (barbers). Included among sojourners who had arrived on different ships were charcoal burners, wood choppers, carpenters, blacksmiths, farm hands, and additional common labourers. City newspapers claimed that at least 1,400 of these men were found in the area of Broadway and Broad streets engaged in the most abject begging. When asked why they came and what they now wanted, the answer was the same: "We want to work."[24]

There were men in the district able to supply just this commodity. Using small enterprises such as saloons, groceries, lodging houses, and immigrant banks as springboards, men like Barsotti, Fugazy and dozens of others made the necessary first contacts with American employers. More often than not in these early years, the burgeoning railroad industry was the first to explore the advantages of *intermediarismo*. Clustered in the Mulberry district, the most successful of these individuals had already erected the skeletal core of institutions and services designed to meet the needs of the great temporary migration. As different waves of Italian sojourners arrived in the district, the men who frequently rested at the apex of the commerce of migration were those longer-settled northern Italian *bossi* and bankers who traced their beginnings to the early years.[25] Scores of enterprises operated by members of the southern migration, however, soon competed in the business, and offered a challenge to the wealth, power and influence of this initial contingent.[26]

The wider public often missed the dynamics that were taking place. As Robert Foerster perceptively pointed out, "When rag pickers and street musicians still seemed to many the very quintessence of Italian immigration, the pick-and-shovel labourers were silently being carried to the remoter places and set to work on railways."[27] Very often the steamship agent who booked the sojourner's passage, the banker who extended him credit and provided temporary lodging, and the labour agent who first inserted him into the wider economy lived in the Mulberry district. By the 1870s, with only a short dip occasioned by the depression, New York *bossi* were securing gangs of labouring sojourners numbering into the hundreds for railroad work work and construction projects. In the next decade crews often numbered into the thousands and the geographic range of their work sites extended to nearly every part of North America.[28] The district became the great clearing-house for the temporary housing and transshipment of Italian migrants—and thereby became indirectly the spawning ground for hundreds of settlements elsewhere in the United States.

The district's population swelled and shrank according to the seasonal variations of employment. Unskilled workmen flocked to the city during winter months and ventured forth again into the interior when warmer weather returned. Large tenements owned by bankers dotted Mott and Mulberry streets and served as winter headquarters for large numbers of sojourners who chose not to return to Italy. One 1884 investigation found nearly five thousand unemployed Italians in the Sixth Ward waiting out the winter until railroad work began anew.[29] With intercity work opportunities inadequate to the numbers at hand, many migrants remained idle through the cold season, often spending their hours at neighbourhood saloons. These conditions led outsiders, unfamiliar with the customs and work patterns of sojourners, to excoriate Italian men as "lazy and unproductive."[30] As recurring waves of sojourners arrived for seasonal "campaigns," their unique demands generated a special set of characteristics.

The favourable geographic location relative to docks and train stations and the clustering of banks and labour agencies meant that the Mulberry district attracted an uncommonly diverse cross-section of the sojourning population. "Nearly all who come here for the first time and have no relatives to join," one study noted, "make at least a temporary halt in New York."[31] The large number of steamship lines linking the city directly with Italian ports facilitated this pattern. Not a few sojourners arrived "in a robbed and plundered condition" and found themselves stranded in the city.[32] There were, of course, those who were willing to add to the vagaries of the migration process. Owners of service institutions in the district sent hordes of runners, "steerers," hackmen and "guides" to prey upon greenhorns. So aggressive were they that not even the protective webs of family and friends were absolute guarantees of safety.[33] Indeed, the range of swindles these individuals perpetrated on newcomers was limited only by their imaginations; no effective control over their activities existed until well after the turn of the century. Thus stranded, many migrants sank roots and established new chain networks linking additional villages to the new world.

Fortunes were made in this commerce of migration and, as the momentum increased—much as news of a gold strike draws the most ambitious and aggressive of any population—the streets of the district attracted the most enterprising intermediaries.[34] Just as the presence of large numbers of sojourners, even if only briefly, brought benefits to middlemen, so too did the clustering of immigrant institutions bring advantages to migrants. Surely the chances of finding employment opportunities were enhanced by the concentration of banks, lodging houses and labour agencies. A random overhearing of a conversation among *bordanti*, a glimpse at employment bulletins in an agent's window, or word-of-mouth news of a new project might mean extra wages for savings-conscious sojourners. That these informal communications lines existed and were important is attested to by the efforts of *bossi* and bankers to use them for their own advantage. Saverio Merlino, among others, documented the process at work in the district. The job-seeker, he noted, "walks through Mulberry Street and sees a crowd around a bar in a basement."

He enters the basement and finds a man employing men for a company. He adds his name to the list without knowing anything about the work he will be called upon to do, or about the places where he is to be transported, or about the terms of his engagement. Perhaps, however, he passes a banker's establishment and stops to read on a paper displayed at the window a demand for two hundred laborers, ...he enters, enlists, takes his chances, and falls in the snare set for him.[35]

Most larger banker/padroni of the district did not have to rely on such measures to acquire the men they desired. Several employed extensive agent networks in Italy to funnel men to their businesses as well as runners in the city who were trained to *fare gli uomini*. Others relied on kin and village networks to send foremen back to Italy and recruit among their *paesani*.[36] Felice Tocci, a prominent Mulberry banker, followed the first course of action. A congressional investigation in 1887 found that Tocci's bank at 28 Mulberry Street operated an agency in Naples which coordinated prepaid tickets and requests for labour. Testimony of one New York Italian revealed, "A lot of the passports of the immigrants were stamped with his address."[37] The address of a New York banker appears to have been almost as common as a suitcase among migrating Italians.

By the late nineteenth century the district had no rival as a centre of padrone/banker operations. Each wave of newcomers tended to form new layers of service institutions, although the more established units always attracted some clientele from each group.[38] John Koren's 1897 analysis of bankers showed that the district was crowded with "shabby little affairs, run in connection with lodging houses, restaurants, grocery stores, macaroni factories, beer saloons, cigar shops, etc., but under imposing names, such as Banca Roma, Banca Italiana, Banca Abbruzzese, and the like."[39] There were scores of these "shabby little affairs" which catered to the *paesani* of a single village or valley region and defied the efforts of city directories to record them. Antonio Mangano walked the district's streets and observed in 1904, "They are constantly springing up to meet the needs of this or that group of persons, coming from a particular town or village." Many of these businesses were little more than forwarding agencies, but even in these limited capacities, they manifested a high failure rate. Banca Termini, a small bank located at 3 Mulberry Street, was said to have failed because it did not have enough *compari* in the area to compete with rivals.[40]

Though by 1890 there were several sizable Little Italies in other sections of the city, the Mulberry district remained the largest concentration of Italian settlement. With the exception of a cluster of Genoese shopkeepers and artisans who remained at the lower end of Baxter Street, the region was overwhelmingly southern Italian in composition. And with them existed all the appurtenances of the temporary migration which continued to stamp the district as a great sojourning base camp. But the lodging houses, banks, labour and steamship agencies and import stores were only the most obvious of the enterprises available to residents of the district. The Mulberry population was large and diverse enough to support a proliferation of trades. Organ grinders had access to repair shops, rental agencies and sales outlets which supplied their needs. Some tenements gave over entire floors to the raising, selling and renting of monkeys. Among the ever-present pushcarts upward mobility was at work as well. Aggressive businessmen attempted to bring order to even this individualistic trade. One 1906 report noted the presence of "pushcart tycoons" who supplied licences, stock and weekly wages to scores of peddlers who worked under their control.[41] Nor were women idle. An 1888 investigation of the Mulberry district found that Italian women had turned stale bread into a "systematized industry." Bakeries took old bread which had formerly been thrown away and sold it to immigrant women who in turn retailed it "at from one to three cents a loaf from the curbstone."[42]

The nature of the district as a massive way station for migrants gave rise to a galaxy of specialized trades and services designed to cater to their particular needs. In this sense sojourners indirectly provided a rich array of investment and business opportunities for those who chose to stay permanently. There were undertakers who specialized in shipping bodies back to the homeland, lawyers who featured an expertise in settling estates and forwarding money, photographers who earned reputations for taking stylized formal portraits which could be sent back to relatives and friends (and perhaps potential brides), fireworks and statuary distributors who supplied the numerous local saint's day celebrations, marriage brokers and matchmakers who acted as go-betweens for the distant village, and so on.[43] For people who resided in the district with one eye firmly fixed on the homeland, these new *mestieri* filled

important roles. They joined company with numerous localized establishments—such as small importers who thrived on supplying familiar
village foods and wines—to provide additional avenues of occupational
progress. It was possible, therefore, for enterprising individuals to
experience upward mobility comfortably within the immigrant community framework.

The growth and perpetuation of these businesses was aided by the
settlement patterns characterizing the district. Although there were
unusually large numbers of isolated travellers docking at New York
relative to other locations, the great majority of arrivals came as part of
larger family, kin or village networks. These considerations shaped
settlement decisions in important ways. Contemporary documents record an unmistakable pattern of block settlement by *paesi*. Luigi Villari,
to cite but one of many observers, noted:

> Alcuni quartieri sono abitati esclusivamente dagli oriundi di
> una data regione; in uno non traviamo che Siciliani, in un
> altro i soli Calabresi, in un terzo gli Abruzzesi; vi sono poi
> certe strade dove non si trova che gente di un dato comune: in
> questo vi è la colonia di Sciacca, in quello la colonia di San
> Giovanni in Fiore, in quell' altro la colonia di Cosenza.[44]

Although Italian consular officials were fond of referring to the area as
an Italian "colony," it was in fact a hodge-podge collection of small
village clusters. Residents of Sannicandri in Apuglia settled in a line
running for two blocks along Hester Street between Mulberry and
Elizabeth. Both sides of Mulberry, from Canal to Broome streets, a
distance of four blocks, were composed entirely of "Neapolitans" coming from a variety of small interior villages (most from the province of
Salerno) such as Padula, Sant'Arsenio, Ricigliano, Sarno and Teggiano.
The Abruzzi contributed a cluster of its sons and daughters to a section
of upper Mulberry Street near the crossing of Spring and Mott. These
settlers came from the village of Arpino. Calabrians from San Donato di
Ninea, Cosenza and Catanzaro inhabited a block of Mott Street between Grand and Broome. Basilicatans from Bella, San Fele, Balvano,
Accettura and Calvello were scattered in small pockets in the district
(occasionally inhabiting all the rooms of one or two tenements), but one
side of Mott Street between Prince and Houston was given over to
them.[45]

After 1890 these streets took on an increasingly Sicilian hue, with
a great influx arriving after the turn of the century. During the decade
1897-1907, several hundred thousand of the "dark people" came
through the city and pushed into the Mulberry district. Residents of
Marineo clustered along Mott Street near the Children's Aid Society
school. Along Grand Street, in a three-block stretch where it interse-
sected Mulberry, Mott, and Elizabeth, were natives of Enna and the
small interior village of Polizzi Generosa. Natives of Sciacca totally
occupied a two-block area of Elizabeth, between Hester and Broome
streets. Indeed, Elizabeth Street become the great haven of Sicilians;

along its length were found former residents of Misilmeri, Baucina, Catania, Girgenti and Messina.[46]

Each village cluster attempted to reproduce the pace and patterns of its homeland setting. In many cases the district possessed sufficient numbers of *paesani* to allow a strict retention of old world customs, and some villages were able to support more than one settlement in the city. The uptown Cinisi colony of East Sixty-Ninth Street followed a pattern typical of many. Composed of some two hundred families from the Sicilian village of Cinisi, the cluster was held together by the force of custom. "People do exactly as they did in Cinisi," reported one authority, "if someone varies, he or she will be criticized." Since the majority intended to return, their reputations had to be guarded in New York as zealously as in the homeland. A few enterprising individuals establi hed roots with small import businesses built on the foundation of this localism, but the mentality of most was firmly rooted in Sicily. Little concern for American politics or citizenship existed; instead the festas, local elections and harvests of Cinisi occupied their minds.[47] Yet, over time, day-to-day contacts with others in the market, the work place and tenements tended to break down the most extreme *campanilismo* and forge a wider identification for those who remained.

The fragmentation of the Mulberry district was also reflected in the proliferation of mutual aid clubs, burial societies and benefit clubs. Such organizations had existed since the early part of the nineteenth century. Some were small, regionally based entities (Lega Toscani, La Piemontese, etc.) but most were not. As early as 1825 the district possessed various patriotic and philanthrophic societies, the most important of which was the Societa di Unione e Benevolenza Italiana. This organization opened its membership to all Italians and sponsored broad programs of reform and social betterment during the period 1840-1870. Many older clubs adopted the name of famous Italians—Cristoforo Colombo, Galileo Galilei, Giuseppe Verdi, etc.—and aimed at a wide clientele.[48]

The great southern migration flooded the city with narrow societies limiting their memberships to a restricted set of *paesani*. By 1915 the city as a whole possessed between two and three thousand of these organizations, and the greatest single concentration of them was located in the district. This was primarily a testament to the influx of Sicilians. One contemporary strolled down Mulberry Street and noted that before he had gone four blocks he counted "at least thirty placards" of different societies.[49] A representative example of these small clubs was the Societa di Mutuo-Soccorso Isola Salina. Its membership was composed of residents of Salina, a small island north of Sicily, with a total population of about one thousand. The society contained one hundred members, most of whom were fruit vendors in the city. The constitution limited membership to those born on the island or descended from parents born there and living in New York or within three hundred miles of it, and to children or parents from any of the Eolina Islands if they had lived ten years on the island of Salina.[50] But here too the layered nature of the Mulberry district was evident. These extremely localized organizations existed side by side with more broadly based societies which admitted all from a particular valley or province. Some clubs established branches in other clusters located in the city and continued to support organizations in the home village. Others slowly began to drift into various "umbrella" organizations such as the United Italian Societies. All efforts at city-wide unification, however, ended in failure.[51]

Middle-class observers, both Italian and American, viewed the amazing proliferation of these societies with consternation. Gino Speranza captured the essence of their complaints. "Each province, each town, each village, has a society of its own," he explained; "they keep the colony divided, create petty jealousies and prevent beneficient activity on a large scale."[52] While localism undoubtedly cut off some avenues of cooperation and potential group advancement, it also opened others that were frequently lost to public view. The dynamics of growth provided new entrepreneurial access routes for dozens of different ethnic businesses in the district. Saloons, meeting halls, grocery stores, and the like benefited from the customer traffic generated by these entities. They also provided employment alternatives for the professionally trained segment of the southern migration. Instead of being hired out as clerks to "half illiterate bankers and contractors," they now had an opportunity to strike out on their own. Hence there existed in the district a class of *avvocati arrivati* and *notai* who owed their livelihood to the trade generated by the mutual aid societies.[53] Looked upon with disdain by longer settled professionals, this form of work provided increased options for a segment of the southern migration often overlooked in the great mass of common labourers.

The force of *campanilismo* was also charted by festas honouring village patron saints. Often working through the agency of local mutual aid societies, recently arrived *meridionali* celebrated these occasions with a fervour that often amazed outsiders.[54] Variations on traditional customs were numerous as Italians adjusted to life in the district. Some small village groups continued to send funds back to the homeland to support festas and never conducted formal celebrations in America. Many held commemorations here and simultaneously helped fund events in the home village. Finally, there were those who lost connection with the village over time, but continued the festa in the district.[55] Sicilian villagers from Misilmeri made obvious the symbolic links tying them to the homeland by building a papier-mâché replica of their village and marching with it next to the statue of their patron saint, San Giusto. Baucinesi living along Elizabeth Street held their first festa to St. Fortunata in 1900, raised $1,000, and sent it back to the home village for the erection of a permanent shrine—again the influence of the old world.[56]

Though each festa possessed its own peculiarities, most included an elaborate procession involving public display of the patron saint's statue accompanied by fireworks, bands, flags and portable shrines. Here too ethnic enterprise surfaced. Vendors circulated through crowds selling *gelati Italiani, lupini, carciofi*, and *ceciretti* as well as more specialized products relating to particular celebrations.[57] The festa of St. Rocco, featuring a processional march between the Church of the

Transfiguration at 25 Mott Street and the Baxter Street Church at 115 Baxter, supported a variety of petty merchants. Since St. Rocco reputedly protected against diseases and pests, the festa procession featured supplicants who carried wax arms, legs, hands and, as the *New York Tribune* reported with a whiff of scandal, "other portions of the body not normally exposed to view." Several small stands and shops did a brisk business in the manufacture and sale of wax impressions to the faithful.[58] Many Americans and longer settled Italians could not reconcile the considerable sums of money spent on fireworks and festivities, given the poverty so characteristic of these newer arrivals. Yet these expenditures were not out of step with their mentality and values. In the context of the migrant's pre-industrial world view, these costs were entirely appropriate.

Various church groups perceived the district as a fertile ground for converts and communicants, but the area was remarkably resistant to the ministrations of priests and ministers. The great transience of the population, as well as traditional Italian cultural attitudes toward religion, proved to be formidable barriers to the organized work of Protestant and Catholic missionaries.[59] Two small Catholic missions located on Centre and Mulberry Streets began in 1888, but these units were amalgamated into a larger parish (St. Joachim) located on Roosevelt Street to the east.[60] The most successful Catholic parish emerged from Missione Italiana della Madonna di Loreto begun in 1892 by Father Nicholas Russo. His first years were trying. "We [priests] were oftentimes received with the coldest indifference," he reported, "not seldom avoided; at times even greeted with insulting remarks. The word *pretaccio* [priestling] as we passed by, was one of the mildest."[61] But the creation of at least a dozen parishes and Protestant churches in the district after the turn of the century signified the breaking down of the extreme localism and indifference that characterized the early years.[62]

Although city residents often charted the changing patterns of Italian life in the district by such colourful pageants as festas and church dedications, there were more fundamental alterations taking place. Beginning in the 1880s and accelerating rapidly thereafter, Italians began to move heavily into the city labour market. Sojourners continued to engage in the traditional off-season occupations—knife-sharpening, scavenging, snow shovelling, etc.—but these began to give way to more dependable employment. The great physical expansion of New York City merged neatly with the presence of Italians uniquely suited to do the necessary work. Sewer-laying, tunnelling, excavating, subway construction, street-grading, rock work and general construction found an increased Italian presence. As early as 1890 the New York Inspector of Public Works claimed that 90 per cent of the labourers under his jurisdiction were Italians. One police officer in 1895 gave testimony to the changed situation. "We can't get along without the Italians. We want somebody to do the dirty work, the Irish are not doing it any longer."

By 1904 more than 1,200 Italians were sweeping New York's streets.[63] After 1900, when work on the Lexington Avenue subway began, newly arrived Sicilians almost totally replaced other nationalities at this labour. On the longshoremen's docks even more striking events were taking place. Irish workmen were elbowed aside in what has been described as "one of the most striking examples of racial displacement in American history." And although unskilled labour was always the great beachhead, even the factories began to feel the movement. Gino Speranza noted the phenomenon in 1908: "Many an Italian who would have never thought of doing anything but outdoor labour hears of a man who is working in a factory...and making good money. Soon, the entire gang goes over to the factory."[64]

By 1903, when the Society for the Protection of Italian Immigrants established its Labour Bureau in an effort to combat the boss system, it listed as a primary stipulation that anyone using its services must agree to accept employment out of the city.[65] The irony is, of course, that so often in the past Italians were criticized for their transience in pursuing out of town, seasonal employment. The impact of this shift on the district was significant. Men could now begin to adopt a more normal lifestyle. No longer were many isolated for long periods of time in remote work camps. They were able to send for family, even if only for short stays, and spend more time in a neighbourhood setting. Hence, the great transiency of the past decades slackened. The change in work area also affected labour contractors. Their ability to establish links with such agencies as city street, park and sanitation departments and large urgan construction projects often necessitated a growing political profile.[66]

Increased permanence also meant an upsurge in the number of women who joined their spouses, fathers and brothers in New York. As women joined the floodtide to America and closed the links of family chains, they too added to the economic vitality of the district. Women, of course, laboured diligently as child-rearers, housekeepers, boarding-house padrone, and the like, but by the late 1880s the sight of Italian women walking through the district carrying huge bundles of coats and trousers for home finishing was not uncommon. This sight signified the entrance of Italians into the garment trades which bordered the district. Based on licence applications for home work in 1901, the area of greatest concentration in the city was "that including Mulberry, Mott, and Elizabeth Streets and the other side with Bowery, Chrystie and part of Forsyth."[67] Located within walking distance of the factories and contractor shops, Italian women had absorbed 95 per cent of the "home finishing" work in the city by 1901. They were concentrated most heavily in the ready-made, men's clothing trades, but large numbers were found in the women's clothing and custom-made fields as well. Although the total number of homeworkers in the city declined by 1908, Italians claimed 98 per cent of this work. Other "sweated trades," such as the making of artificial flowers, paper boxes and willow plumes, attracted Italians by the thousands.[68] Despite advertisements in Italian newspapers promising "buona paga, lunga stagione, Si da lavoro a casa," the seasonal wages earned by these women were depressingly low. Yearly totals of $50 to $100 testified to the economic precariousness existing among some of the *contadini* seeking a better life.[69]

The practice of mixing residence with work place was not unique to homeworkers nor was it out of step with Italian cultural mores. As early as the 1860s various city reports noted that Italian ragpickers and scavengers in the district operated their businesses out of tenement homes. The New York Association for Improving the Condition of the Poor investigated a settlement along Jersey Street in 1879 and found it "swarming with Italians of the ragpicker class." This concentration was composed of approximately two hundred families who filled their back yards and open spaces with lines for drying rags and with bones, bottles and papers. In a cellar apartment, used in part to house boarders, investigators noted "heaps of bags and rags, and right opposite to them stood a large pile of bones, mostly having meat on them, in various stages of decomposition."[70] Similar conditions were found on Crosby Street to the south. Italian residents here occupied the most squalid rear tenements and filled homes with the products of their trade. An inspection of one cellar unit found the area divided into twenty-one compartments packed with rags, bones, and "immense heaps of what even the ragpickers refuse." The old rural life rhythms apparently died slowly, as city reports documented numerous cases of district Italians keeping birds, chickens, goats and pigs in their tenement dwellings.[71]

Just as Mulberry Street became synonymous with America in the minds of many Italians, so too did it become synonymous in the opinion of many Americans with Italian settlements. The v 'llingness of district residents to exist under what others regarded as debased living conditions generated negative stereotypes. Lurid descriptions of Italian life in the district were significant in shaping employment opportunities, social receptions, nativist legislation, and more. By the mid-1880s unfavourable impressions had largely crowded out the occasional positive views that had surfaced earlier. One 1885 expression was characteristic:

> By all odds the most vicious, ignorant and degraded of all the immigrants who come to our shores are the Italian inhabitants of Mulberry Bend and the surrounding region of tenements. . . . [here] is an eddy in the life of the city where the scum collects, where the very offscourings of all humanity seem to find lodgement . . . a seething mass of humanity, so ignorant, so vicious, so depraved that they hardly seem to belong to our species. Men and women; yet living, not like animals, but like vermin![72]

Negative assessments of district Italians increased dramatically when the ugly reality of crime became commonplace starting in the 1890s. Bombings, extortion attempts, Black Hand kidnappings and threats, shootings, stabbings and counterfeiting operations garnered the headlines of city newspapers on an almost daily basis after the turn of the century.[73] Northern Italians, ever anxious to protect the "good name" of Italians, rushed to disassociate themselves even further from their more recently arrived countrymen. Italian Chamber of Commerce President Antonio Zucca put the matter succinctly in 1904: "Practically all crime comes from the South, and it would not surprise me to see a race war between the two factions if the crime continues."[74]

Despite the impressions of social pathology and family and cultural disorganization that issues such as crime generated, the district possessed a stable social structure. The behaviour and social priorities of residents differed from those of outsiders, but they underpinned an elaborate social and economic structure that fitted the needs of the area. In fact, the district was an institutionally complete sub-society. A few perceptive viewers were able to see the wider patterns existing. One 1896 description caught some of the essence:

> Today the Sixth and Fourteenth Wards are still peopled by the Italians. They are laborers, toilers in all grades of manual work. They are artisans, junkmen, ragpickers.... There is a monster colony of Italians who might be termed the commercial and shopkeeping community of the Latins. All sorts of stores, pensions, groceries, fruit emporiums, tailors, shoemakers, wine merchants, importers, musical stores, toy and clay molders, are found and abound here. There are notaries, lawyers, doctors, apothecaries, undertakers—followers of every profession and business, in fact, found in a great city.[75]

Unrecorded by this observer, but present as well, were *lupanari* (brothels keepers), *strozzini* (loan sharks), and *giocatori* (gamblers).[76]

Although middle-class reformers and journalists may have viewed the streets twisting through the Mulberry district with alarm, the residents themselves had a far different image of their thoroughfares. Streets were the meeting places providing a setting for an intricate network of social relationships. Indeed, it was in the streets that much of the explosive vitality of the district was revealed. Here was where fruit and vegetable carts, lined wheel to wheel, clogged the curbsides and offered an endless variety of fresh goods for sale. Wives and boardinghouse keepers gathered to do their daily shopping and gossiping. Hordes of children ran, jumped and brawled while peasant-garbed women balanced baskets on their heads filled with grocery supplies for the evening meal. As Jacob Riis recorded in 1890, "when the sun shines the entire population seeks the street, carrying on its household work, its bargaining, its love-making on street and sidewalk, or idling there when it has nothing better to do."[77] On the pavement proper hacks, delivery trucks and pushcarts jostled for space and right of way, while peddlers worked their way through the crowd offering wares. Dozens of shops occupied the first floors of tenement buildings and oftentimes their goods spilled out onto the sidewalks. Above the walkways, fire escapes created an elevated metal lacework frequently festooned with freshly cleaned laundry and chattering neighbours leaning over to obtain the latest news.

On such streets residents could obtain everything they required. An incredible variety of shops lined the avenues. Despite nativist contentions of Italian mental inferiority and often-quoted statistics on illiteracy, bookstalls and small libraries abounded in the Mulberry district. The reading fare offered by these institutions ranged widely, from the great literature classics to "commic sheets and Neapolitan dialect love songs by the score, and innumerable tragic or amorous novelettes by Carolina Invernizio and other popular writers." One banker/bookseller in the city published a copiously illustrated catalogue book of 176 pages to advertise his merchandise.[78] Saloons also attracted a steady clientele, and men engaged in endless games of *mora, briscola* and *tresette* or discussed the latest lottery drawing. Restaurants attracted customers from outside the district by featuring the tasty, inexpensive food that still characterizes the Italian *trattoria*. Such variety existed in the district that someone could "make a tour of the provinces and chief towns of Italy" by visiting restaurants.[79] Italian professionals also claimed space: funeral directors, dentists, pharmacists, lawyers, notaries, the *levatrice* (midwife) and medical doctors. Not a few of the latter were quacks who conducted a thriving business in bogus cures. One bold imposter at 91 Mulberry Street pledged the sum of $1,000 to anyone who could disprove his claims after his cure-all was condemned in the press as "falso come un soldo papalino". History has not recorded if this money was claimed.[80]

Unless drawn out by work opportunities or a roving spirit, many Italians spent their entire stay in America within the confines of the district. In her investigation of the Mulberry area, social worker Lillian Betts found numerous residents who had never ventured beyond this inclusive little world. Every possession owned by one family of nine had been purchased within the borders of the district. "Within this limit of territory," Betts claimed, "all worked, all their social affiliations were established, and it was all of America they knew."[81]

The attractions of the district were not limited to shops and job opportunities. The area earned for itself a reputation as a centre of theatre and music that regularly attracted Italians from all sections of New York and other cities as well. For years small theatres were maintained in the rear of saloons or in coffee houses. In the cheaper ones marionettes took the place of paid actors.[82] These were gradually overshadowed by the more established entities with permanent stages and regular lists of performances. By 1915 social worker Lillian Wald reported that almost all of the older impromptu meeting halls had been abandoned in place of the more structured theatre and "we can no longer find on Mott, Elizabeth, and Spring streets the stuffy little theaters filled with workingmen and an occasional woman."[83]

Enjoyment of music was not confined to the stage. Music concerts, band performances and choral societies all enjoyed a flourishing existence in the district. As early as 1890 an Italian American Musicians Union was incorporated, followed in 1893 by an Italian Choral Society. Musicians played regularly in Mulberry Park and by 1908 the park boasted a permanent band for entertainment. Each concert attracted large crowds of listeners "who pour forth from a hundred tenements, and stand listening in rapt delight by the hour to the strains of 'Il Trovatore'...."[84]

Sharing popularity with the theatre and band concerts were the twice-daily lotteries. A grocery, cigar shop, candy store or dressmaker might serve as a centre for bets on *lotto*. Some bets were restricted to small clusters of *compari*, but the system soon grew to incorporate a much wider clientele. One report in 1893 already noted that "at every corner of Mulberry and the neighboring streets there is a betting place bringing on the average a net revenue of two hundred dollars per day."[85] *Campanilismo* could not have supported such widespread dispersion.

The texture of life in the Mulberry district included a much grimmer side. Living conditions were among the most congested and disease-ridden in the world throughout the period under review. Dr. Antonio Stella, a pioneer in health care among Italians, conducted an investigation of a one-block section of the district (bounded by East Houston, Prince, Mott and Elizabeth) which can be taken as being representative. The majority of families there lived in apartments of one or two rooms and at least one-third took in boarders. "In most cases," Stella found, "the number of cubic feet of air for occupants of sleeping rooms was less than is provided in hospitals and prisons." Among *bordanti* packed into these tenements Stella found instances of mixing the sexes in sleeping arrangements.[86]

The density of settlement in the district necessitated the use of all possible living space. In that portion of Elizabeth Street, between Houston and Prince, known as the "Barracks," there were reputed to be 1,110 people to the acre.[87] The structures characteristic of this area were the older "front and rear" buildings with ancient frame units scattered throughout. Three, four, five and six storey tenements were indiscriminately joined together to create a mixed clustering of units— unlike the more uniform and newer "dumbbell" tenement sections which characterized the areas of Jewish settlement to the east.

When these congested conditions combined with Italian cultural practices and employment patterns, they produced abnormally high death rates in the district. For the year 1905-6, the block examined by Stella possessed the highest death rate for adults and children in the entire city (a distinction that Italian sections had held since 1894). Children under five were the most affected; bronchial pneumonia, measles, and various disorders of the digestive tract were the biggest killers. Stella estimated that during the 1890s rickets affected between 75 and 80 percent of all Italian children below the age of five.[88] For adults, tuberculosis was the scourge. Among eight hundred cases investigated in one survey, former residents of southern Italy predominated, a situation which reversed conditions in Italy itself.[89] Luigi Villari estimated that of five thousand Italian street sweepers in 1912, one-third were *tisici*. Official statistics and contemporary observation, however, failed to capture the true extent of the disease. Many mutual aid societies and benefit clubs provided for the passage home of infected members. So great was the outpouring of diseased *ritornati* that not a few Italian villages were faced with outbreaks of tuberculosis. The coastal town of Sciacca opened a sanitorium just outside city limits for returned emigrants as a means of protecting the community from infection.[90]

As with many other urban problems, reformers and middle-class analysts often confused cause with effect. Flaws in Italian diet and constitutions, living conditions, and work preferences often emerged in the literature as being the chief causes of disease, but these assessments overlooked other considerations. Tenements along Elizabeth and Mulberry streets had long records of infection—some rear tenement apartments, for example, reported up to forty cases per year—but they remained occupied by different families year after year. Italian transiency played a role in perpetuating these conditions, but landlord avarice and greed must be considered as well.[91] Not until several formal education programs were launched in the district and the population began to settle more permanently did infection rates begin to drop. Antonio Stella and housing reformer Lawrence Veiller organized efforts in 1908 and 1910 with the aid of an Italian Committee on the Prevention of Tuberculosis. Agents visited every family in the Mulberry district and passed out some thirty thousand Italian-language pamphlets entitled "How to Avoid Consumption." Bright-coloured posters containing basic information on preventive measures set against a backdrop of Italian scenes appeared throughout the area. A travelling exhibition with signs in Italian and English visited the streets during an eleven-week climax to the campaign and claimed that 132,652 people registered at the display for materials and information.[92]

Ironically, as infection rates began to drop, a variety of forces intersected to shift the locus of population away from the district. Though considerable numbers of newcomers continued to move into the area, the composition of the movement was beginning to change dramatically after 1900. Women assumed an increasing presence among the newest arrivals, and as they tied together previously splintered family chains, the orientation of the district changed. The "family stage" of Italian immigration gained ascendency. As the Society for Italian Immigrants noted in 1912, movement now was beginning "to fill the gaps of Italian families and communities already established here. . . . "[93]

Considerations such as housing assumed enhanced importance in this context. The crowded and crumbling tenements found in the district were among the most dilapidated in the city. As permanent immigration increased, there was an almost irresistible urge to find better accommodations. The Mott Street Industrial School observed this tendency in 1907. "As soon as they learn the city and its ways and find they can better themselves," the school reported, "they move to other quarters [in the city]."[94] In some cases, of course, the choice was dictated by the wrecking ball. The creation of Mulberry Park in 1897 was indicative of continuing efforts of reform and business groups to clean up the worst slum areas.[95] The alternative for many who were faced with this choice was to leave the district and find better housing elsewhere.

Developments after 1900 affecting the city's transportation and communications networks made it easier for Italians to accomplish precisely these goals. The massive rapid transit building programs taking place in the metropolitan area, as well as the addition of new bridges, tunnels and roadways, allowed far more settlement options.[96] Many new arrivals now by-passed the Mulberry district entirely and proceeded directly to other sections of New York. Dozens of locations now duplicated the service and institutional bases previously only available in the district. The "hospitality of place" that attracted Italians to the streets surrounding Mulberry for decades was now no longer an exclusive commodity of the Lower East Side. Similarly, the dispersal of commerce and industry away from the confines below Manhattan's Fourteenth Street opened new areas of employment for city Italians.[97] Hence, the centrality of the Mulberry district as a supplier of employment was diluted and the pressure to settle there suffered another diminution. The region peaked in its population in 1910; by 1930 it contained about one-half of its former total.[98]

The experience of the district in the years before 1914 revealed that the area did not develop along a linear continuum; the experience was multi-layered. Different immigrants arrived at different times with quite distinct backgrounds, goals and skills. Job area, residence, community life and culture were, in turn, vitally affected by these distinctions. From the time northern Italian merchants, professionals and workmen first arrived, the district underwent a process of change. This initial contingent desired permanent settlement and achieved a measure of stability and acceptance that largely eluded later arrivals. By the 1870s the district was essentially shaped by a massive infusion of temporary migrants. Composed in the early years primarily of *contadini* from Campania, Basilicata and Calabria, these Italians brought their unique perspectives to the migration process. In a dynamic transformation, the district became a great way station serving the needs of sojourners. But even here diversity existed. Italian migrants defined much of their life in New York based upon aspects of their old world culture. A wide variety of religious festas, mutual aid societies, language dialects and settlement patterns gave testimony to the enduring importance of these old loyalties. The huge Sicilian influx arriving after the turn of the century continued these themes. Though by no means unaffected by the wider society, district residents defined largely for themselves their own particular lifestyle and culture. The *ambiente* which existed varied from time to time, but it did not shift in an unpredictable manner. It changed to meet the specific needs of the diverse Italian populations which inhabited the district's streets.

Notes

1. Kate Holladay Claghorn, "The Foreign Immigrant in New York City," in U.S. House, Report of the Industrial Commission, vol. 15, *Immigration*, 1901, p. 465. Census figures for foreign-born Italian residents of New York list the following totals: 1860—1,463; 1870—2,793; 1880—12,223; 1890—39,951; 1900—340,770; 1920—390,832. Greater New York was not formed until 1898; early figures are for Manhattan.

2. Luigi Villari, *Gli Stati Uniti d'America e l'Emigrazione italiana* (Milano, 1912), p. 216.

3. The careers of these early exiles have been ably recorded in Howard Marraro's essays, the most important being, "Italians in New York during the first half of the Nineteenth Century," *New York History*, 26 (July,

1945), pp. 278-306; "Italo-Americans in Eighteenth-Century New York," *New York History*, 21 (July, 1940), pp. 316-323; "Italians in New York in the Eighteen Fifties," *New York History*, 30 (April-July, 1949), pp. 181-203. Not to be overlooked are Giovanni E. Schiavo, *Italian-American History*, 2 vols. (New York, 1947-49) and *Italians in America before the Civil War* (New York, 1924). New York possessed the largest concentration of exiles in America.

4. The works cited above supply much information on these early arrivals, as do the pages of New York's first Italian-language newspaper, *L'Eco d'Italia*. Marraro, "Italians in 1850s," p. 185, for example, documents the arrival of twenty-two Italian tailors in 1853.

5. Most of this biography is contained in *Il Progresso Italo-Americano*, April 2, 1893. See also, *L'Araldo Italiano*, November 6, October 13, 1898; *Trow's Business Directory of New York City, 1882-1883* (New York, 1883), p. 39; *Hunt's New York City Business Directory* (New York, 1890), p. 24; *Trow's Directory, 1890-1891*, p. 279.

6. The most ubiquitous of these early settlers were the fruit vendors, a trade dominated by Genoese. They were found in practically all areas of Manhattan, though the majority were located below Fourteenth Street. Two large clusters existed in the early decades; one on lower Baxter Street and another on Sixth Avenue near Grand Street. The Zucca family was among the most successful. The father Antonio Zucca, owned a large wholesale business, which provided a base for several sons. He was a guiding force in the organization of the Society of Italian Fruitvendors and served as President of the Italian Chamber of Commerce and many mutual benefit societies. Ultimately he became a power in Tammany politics. Fellow Genoese in the trade included Louis Botto, A. L. Cella and Paolo A. Arata, all of whom became prosperous merchants. See *L'Eco*, 27 February, 1896; *L'Araldo*, 2 September, 1898; *Corriere della Sera*, 30 December, 1910; 15 April, 17 March, 1911; *Wilson's Business Directory of New York City, 1880-1881* (New York, 1881), p. 297; *Business Directory of New York, Brooklyn, and Newark, 1885* (New York, 1886), p. 225.

7. Industrial Commission, p. 452; Charles Loring Brace, *The Dangerous Classes of New York* (New York, 1880, 3rd edition), pp. 196-97; Carroll Smith Rosenberg, *Religion and the Rise of the American City* (Ithaca, New York, 1971), p. 35; James Ford, *Slums and Housing* (Cambridge, Mass., 1936), pp. 100-108.

8. Brace, *Dangerous Classes*, p. 197. Brace described these Italians as being "generally from the Ligurian coasts." There were plaster workers from Lucca, fruit dealers from Palermo, and ragpickers from Pavia as well.

9. This breakdown is based upon Robert Ernst's analysis of the New York State Census of 1855. The employment classifications mentioned accounted for 85 per cent of all gainfully employed Italians. Robert Ernst, *Immigrant Life in New York City* (Port Washington, 1949), pp. 69, 74-78, 86, 95.

10. Interviews in author's possession; Schiavo, *Italians before Civil War*, p. 207; Marraro, "Italians in 1850s," pp. 196, 198, 283-84; Valentine Winsey, "A Study of the Effects of Transplantation upon Attitudes Toward the United States of Southern Italians in New York City" (Ph.D. dissertation, New York University, 1966), p. 100; *L'Eco*, 18 March, 1865; 25 April, 1884; *New York Herald Tribune*, 16 September, 1908; *New York Times*, 31 May, 1896; Charlotte Adams, "Italian Life in New York," *Harper's Magazine*, 62 (April 1881), pp. 676, 679.

11. Alan F. Harlow, *Old Bowery Days: The Chronicles of a Famous Street* (New York, 1931), p. 391; George J. Manson, "The Foreign Element in New York City," *Harper's Weekly,* 34 (October, 1890), p. 818; Federal Writers Project, *The Italians of New York* (New York, 1938), p. 18; *New York Times,* 31 May, 1896. As late as 1892 Jacob Riis noted, "The Italian who comes here [the Bowery] gravitates naturally to the oldest and most dilapidated tenements in search of cheap rents." Jacob Riis, *The Children of the Poor* (New York, 1892), pp. 9-10.

12. *L'Eco,* 7 January, 1865; 30 July, 1869; Ernst, *Immigrant Life,* p. 157; Silvano Tomasi, *Piety and Power: The Role of Italian Parishes in the New York Metropolitan Area* (Staten Island, 1975), p. 73. Founded in spring 1866, St. Anthony of Padua was located on Bleecker Street near a large concentration of Genoese.

13. *Il Progresso,* 16 October, 1892; *L'Araldo,* 13 October, 6 November, 1898; *Trow's Directory, 1880-81,* p. 533. The more prosperous northern Italians who abandoned the lower ward tended to cluster in the Washington Square area, along Bleecker, Sullivan and MacDougal streets, where they formed a fairly homogeneous settlement. Most of the earliest residents of this section had gained their initial footholds in the cluster to the south.

14. *L'Eco,* 25 October, 1879; 5, 12 March, 1896; *Il Progresso,* 20 July, 1890; 19 January, 2 February, 1892; *New York Times,* 31 May, 1896. For more discussion on Fugazy's stature in the community, see Victor Greene, "'Becoming American': The Role of Ethnic Leaders—Swedes, Poles, Italians, Jews," in M. G. Holli and P. d'A. Jones, eds., *The Ethnic Frontier* (Grand Rapids, Michigan, 1977), pp. 162-64.

15. *New York City Directory, 1880-81* (residential directory), p. 80; *Trow's Directory, 1881-82,* p. 82; *Business Directory of New York, Brooklyn, and Newark, 1885,* p. 21; *Hunt's Directory* (1890), 410; Robert E. Park, *The Immigrant Press and its Control* (New York, 1922), pp. 342-44; George P. Rowell, *American Newspaper Directory* (New York, 1890), p. 649; N. W. Ayer and Sons, *American Newspaper Annual* (Philadelphia, 1890), p. 670.

16. *Il Progresso,* 16 January, 1890, affords examples of advertisements for many of these enterprises, but virtually every issue mentioned some. See also *Il Progresso,* 16 October, 1892; 18 February, 12 November, 1893; 24 June, 1893; 16 February, 1909.

17. *Il Progresso,* 25 July, 1890; 16 October, 1892; 26 March, 1893; 26 March, 1909; *Corriere della Sera,* 10, 28 January, 1910; *New York Times,* 17 March, 1890. When Secchi de Casali died in 1884, control of *L'Eco* passed to Felice Tocci, a prominent banker and labour contractor. Tocci soon became a bitter rival of Barsotti and the pages of *L'Eco* carried vicious attacks on *Il Progresso* and its editor. For a time in 1893 *L'Eco* carried cartoons depicting Barsotti in the form of a pig; arrests for libel were commonplace among the *prominenti.* See *L'Eco,* 20 August, 1 October, 24 September, 1893; *La Parola del Medico,* 15 September, 1916.

18. Katharine Anthony, *Mothers Who Must Earn* (New York, 1914), p. 8; Autobiography of Robert Ferrari, 19, Box 1, Ferrari Papers, Immigration History Research Center, University of Minnesota; J. Gilmer Speed, "The Mulberry Bend," *Harper's Weekly,* 36 (30 April, 1892), p. 430; *Il Progresso,* 10 July 1890; 3 February 1892; *New York Tribune,* 9 September, 1901; 24 November, 1903.

19. *L'Eco,* 23 July, 6 August, 1869; *New York Times,* 20, 21 June, 1873; Robert Foerster, *The Italian Emigration of Our Times* (Cambridge, Mass., 1919),

pp. 102, 324. Villages such as Viggiano, Corlito, and Laurenzana were sources of supply.

20. Brace, *Dangerous Classes*, p. 194f. See also *16th Annual Report of the Children's Aid Society* (New York, 1869), pp. 41-42; *21st Annual Report of the Children's Aid Society* (New York, 1873), pp. 30-35.

21. Brace, *Dangerous Classes*, p. 203. The story of the Italian school and its war against the padroni, as related by Cerqua, is contained in ibid, pp. 195-211. Also see *L'Eco*, 30 April, 30 July 1869; 24 April 1872; 23 July, 1879; 27 April, 1884.

22. Foerster, *Italian Emigration*, pp. 328-29.

23. *New York Times*, 13, 14 December 1872. One agent in Naples, Giovanni Tedeschi, received $22 for "passage" but the receipt slip he dispensed did not specify a destination. A report from Basilicata at this time indicated that emigration to America was "constantly increasing" and some villages had lost most of their artisans.

24. *New York Times*, 15 December 1872. A three-month strike in New York at the time affected thousands of workers and perhaps afforded opportunities for both sojourner and padroni to gain footholds. Edwin Fenton, *Immigrants and Unions, A Case Study: Italians and American Labor, 1870-1920* (New York, 1975), pp. 78-79, discusses the timing. One wonders if indeed the arrival of these sojourners was a coincidence.

25. See the following for representative careers of early arrivals: *L' Eco*, 18 March, 1865; 14 August, 1889; 25 April, 1884; 14 August, 1889; *La Follia di New York*, 28 April, 1907; *New York Tribune*, 16 September, 1908.

26. Francesco Sabbia, a Sicilian from Catania, was representative. Arriving in the late 1870s, he settled at 92 Mulberry Street and opened a small grocery and "stale beer dive." From this base he began finding railroad jobs for *paesani*; by the 1890s he was sending men throughout the east coast. His specialty became the supplying of railroad labourers and "colonists" to the southern states. In 1907 he owned a sizable bank at 177 Mulberry, from which he sent hundreds of workers to the Florida East Coast Railway. These activities involved him and his commissary agent, Angelo Schrione, in one of the largest peonage cases investigated by the United States government. *La Follia di New York*, 5 May, 16 June, 1907; Pete Daniel, *The Shadow of Slavery in the South, 1901-1961* (New York, 1972), pp. 95-107. Daniel relates the essential story of the peonage case; railroad records on the case (not used by Daniel) are contained in "Peonage File," Henry M. Flagler Pagers, Flagler Museum, Palm Beach, Florida. Interestingly, despite the court case, the railroad continued to use Sabbia's services until 1911.

27. Foerster, *Italian Emigration*, p. 358.

28. For a sampling of recruiting experiences see, *L'Eco*, 24 May, 1873; 24 March, 1874; 31 May 1881; *New York Tribune*, 23 January, 1887.

29. Charlotte Erickson, *American Industry and the European Immigrant* (New York, 1967), p. 104; Adolfo Rossi, *Un Italiano in America* (Treviso, 1907), pp. 65-71; *New York Times*, 6 October 1895; John Koren, "The Padrone System and the Padrone Banks," *U.S. Bureau of Labor, Special Bulletin*, no. 9 (March 1897), p. 119. The extreme transiency of Italians has been documented by Thomas Kessner, *The Golden Door: Italian and Jewish Immigrant Mobility in New York City, 1880-1915* (New York, 1977), who found for the decade 1880-1890 a persistence rate of only 8 per cent.

30. *New York Tribune*, 12 July 1903; *New York Times*, 6 October 1895.

31. Koren, "Padrone System," p. 116.

32. Adams, "Italian Life," p. 677. By 1907 thirteen steamship lines connected Naples with New York City; other Italian ports also possessed direct routes. U.S. Congress, House, *Monthly Consular and Trade Reports*, 59th Cong., 2nd Sess., 1907, 37; U.S. Senate, Reports of the Immigration Commission, *Emigration Conditions in Europe*, 61st Cong., 2nd Sess., 1911, p. 115.

33. The *Annual Reports* of the Society for the Protection of Italian Immigrants, a philanthropic organization begun in 1901, provide the best picture of conditions at the landing areas. A nearly complete set of these reports is contained in the Gino C. Speranza Papers, New York Public Library, New York. The Society's first effort to control runners occurred in early 1902. A manager of the Society plus three other individuals met a party of thirty-two immigrants at Ellis Island. With these representatives on all sides, the group attempted to reach the elevated trains at the Battery. Runners managed to pounce on fourteen new arrivals and physically drag them away. See also *New York Tribune*, 3 March, 16 November, 1902; 4 March 1903; "Protection of Italian Immigrants," *Charities*, 8 (1902), p. 247.

34. The careers of many *prominenti* testify to the attracting power of the district. Antonio Maggio (James E. March) is illustrative. He arrived in New York in 1872 as a 12-year-old boy, but soon left the city for several up-state locations. Sometime between 1878 and 1880 he returned and began working for the Erie Railroad. By 1882 he owned a bank/employment agency at 35-37 Marion Street, and held positions as superintendent of immigrant trains and chief labour contractor for the railroad. In these capacities he supplied thousands of Italians to track crews and built a political base from which he carved a colourful career as Republican "Boss" of Italians in the Third Assembly District. *New York Tribune*, 7 December 1902; *Il Progresso*, 19 September, 1894; *L'Eco*, 31 August, 1894; *Corriere della Sera*, 15 September, 19 October, 1910.

35. Saverio Merlino, "Italian Immigrants and their Enslavement," *Forum*, 15 (April, 1893), pp. 185-86. The list of swindles pepetrated by unscrupulous agents was almost limitless. See Frank J. Sheridan, "Italian, Slavic, and Hungarian Unskilled Laborers in the United States," *U.S. Bureau of Labor Bulletin*, no. 15 (September, 1907), pp. 445-47; Gino C. Speranza, "Italian Foreman as a Social Agent," *Charities*, 11 (1903), pp. 84-89; Francis A. Kellor, "Who is Responsible for the Immigrant?" *Outlook*, 107 (1914), p. 912; *L'Araldo*, 6 November, 1898. The Speranza collection contains dozens of affidavits of New York Italians who had been cheated by bankers and labour agents.

36. *L'Araldo*, 6 November, 1898; State of New York, *Report of the Commission of Immigration* (Albany, 1901), p. 122. One instance in 1907 saw eight Italians from the village of Sannicandri, Province of Bari, engage themselves to a banker on Mulberry Street. They paid one dollar each for employment and all were swindled. See Sheridan, "Unskilled Laborers," p. 445.

37. U.S. House, Diplomatic and Consular Reports on Emigration, 50th Cong., 1st Sess., 1887-88, *Miscellaneous Documents*, pp. 84, 94. See also U.S. House, *Letter from the Secretary of the Treasury ... Immigration to the United States*, 52nd Cong., 1st Sess., 1892, p. 251; Broughton Brandenburg, *Imported Americans* (New York, 1903), p. 21.

38. New York Commission of Immigration, *Report*, p. 26; Report Immigration Investigating Commission, 1895, p. 26, quoted in *Industrial Commission*, p.

435; Gino Speranza, "The Assimilation of Immigrants," typewritten copy, Speranza Papers. Sheridan dates the beginning of the padrone system in 1885. This is surely too late. By 1915 New York City still possessed in excess of one thousand employment centres, many of which were classified as padroni or "steerers." See "The Distribution of the Immigrant," *Immigrants in America Review*, 1 (1915), p. 29.

39. Koren, "Padrone System," p. 126; Reports of the Immigration Commission, *Immigrant Banks*, 1911, p. 225; Charles F. Speare, "What America Pays Europe for Immigrant Labor," *North American Review*, 187 (1908), p. 108. For efforts to combat the padroni/banker system, see *Bollettino dell'Emigrazione*, 3 (1907), pp. 10, 62-67; 8 (1909), pp. 28-29; 18 (1910), pp. 112-25.

40. Mangano, "Associated Life," 481-82; *L'Eco*, 3, 4 December, 1896; *Corriere della Sera*, 18 June, 9 July 1909; 1 February, 20 August, 8 September, 1910. The amazing number of abscondings of district bankers added to the failure rate. See New York Commission on Immigration, *Report*, pp. 30-34, for a list covering the year 1907-8.

41. *Report of the Mayor's Pushcart Commission* (New York, 1906), p. 17, quoted in Kessner, *Golden Door*, p. 55; Adams, "Italian Life," pp. 680-82.

42. Viola Roseboro, "The Italians of New York," *Cosmopolitan*, 4 (January 1888), p. 398.

43. Interview; Gino Speranza, "The Meanest Fraud of All," typewritten copy, Speranza Papers; Gino Speranza, "The Handicaps of Immigration," *The Survey*, 25 (1910), p. 470; *L'Eco*, 9 January, 1896; Speed, "Mulberry Bend," p. 430.

44. Villari, *Gli Stati Uniti*, p. 216; Alberto Pecorini, "The Italians in the United States," *The Forum*, 45 (January 1911), p. 17; Gino C. Speranza, "Italian Characteristics," typewritten copy, Speranza Papers; *New York Times*, 6 October 1895.

45. Interviews; *Il Progresso*, 22 June, 1893; *L'Eco*, 13 February, 5, 12 March, 1896; *Corriere della Sera*, 15 March, 1912; Gino C. Speranza, "Industrial and Civil Relations of Italians in Congested Districts," 4, Speranza Papers, Winsey, pp. 201, 234.

46. Interviews; Tenement House Department of the City of New York, *First Report, 1902-1903*, 2 vols. (New York, 1903), I, pp. 27ff; Robert E. Park and Herbert A. Miller, *Old World Traits Transplanted* (New York, 1921), pp. 95, 242.

47. Gaspare Cusumano, "Study of the Colony of Cinisi in New York City," in Park and Miller, pp. 147-58. See also, Gino C. Speranza, "Italian Characteristics"; Thomas Jesse Jones, "The Sociology of a New York City Block," *Columbia University Studies in History, Economics, and Public Law*, 21 (1904), p. 102; Philip Rose, *The Italians in America* (New York, 1922), p. 61.

48. Marraro, "Italians 19th Century," p. 26; *Il Progresso*, 26 April 1892; 22 June, 2 July, 11 August, 1898; *L'Eco*, 5, 12 March, 1896. The city's largest mutual aid society, La Fraterna, was founded in 1887 by the redoubtable Luigi Fugazy. Composed primarily of northern Italians, it took the lead in sponsoring Garibaldi Day parades. By the turn of the century, La Fraterna's membership was over two thousand and in the year 1902 it paid out over $14,000 in sick and death benefits to its members. See *Il Progresso*, 2, 20 February 1890; *L'Eco*, 20 February 1896; *Corriere della Sera*, 3 July, 29 September, 1909; 13 March, 1912.

49. John Mariano, *The Italian Contribution to American Democracy* (Boston, 1921), p. 140; William E. Davenport, "The Italian Immigrant in America," *Outlook*, 73 (1903), p. 32; Antonio Mangano, "Associated Life of Italians in New York," *Charities*, 12 (1904), p. 479; *New York Times*, 13 June 1913. Edwin Fenton's estimate of mutual aid society numbers in New York projected the following totals: 1879—15; 1885—15; 1889—48; 1890—78; 1896—145; 1902—200; 1910—2,000. Fenton, *Immigrants and Unions*, p. 50.

50. Mabel Hurd Willet, "The Employment of Women in the Clothing Trades," *Columbia University Studies in History and Political Science*, 16 (1902-1903), p. 132; *New York Times*, 13 June 1913; *Il Progresso*, 2 July, 1892; *L'Araldo*, 27 August, 16 November, 1898; *Corriere della Sera*, 7 July 1909.

51. John Daniels, *America via the Neighborhood* (New York, 1920), p. 101-3, 197-99; *L'Eco*, 23 April, 1896; *Corriere della Sera*, 4 January, 1 February, 1910; *La Fiaccola*, 12 December 1912.

52. *New York Times*, 8 March, 1903; Foerster, *Italian Emigration*, pp. 393, 399, 436; Mangano, "Associated Life," p. 479; Villari, *Gli Stati Uniti*, p. 31.

53. Antonio Mangano, "Italian Colonies of New York City," (M.A. thesis, Columbia University Teacher's College, 1903), p. 48; *Il Progresso*, 14 July, 1912; *Corriere della Sera*, 3 July 1909.

54. *Il Progresso*, 6, 8 September 1894 (Madonna del Lauro), 13 May, 1893; 30 September, 1894 (St. Michael), 22 July, 1890 (San Arsenio); 20 September, 1894 (San Gennaro); *New York Times*, 13 June 1913 (San Giovanni Battista); Phyllis H. Williams, *South Italian Folkways in Europe and America* (New Haven, 1938), p. 149 (San Gandolfo); "Italian Festivals in New York," *Chautauquan*, 34 (1901-2) p. 228.

55. Interviews; *New York Tribune*, 12 July, 1903; 18 July, 1904; *New York Times*, 13 June, 1913.

56. *New York Tribune*, 9 September, 1900; 10 September, 1901; 14 September, 1902; *New York Times*, 13 June, 1913. San Guisto was the patron saint of fishermen. The *New York Tribune* offered the opinion that celebrants were praying for protection from New York food inspectors not ocean storms.

57. Interviews; Mangano, "Associated Life," p. 480; *New York Tribune*, 12 July, 1903.

58. At least three different villages honoured St. Rocco as their patron saint and celebrated his feast day on August 16. The largest apparently was that taking place along Mott Street, organized by villagers from Savoia di Lucania. See *Il Progresso*, 18 August, 1892; *New York Tribune,* 17 August, 1901; 17 August, 1902; 18 July, 1904, *Corriere della Sera*, 17 August, 1909.

59. Though there was a significant anti-clerical tradition among Italians, most sojourners appear to have shaped their responses to religion on other considerations. The accumulation of a nest-egg and a quick return to the homeland occupied first priority. As one commentator noted, "The Italian did not come here to get anything but a decent living. He is not interested in politics, sociability, or religion." The 1886 Catholic Census of New York estimated that only 1,200 of some 50,000 Italians were attending mass regularly. Henry J. Browne, "The 'Italian Problem' in the United States," U.S. Catholic Historical Society; *Historical Records and Studies*, 35 (1946), p. 53; Antonio Mangano, "Italian Colonies," pp. 36-38; Stefano L. Testa, "Strangers from Rome in Greater New York," *Missionary Review*, 31 (1908), p. 217; "Catholic Italian Losses," *Literary Digest*, 47 (1913), p. 636.

60. St. Joachim's was known as the "Rag Shop Church" because it occupied a

building formerly housing the largest rag shop in the city. A contemporary description of the church noted that it "stands with a cheap lodging house on one side and a typical slum grocery store on the other. A nest of tough saloons is near by, up and down the street." Quoted in Tomasi, *Piety and Power*, pp. 106-7.

61. George J. Hoffman, "Catholic Immigrant Aid Societies in New York City from 1880-1920," (Ph.D. dissertation, Syracuse University, 1966), pp. 84-89; Giovanni Schiavo, *Italian American History: The Italian Contribution to the Catholic Church in America*, (2 vols. New York, 1949), II, pp. 757, 770; "Diocesan Bureaux for the Care of Italian, Slavic, Ruthenian and Asiatic Catholics in America," *Ecclesiastical Review*, 48 (1913), p. 221.

62. George E. Pozzetta, "The Italians of New York City, 1890-1914," (Ph.D. dissertation, University of North Carolina, 1971), pp. 287-89, 295-302.

63. U.S. House, 58th Cong., 3rd Sess., *Report of the Commission General of Immigration, 1904* (Washington, 1905), pp. 853-54; J. F. Carr, "The Italian in the United States, *World's Work*, 8 (1904), p. 5403; Industrial Commission, 474; Foerster, *Italian Emigration*, p. 360. *Corriere della Sera*, 2, 4 June, 1909, reported a street sweeper's parade composed of more than six thousand Italians.

64. Charles B. Barnes, *The Longshoremen* (New York, 1915), pp. 4-10; *New York Tribune*, 20 August, 1901; Gino C. Speranza, "The Italian in Congested Districts," *Charities and the Commons,*" 20 (1908), p. 55. Among the larger construction projects absorbing Italian labour after the turn of the century were the Bronx Aqueduct, Grand Central Station and the Jerome Park Reservoir.

65. Eliot Norton, *Open Letter to the Society for the Protection of Italian Immigrants*, 1902, Speranza Papers. The society operated its main employment office at 17 Pearl Street, and a branch at 159 Mulberry Street. The latter location had to be closed in 1904 as an unprofitable venture; the entire plan was judged a failure by 1910. See Norton to Speranza, 27 October, 1904; J. Phipard to Norton, 29 November, 1904.

66. *New York Tribune*, 30 November, 1903. Andrew Barbieri followed this path. Starting with a fruit stand on Bowery Street in the late 1860s, he soon became a saloon keeper. This business proved to be a cornerstone for a career in politics among Italians of the Second Assembly District. In the 1880s and 1890s he was able to use his political influence to obtain contracts for removing ashes and scow trimming. By the time of his death in 1903 he had employed hundreds of Italians in city work.

67. Willett, "Clothing Trades," p. 96; George E. Walsh, "Immigration and the Sweating System," *Chautauquan*, 18 (1893-94), p. 177; Industrial Commission, pp. 324, 329, 369; Joel Seidman, *The Needle Trades* (New York, 1942), p. 36.

68. Mary Van Kleeck, *Artificial Flower Makers* (New York, 1913), pp. 29-34; Mary Van Kleeck, *A Seasonal Industry: A Study of the Millinery Trade in New York* (New York, 1917), pp. 66-67; Foerster, *Italian Emigration*, p. 348.

69. Louise C. Odencrantz, *Italian Women in Industry: A Study of Conditions in New York City* (New York, 1919), pp. 32-35, 348.

70. Industrial Commission, p. 472, extracted from *Report of New York Association for Improving the Condition of the Poor*, 1879, p. 64. An earlier report in 1864 noted that the area was composed primarily of very poor blacks; by 1879 they had been supplanted by Italians.

71. Ibid., 473; Florence Kitchelt Journal, 6 May, 1905, Florence L. Cross Kitchelt Papers, Arthur and Elizabeth Schlesinger Library, Radcliffe College, Cambridge, Massachusetts. For a report of four goats and a 200-lb. hog, see Tenement House Department, *First Report*, I, pp. 110-111, 115.

72. Allan Forman, "Italians in New York," *The American Magazine*, 9 (1885), pp. 46-52; *New York Tribune*, 2 June, 1895; 26 September, 1890.

73. Pozzetta, "Italians of New York City," pp. 185-87, 194-206, 225-30.

74. *New York Tribune*, 18, 19 August, 1904. The New York City Police Department gave graphic evidence of the district's reputation by placing its headquarters at 300 Mulberry Street. See William McAdoo, *Guarding a Great City* (New York, 1906), p. 3.

75. *New York Times*, 31 May, 1896.

76. A very revealing picture of the Mulberry district through the eyes of an immigrant is offered in C. Cianfarra, *Il diario di un Emigrato* (New York, n.d.), pp. 51-55, 64-65, copy in Immigration History Research Center, University of Minnesota.

77. Jacob Riis, *How the Other Half Lives* (New York, 1890), p. 43; William P. Shriver, *Immigration Forces: Factors in the New Democracy* (New York, 1913), p. 93; Helen Campell, *Darkness and Daylight* (New York, 1893), p. 402.

78. Elliot Lord, John Trenor, and Samuel Barrows, *The Italian in America* (New York, 1906), pp. 246-47; Society for Italian Immigrants, *Seventh Annual Report*, 1908-9, 7-8; Davenport, "Italian Immigrant," p. 32.

79. Peter Roberts, *The New Immigration* (New York, 1911), p. 270; T. J. Jones, "Sociology of a City Block," p. 110; Manson, "Foreign Element," p. 818; *New York Tribune*, 19 March, 1893; *Corriere della Sera*, 15 July, 1910.

80. *La Parola del Medico*, 15 August, 1 November, 1916; *Il Progresso*, 23 January, 1890; 25 April, 1908; *Corriere della Sera*, 9 June, 1909.

81. Lillian W. Betts, "The Italian in New York," *University Settlement Studies*, 1 (1905), pp. 90-91; Enrico Sartorio, *Social and Religious Life of Italians in America* (Boston, 1918), p. 18.

82. *L'Eco*, 29 October, 1896; Davenport, "Italian Immigrant," p. 32.

83. Lillian D. Wald, *The House on Henry Street* (New York, 1915), p. 272; *Corriere della Sera*, 12 April, 1911. New York's first Italian coffee house with a regular stage, Villa Vittorio Emanuele, opened on Mulberry Street in 1890. It presented a varied bill of fare including light comedies, heroic tragedies and dialect plays. The Villa, and dozens of similar houses, were immensely popular. They were typically crowded each night as they played hosts to numerous touring actors and troupes. See Giuseppe Cautela, "The Italian Theatre in New York," *American Mercury*, 12 (1927), pp. 106-12; Stephen Graham, *With Poor Immigrants to America* (New York, 1927), p. 77; Elisabeth A. Irwin, "Where the Players are Marionettes . . . in Mulberry Street," *Craftsman*, 12 (1907), pp. 667-69.

84. *Il Progresso*, 8 July, 1890; 12 March, 1893; 6 August, 1908; *Corriere della Sera*, 19 January, 31 May, 1912.

85. Vincent Van Marter Beede, "Italians in America," *Chautauquan*, 34 (1901-2), p. 423; Brandenburg, *Imported Americans*, pp. 18, 25.

86. Antonio Stella, "The Effects of Urban Congestion on Italian Women and Children," in *Italians in the City: Health and Related Social Needs* (New York, 1975), pp. 4-6.

87. *Report of the Tenement House Committee of 1894* (Albany, 1895), pp. 11, 19-26; Jacob Riis, *The Children of the Poor* (New York, 1892), pp. 14-15; Thomas Adams, *Population, Land Values, and Government*, 2 vols., (New York, 1929), II, p. 17; Foerster, *Italian Emigration*, p. 382.

88. Stella, "Urban Congestion," pp. 11-12, 21-23. See also Board of Health of the Department of Health of the City of New York, *Annual Report*, 1901 (New York, 1902), p. 8; Louis H. Pink, "Old Tenements and the New Law," *University Settlement Studies*, 2 (1907), pp. 8-9.

89. Stella, "Urban Congestion," pp. 31-32. The report concluded: "Peasant women from Calabria and Basilicata and those from the strictly primitive provinces of Girgenti and Caltanisetta, give New York a very high percentage of tuberculosis compared to other regions of Italy."

90. Stella, "Tuberculosis and the Italians in the United States," *Charities*, 12 (1904), pp. 486-87; Stella, "Urban Congestion," pp. 25-26; Villari, *Gli Stati Uniti*, p. 200.

91. Charity Organization Society of New York, *First Annual Report of the Committee on the Prevention of Tuberculosis*, "A Handbook on the Prevention of Tuberculosis" (New York, 1903), pp. 55, 91; Rocco Brindisi, "The Italian and Public Health," *Charities*, 12 (1904), p. 486; *A Report of the Board of Health of the City of New York to Honorable William L. Strong on Pulmonary Tuberculosis* (New York, 1897), pp. 28, 38-42.

92. *Reminiscences of Lawrence Veiller*, pp. 187-88; 199-200, Columbia University Oral History Project, Columbia University, New York; R. L. Breed, "Italians Fight Tuberculosis," *The Survey*, 23 (1909-10), p. 702; *Corriere della Sera*, 20 June, 7 July, 11 October, 1910; 15-25 January, 1911.

93. Society for Italian Immigrants, *Tenth Annual Report*, 1912, pp. 2-3.

94. Children's Aid Society of New York, *Fifty-Fifth Annual Report*, 1907, pp. 94-95. See also Kellogg Durland and Louis Sessa, "The Italian Invasion of the Ghetto," *University Settlement Studies*, I (1905), p. 109.

95. *New York Times*, 7 December, 1894; 12 July, 1896; 15, 16 June, 1897.

96. Kessner, *Golden Door*, pp. 144, 149-50; David McCullough, *The Great Bridge* (New York, 1972), pp. 480-84, 514-15.

97. Edward E. Pratt, *Industrial Causes of Congestion of Population in New York City* (New York, 1911), pp. 84-86; Kessner, *Golden Door*, p. 149.

98. Donna R. Gabaccia, "Why do People Move? Residential Choice and the Search for Housing, Little Italy, 1905-1925," paper read at American Historical Association, San Francisco, 28 December, 1978; Gwendolyn Berry, *Idleness and the Health of a Neighborhood: A Social Study of the Mulberry District* (New York, 1933), pp. 6-8; Walter Laidlaw, ed., *Population of the City of New York, 1890-1930* (New York, 1932).

Bibliographic Note

There is a large secondary literature dealing with the New York Italian experience, a cross-section of which is included in the footnotes of this study. The intention of this bibliographic note is not to discuss these materials. Readers interested in a more complete listing are directed to my dissertation, "The Italians of New York City, 1890-1914," completed at the University of North Carolina in 1971. This essay will offer instead an overview of primary research materials that may be consulted in examining the New York Italian past. Two additional studies which supply guidance on a wide variety of sources and are helpful to the student beginning such work are Harold Eiberson, *Sources for the Study of the New York Area* (New York, 1960) and Thomas Kessner, *The Golden Door: Italian and Jewish Immigrant Mobility in New York City, 1880-1915* (New York, 1977).

An unusually large number of Italian-language newspapers printed in New York City have survived. These journals represent the entire spectrum of commercial, ideological, political and religious interests. The newspaper annex of the New York Public Library has the largest single holding of these papers. Newspapers which are particularly valuable include long runs of *L'Eco d'Italia* (1862-1896); *Il Progresso Italo-Americano* (1886-   ); and *Il Proletario* (1905-1942), although there are many other journals from which to sample. The Immigration History Research Center, University of Minnesota, contains a wide variety of New York radical and labour newspapers, among them *L'Adunata dei Refrattari* (1922-1971, incomplete) and *Giustizia* (1919-1974, scattered). Other important holdings can be found at the Center for Migration Studies, Staten Island, which lists among its collection *Il Lavoro* (1916-1930) and *Il Fuoco* (1914-1915). *The New York Times* is available on microfilm in numerous locations and, because of its comprehensive *Index*, is an unusually helpful research tool for all New York topics. Less well known, but useful for earlier dates, is the *New York Daily Tribune Index*, (1875-1906).

The reports of various city agencies, boards, bureaus, and departments offer much information on the Italian condition. Eiberson's study is perhaps the best place to begin an investigation of the voluminous amount of material existing in these sources. The New York City Health Department *Annual Reports* 1842-   ) document death and sickness rates and contain various narrative commentaries on the condition of immigrants. The New York City Tenement House Department issued fact-filled studies of housing among the poor and its *First Report* (1902-1903) remains as a classic investigation of the causes, extent and characteristics of congestion and tenement life. Police Department and Public School records, though poorly organized and difficult to use, also offer insights into the nature of Italian immigrant life. The *City Record: Official Journal of the City of New York* (1873-   ) documents the day-to-day operation of the city. *Annual Reports* of the Commissioner of Licenses (1905-1913), the City Inspector, and the New York City Bureau of Buildings all supply important data on the changes wrought in the city landscape by the immigrant presence. Voting patterns can be followed, in part, through the pages of the Board of Elections, *List of Registered Voters, 5 Boroughs* (annually).

New York State agencies often contain materials relevant to the city experience. The New York State Board of Charities *Annual Reports* touch upon various charitable activities taking place in New York City. The *Annual Reports* of the State Commissioner of Immigration and the Commissioners of Population contain data of obvious relevance. Beginning in 1825 the State of New York conducted censuses of its population and many of these efforts have survived. These materials in many cases can be effectively supplemented by federal census information.

Published federal census materials provide a rich lode of information on many different topics touching upon the New York Italian experience. Statistics on health, population, manufacturing, literacy, income and much more can be obtained from these sources. Manuscript schedules are not plentiful for New York City, but the 1880 returns have benefited from an extremely useful guide prepared by the New York Public Library, Main Research Branch. This guide ties the census returns (by microfilm reel) to specific locations in Manhattan. Not to be overlooked are two published volumes which present census statistics: Walter Laidlaw, ed., *Population of the City of New York, 1890-1930* (New York, 1932) and Dr. John S. Billings, *Vital Statistics of New York City and Brooklyn Covering a Period of Six Years Ending May 31, 1890* (Washington, 1894).

Various private agencies existing in the city have saved records which provide very useful insights into the Italian presence. The New York Children's Aid Society *Annual Reports* (1854-   ) are in a published state and available in several locations including the New York Public Library and Columbia University. The Society for the Protection of Italian Immigration *Annual Reports* (1903-1923) are contained in the Gino Speranza Collection located in the New York Public Library. The Records of the Charity Organization Society of New York are housed at the New York State Historical Society. These records contain a series of disease and poverty maps of the city.

Researchers interested in using city directories to explore the city fabric have a variety to choose from in New York. Of the business directories, the most consistent and useful are those published by Trow Publishing Company. Others appear to have reported on ethnic enterprises in an erratic manner. The *New York City Business Directory with Brooklyn Appendix* (New York, 1896), for example, seems to have avoided listings of Italian businesses entirely. Residence directories of the city are comprehensive, but they list residents alphabetically by name rather than by street. Their great size limits the ability to use them without computer assistance. Map resources are available in two helpful publications. For the more recent period G. W. Bromley and Co., Inc., *Manhattan Land Book of the City of New York* (New York, 1955) presents a diagrammatic street atlas which gives details of every house and building in Manhattan. Early maps of Manhattan are contained in Roger H. Pidgeon, *Atlas of the City of New York Lying South of Fourteenth Street* (New York, 1881).

Oral history collections touching upon Italian immigration are scarce. The massive Columbia Oral History Collection contains a handful of interviews which deal with this subject. The most important are those of Aldino Felicani, a publisher of radical newspapers; Lawrence Veiller, noted housing reformer; and Leonard Covello, a pathfinding educator. Herbert Gutman of the City University of New York Graduate Center has compiled a series of interviews focusing on the work experience of Italian and Jewish immigrants in New York City after 1900.

These items are not yet open to the public. Much more needs to be done.

Traditional manuscript sources dealing with Italian immigration are similarly in short supply. The Speranza Collection, already mentioned, stands as the most significant single collection of private papers. Speranza was a second-generation, middle-class Italian-American lawyer practising in New York City. His activities were diverse and he dealt on many levels with the larger problems of Italian adjustment to American conditions. The Immigration History Research Center contains a number of useful collections, including those of several writers, musicians and actors who spent time in New York. The Center for Migration Studies holds the records of the Saint Raphael Society for Italian Immigrants as well as a number of smaller collections.

Italian sources should not be overlooked. The files of *Bollettino dell'Emigrazione, Emigrazione e Colonie, Bollettino Consolare* and *Bollettino del Ministero degli Affari Esteri* have numerous pages devoted to developments in New York City. The *Annual Reports* of the Italian Immigrant Office at Ellis Island (1895-1899) and those of the Labor Information Office (New York City), *Bellettino d'Informazione*, 1910-1915, document the fate of these two offices funded by the Italian government.

An excellent starting point for research into the church history of New York's Italians is the WPA publication, Historical Records Survey, New York (City), *Inventory of the Church Archives of New York City* (New York, 1939-1941). This publication examines the seven major denominations of New York City including the Roman Catholic Church, Archdiocese of New York. Access to parish archives, however, is limited and many are uncatalogued. A full scrutiny of marriage and baptismal records, therefore, will have to await a future date.

On all topics relating to Italians in the city there is much helpful information contained in two massive government reports published in the early twentieth century. The *Reports of the Immigration Commission*, 41 vols. (Washington, 1911) and *Reports of the Industrial Commission*, 19 vols. (Washington, 1900-1902) both suffer from the prejudices of their compilers, but contain vast amounts of data not available elsewhere.

Toronto's Little Italy, 1885-1945

Robert F. Harney

Italian colonies in Canada, unlike those in the United States, have burgeoned rather than withered since World War Two. Differences in immigration policies between the two countries, revived family or village chain migration, and information about job opportunities in Canada brought thousands of new Italian immigrants to southern Ontario after 1947. Toronto is now a metropolitan area with upwards of half a million Italian immigrants and their descendants. It is also a city with visible and massive Italian neighbourhoods and with healthy ethnocultural institutions that afford an Italian Canadian the opportunity to live and die within an immigrant Italian *ambiente*.

This paper, however, deals not with the contemporary immigrant city but with the more threatened history and vanished world of the pre-World War Two Italian Canadian: a world which formed part of the classic turn-of-the-century Italian diaspora throughout the Americas, a space which was neither fully Canadian nor Italian.

Only a few immigrants from the Italian peninsula had reached Toronto by the middle of the nineteenth century; the city did not emerge as a significant location on the cognitive map of Italy overseas until the 1900s. Even then, although the Toronto settlement served as port of entry and base camp for Italian sojourners who worked in the mining, timber and railway towns of the north or along the Welland Canal to the southwest, the city was not generally well known in Italy. As late as 1914, the *Calendario per Gl'Emigranti di Societa Umanitaria* (1914), an influential guidebook for immigrants, included a map of Canada that pinpointed the cataracts at Niagara and the city of Mon-

"THE WARD" - TORONTO

COLLEGE ST.

TORONTO GENERAL HOSPITAL

HOSPITAL FOR SICK CHILDREN

CENTRAL MILITARY CONVALESCENT HOSPITAL

BUCHANAN ST.

LA PLANTE AVE.

HAYTER ST.

ELIZABETH STREET PLAYGROUND

GERRARD ST. WEST

HESTER HOW SCHOOL

WALTON ST.

UNIVERSITY AVENUE

ELM ST.

HOUSE OF INDUSTRY

ELIZABETH ST.

PRICE'S LANE

TERAULEY ST.

Y.W.C.A. ST. GEORGES HALL

ELM PL.

EDWARD ST.

CENTRE AVE.

NATIONAL THEATRE

YONGE ST.

CHESTNUT ST.

DUNDAS ST. W.

ALICE ST.

FOSTER PL.

ARMOURY ST.

HAGERMAN

HOLY TRINITY CHURCH

TRINITY SQ.

T. EATON CO.

AMOURIES

REGISTRY OFFICE

LOUISA ST.

JAMES ST.

T. EATON CO.

OSGOODE

ALBERT ST.

SHEA'S THEATRE

OSGOODE HALL

CITY HALL

T. EATON CO.

QUEEN ST.

COLLEGE ST.

GORE ST.

CLINTON ST.

HENDERSON AVE.

ST. FRANCIS CHURCH

MANSFIELD AVE.

CLAREMONT ST.

MANNING AVE.

GRACE ST. SCHOOL

BELLWOODS AVE.

TREFORD PL.

EUCLID AVE.

GRACE ST.

ST. FRANCIS SCHOOL

ST. AGNES CHURCH

PLYMOUTH AVE.

DUNDAS ST. W.

TORONTO

treal but not Toronto.[1] It was as if the migrant labourers sent into the Ontario bush by padroni in Montreal and storekeeper/labour bureaus in Buffalo fell off the face of the known earth.

However, there were by the 1890s some places in Italy, ironically enough in rural and isolated areas, in which Toronto as a target of migration was much discussed. For potential migrants from Laurenzana and Pisticci in Basilicata, Pachino, Vita, and Termini Imerese in Sicily, and later, Modugno and Monteleone in the Puglia, from areas around Chieti in Abruzzi, Cosenza in Calabria, Udine in Friuli, Caserta near Naples, Toronto was a familiar destination. Information about transportation to and job opportunities in Ontario, about Anglo-Canadian mores, was commonplace among the populace of those areas.[2]

In a sense, Toronto's Italian settlement can be understood best not as a Little Italy but rather as the terminal or way station for a variety of colonies serving the transatlantic networks of many small towns in Italy. The immigrant quarter in Toronto was St. John's Ward, known simply as "The Ward," stretching up from the train station, and west of Yonge Street. By the turn of the century it had become a cluster of *colonie*, little outposts of Europe's rural towns, each trying to cope in their own way with the intrusion of a cash economy, over-population, rising levels of expectations, and all the other disruptions unleashed by modernity.

If we understand the so-called Little Italy in these terms rather than assuming its Italian national identity, the attitudes and behaviour of its people become more comprehensible, and the occupational pattern of the early settlers emerges as an aspect of the venturesomeness and initiative of each small-town chain of migration. For example, Laurenzana in Basilicata provided a disproportionate number of the city's bandsmen and musicians. Laurenzanese youth, migrating to Toronto, were slotted into specific orchestra and band positions by those who came before them.[3] In that town, prospective immigrants were pre-trained for insertion into the Canadian occupational structure. Such a flexible approach to occupation gives a sophistication and specification to the idea of all migration as a flow of labour to capital and opportunity; it also shows the limitations of studies which use only North American census information to understand *mestiere* (occupation) and status. Migrants depended on relatives, *paesani* and ethnic brokers for intelligence about job opportunities, but, in a sense, each small town in Italy and its *colonia* in Toronto mediated the occupational as well as the family flow. Monteleonesi dominated the shoeshine business. Sicilians moved easily from railway work to banana peddling to domination of fruit and greengrocer enterprise in the city. A Canadian-English grammar for adult foreign students contained a lesson about Mr. Conti, the Italian fruit dealer, but the banana men themselves knew that they were Sicilians from Termini Imerese or Vita and fraternized little with Italians.[4]

It would be wise then for the historian to approach the immigrant settlement, before World War Two, without either the nationalist prejudice of Italian officials and intelligentsia, or the prejudice of the host society, which in its acceptance of stereotypes ignored sub-ethnic or regional differences. The people of Toronto's Ward before 1914 were not Italians manqué, torn asunder by *campanilismo*, regional rivalries and local factionalism. That view of them is only possible if one ignores their self-identity and their true ethnoculture. Thirty or so years of political unity in Italy had produced a litany of rhetoric, misgovernment, disappointment and official *Italianità* but not an Italian nationality. The newcomers to Toronto in 1900 were first of all men of their *paese*, and the larger immigrant neighbourhood was not initially a warmly ascriptive urban village of people who had known one another for generations.

Those in the colony who emphasized *Italianità* rather than *paese* loyalty—the newspaper editor, the Methodist preacher, the court translator, a little group of immigrants with more education than the rest— were atypical in both their literacy and influence. Plain folks may have applauded anyone who started a speech with "Noi italiani," as the newspaper editor did, or "connazionali," as the apostolic delegate did, but such an Italian national view of themselves grew slowly in Toronto. The exigencies of life in the new world, the advantage of widening ethnic contact for enterprise, the surge of patriotic feeling for endangered Italy that came with World War One, did help a larger Italian or Italian-Canadian identity to evolve, but that was a North American historical process, not a fact of immigration and it never fully replaced the ascriptive world of the *paese* and its *colonia*.

In the first decade of settlement, the newcomers' networks were not Italian, but specific to their *paese*. For example, Toronto's Pachinesi knew more about events in their hometown and that hometown's other major *colonie* in Lawrence, Massachusetts, and Caracas, Venezuela, than about "other Italians" in Toronto. Until World War One, only a few institutions in Little Italy contained the word "Italian" in their title, and prominent among them were a Methodist mission and a market run by a man with no *paesani* in Toronto.

Italian identity and inter-*paese* contact grew slowly as a result of proximity and shared experience in Canada, and the formation of a single national parish in 1908, Our Lady of Mt. Carmel, did force consolidation of identity (although two communities continued to war over possession of San Rocco as patron.) So there was an Italian National Club and the city's first three mutual aid societies bore national or monarchist names: the Umberto Primo, the Vittorio Emanuele, and the Operaia Italiana, and by their statutes were open to all Italians. However, when those societies reacting to the decline in membership and the patriotic fervour of the war effort, merged in 1919, to form the Societa di Mutuo Soccorso Italo-Canadese, their records show that the majority of the fraternal members came, in fact, from several towns in Basilicata and Calabria. Nor was there any inevitable urge to create a single Italian or Italian-Canadian identity. When the *colonia* of a given *paese* in the city reached a critical density, sub-ethnic institutions revived or emerged. When the Trinacria (Sicilian), the Famee Furlane (Friulian), Stella Alpina (Piedmontese) societies were formed, even when the Lucchese walked out of the Circolo Colombo because it was dominated by Modugnese, the men involved were not betraying *Italianità* or

demonstrating the debilitating effects of *campanilismo* and of factious-
ness—they were being who they were.

So even though we use Toronto's Little Italy as our frame, in some
sense we are describing neither Italians nor Toronto. We are talking
about immigrants with loyalties to specific places in Italy and to different segments of the Italian group in Canada. Each *paesano* network
inclined its members to a specific view of Toronto's possibilities, of
other Italians there, and of other ethnic groups in the city. A street
name, a factory location, evoked different images in different Italian
villages.

The fate of separate *paese* chains in Little Italy's later history is
analogous to that of a stream that goes underground. That seems a
sufficient paraphrase of the sociologist's "ethnic-ascriptive solidarities
criss-crossing the lonely differentiations of the urban non kinship Ge-
sellschaftn."[5] Sophisticated use of quantification—city directories, parish
records and fraternal membership cards—in coordination with the
collective memory are producing a complex of typologies within Little
Italy in which hometown networks run like veins—the choice of neighbourhood (on the block scale), of occupation, of solidarity, of mutual aid
society, of stores and businesses to patronize, of the timing of the
transition from a sojourner's to a settler's point of view—all show
telltale traces of paesanism. The number of fellow townsmen in Toronto
affected a man's ability to be an entrepreneur, his ascriptive status in
the community (his political potential), and one can only assume also
had impact on everything from his attitude toward Fascism to his pace
of acculturation.

The first role of this *colonia* as *paesano* collectivity (or *u paesanu*,
as Amy Bernardy has called the sub-ethnic labour broker), was to assure
that Toronto remained a profitable target of migration for the *paese*'s
people.[6] From the earliest music teachers and hurdy-gurdy men to the
banana peddlers and day labourers, the newcomers could only survive,
as sojourners or settlers, if their skill or willingness to work could be
matched quickly to a need of a Canadian employer or a Toronto
clientele.

Chain migration meshed with the fate of goods and services in the
modern city itself. The transition from the immigration of artists and
intellectuals to the immigration of artisans to the immigration of semi-
skilled workers simply followed the industrialization of the North American city—the development of factory-made goods and a mass consumption in which the immigrant was both producer and consumer. Italian
migration to Toronto reflected changes in the city as much as realities
in Italy, and the pre-selection of those who could survive in Toronto
was made by families and towns in the old country where Toronto's
potential as a target in terms of jobs and of friends and relatives was
fully understood.

In effect, as Toronto's Little Italy grew, its versatility as a migration target and its importance to certain towns in Italy also grew. It is
clear that newcomers, often the first generation as well, shared a
common mental landscape with those from their hometown wherever
they were. In 1906, about one-third of Toronto's Italians went back to

their hometowns for the winter.[7] Canadian authorities saw that as a slightly pathological sign of transience; think instead of the transactions —familial, economic, and of knowledge—that return from the *colonie* to the *paeselli* probably entailed.

Italian settlements in cities like Toronto grew for another reason. Toronto's Little Italy could be compared to a coastal enclave on a foreign shore. Most railway work gangs and most small Italian outposts in the mining or railroad towns of the Ontario hinterland fell back on Toronto or Montreal for protection against the hostile countryside. The Little Italy that grew up first around the train yards and the wholesale market and then in the Ward in downtown Toronto was the metropolis, along with Montreal, for small huddled *colonie* throughout the interior of the province.

If one sees Toronto's Little Italy in this light, questions about magnitude and permanence – transience arise. The government census and *Might's City Directory* help only a little; the migrant and non-propertied were always under-enumerated. That was inevitable since the census-taker thought of Toronto as a self-contained entity while the migrant worker treated it only as a base camp. Before 1911, the census was taken in April, after that in June, but many men had already left for the north or the Niagara peninsula by the first thaw. Consequently, the number of Italians in the city was underestimated; also, under-enumeration of navvies produced an impression of permanence and middle-class prosperity among the Italians that was only partially true. Men came and went, unrecorded by the larger society.

> As a rule, a good percentage of them are absent from the city during some months in the year. A number have been employed in the new bridge being built near Brockville, by the Ottawa and New York railroad; others have recently gone to work on the railways near Hull, Muskoka, and Niagara Falls, and a good many others have been employed on the Peterborough canal.[8]

This 1897 description of the Toronto Italian workforce affords a proper perspective on the city's role. The city was a place from which to sally forth, or to fall back on when unemployed and unable to return to Italy. It was the address to which relatives sent mail. It was the location of the importer of pasta and tomato paste; it was the location of the immigrant banker who transmitted savings to loved ones. In fact, it was where one was, even if one were in the bush several hundred miles away.

Although Toronto and Montreal served many thousands of Italian migrants yearly, the stable communities grew more slowly, and the statistics suggest that migrants still outnumbered permanent settlers. The 1911 census of Italian-born in Toronto counted more than 2,200 males to 800 women in Little Italy. The imbalance between males and females was probably even greater than that, and it suggests a world of boarding-houses, where *paesani* or others lived as boarders with established families.[9]

By tracking through city directories and assessment rolls, one can map the development of a settled Italian community in Toronto, a community that was varied and rich in its occupational structure. Seeing what happened is not, however, understanding how it happened. Who were the new class of shopkeepers and professionals who emerged after 1910? Were they all the offspring of that earliest middle-class immigration? Did young migrants begin as navvies, work as peddlers, and succeed as businessmen, or did a different type of immigrant come with sufficient capital to enter directly into the middle classes? The percentage of those who travelled to North America as steerage passengers would seem to suggest otherwise. In other words, we do not know the origins of the bourgeoisie in the first Little Italies.

The emergence of an Italian *ambiente* in Toronto's Ward depended on three circumstances.[10] First, in spite of facile use of the adjective "unskilled," most of the migrants who settled in the city did have a trade, if only at the apprentice level. They worked as navvies but they knew how to make shoes, tailor clothes, barber, and work as stonemasons. Italians in Toronto, like other small-town and village people, brought a number of precise skills to the city's economy. Here are some occupations the Italian peasant newcomers practised: cooper, grinder, cutter, mirror maker, corset-maker, bell hangers, carriage and coat makers, coal and wood dealers, banana peddlers, music teachers, tobacco and cigar retailers, boot-blacks and boot makers, figurine and model makers, chair canists, plasterers, weavers, confectioners, tailors, image makers, carters, blacksmiths, barbers, restaurateurs, hucksters, artists, artificial flower makers, butchers, gun makers, hairdressers, hat manufacturers, boardinghouse keepers, instrument makers, leather and oil dealers, importers of dye, and importers of fancy goods, liqueurs and wines, looking glass and picture framers. And oral testimony refines even further status and occupational variety. At one time the man who sold whirligigs and balloons at parades was the richest money-lender in the Ward; many occupations, from informal boardinghouse keeper to translator and document arranger, of course, never appeared in the records of the host society, although income from them served to launch successful real estate and insurance careers.

The second influence on the Italian character of the Ward was the seasonal nature of outdoor labour in Canada. The natural entrepreneurship of many migrants led to a constant probing of economic possibilities in the city during periods of unemployment. The heritage of chronic seasonal underemployment in rural Italy made it natural to accept a multiplicity of jobs as one's lot. Finally, and most important, the demand for unskilled labour almost imperceptibly passed from the countryside to the city. Not doubletracking the transcontinental railways through remote bush areas but rather digging sewers and laying street railway lines in Toronto became the chief source of work for navvies. After 1905—a great fire the year before had prompted much demolition and building work—more and more navvies became permanent residents of the city, and Toronto's Little Italy achieved the critical mass necessary to support and encourage a kaleidoscope of enterprises and occupations.

The new Italian immigrant workforce was intimately and complexly bound up with the city's growth. Immigrant labour, whether in the form of peddlers, sewer workers, or streetcar-track gangs enabled the middle classes of the city to live away from the commercial core of Toronto. It enabled them to live in a style that scant years before had been the preserve of only the wealthy. (It enabled them to live away from the undesirable newcomers as well.) The Sicilian banana men or the Calabrians and Abruzzians who created a sewer system where there had only been outhouses and cesspools were, through backbreaking labour, supplying amenities to the middle classes. Other Italians who found work in the needle trades in the Spadina area or who rolled cigars and cigarettes all day were also making middle-class life *gentile e civile*, while creating mass production and mass consumption without rapid industrialization.

The relationship of the Italian labourer to the city's economic boom sometimes appears downright providential, if not actually causative. For example, the technological shift, beginning in the 1900s, from wooden boardwalks and dirt roads to cement sidewalks and paved roads corresponds so closely to the arrival of Italians in the urban workforce that it defies coincidence. Italian navvies, through bitter experience in the Ontario North or on rocky farms in Italy, knew about excavating, grading, and shoring up ground. Large numbers of them, from a land where wood was too scarce to be a building material, had apprenticed as stonemasons. (Few were trained as carpenters.) After the great fire of 1904, Toronto emerged as a city of brick, cement and cobblestone, from its sewers to the large new hospitals in the Ward. It is almost inconceivable that the city could have been so transformed without Italian workers.

Beyond the enlarged payroll that the navvies, now an urban workforce, began to bring home to the Ward, the Italian community had several other major sources of income from the receiving society. Ironically, many of those minor trades that had languished in the restricted market of Italian agrotowns flourished in the no-man's land between consumer demand and the slow industrialization of Toronto. Barbers, cobblers, tailors, victuallers could depend on the middle-class desire for service and new luxuries to provide employment. In these trades, too, Canadian stereotyping—the idea that "this is what those people do and are good at"—seems to have aided these enterprises. So much so that entrepreneurship was sometimes more important than apprentice skills. One of the first successful Italian barbershops (ten chairs) on Toronto's main street was started by a man who had apprenticed as a shoemaker in Pisticci.

Nowhere did stereotype and talent interweave more than in the perishable foods trade. From the earliest days of settlement, there had been Italian fruit stores, and after 1900 the navvy-turned-fruit-peddler was ubiquitous. By 1912 at least half of the fruit stores in Toronto were Italian-owned. Contrast that with only about a hundred out of 1,500 grocery stores, and with less than 10 per cent of the barbershops in Italian hands. Syrians, Macedonians and Greeks provided sharp competition in shoeshine work, diners, and the sale of confectioneries.

Two points emerge. By 1905 the Italians in Toronto earned their primary income by performing their stereotyped roles. In other words, they did the jobs that Canadian society expected of them. On the other hand, that money—from navvies, peddlers, and so forth—was spent within the *ambiente* of the Ward on a myriad of goods and services that gave the lie to the stereotypes. A typical intersection of Little Italy might have a steamship agency that doubled as "immigrant banker" or post office, several boardinghouses or inns, a notary and interpreter. These enterprises obviously served as conduits for money, goods and people from Toronto to Italy and to the work sites in the interior. Bakeries and confectioneries, a shoemaker's shop and a newspaper office, along with many little stores selling Italian-style cheese, canned fish, vegetables, and pasta also lined the street. The Ward had few multi-storey buildings, and proprietors tended to live in back or over their shops. The presence of kosher poulterers and fish markets retarded Italian enterprise in those trades. Restaurants, a saloon, the headquarters of several mutual aid organizations were prominent as well. Barbershop steps and the fronts of clubs served as public squares in the evening. The Little Flower Methodist mission was in the heart of Little Italy, while the first Italian parish, Our Lady of Mt. Carmel, was on the fringes of the community.

While the locations of the first clusters of Italian immigrants near the train yards and then in the Ward behind the business district could be explained simply enough, the history of secondary Italian colonies in the city is more complex. Churches, the proximity of work, new public transit routes and cheap housing drew people to new areas, but so did accident and, of course, chain or family migration patterns within the city itself. First we must record the courage and enterprise of men who spoke little English and yet chose to live outside the Ward among their clientele. A high percentage of barbers, tailors, peddlers commuted back to the Ward every evening, but other men dared to move out.

As we have already seen, fruit vendors in particular resided in non-immigrant neighbourhoods. Many such merchants remained isolated. In a number of cases, however, their shops became the nuclei of new Italian residential areas. Men who began in the fruit business became grocers and provisioners. This often meant a change from a Canadian to an immigrant clientele. Sewer or street work near their stores turned them into subcontractors, steamship agents and boarding-house keepers as well. Remarkably, all this activity could go on from the same corner store and upstairs flats that had passed into the hands of a fruit merchant at the beginning of the century.

One sort of distribution that may have been as important as the fruit vendors was that promoted by the street railway development and by the construction of railway sheds in greater Toronto. Just as the railroads played a key role in the settlement of various ethnic groups across the continent, so the substations and junctions created little groups of foreign labourers and later of their dependants in various outlying parts of the city. Track maintenance in the severe winters further attenuated the pattern of settlement. In the city itself the street railway and the radial trolleys served to disperse the original Italian community. Track workers, motormen, and ultimately drivers who worked the long and often split twelve-hour shifts on the street railways found it logical to reside at different turns and junctions on the line.

New settlements patently represented geographical mobility, but it is not clear that any upward mobility was involved. Sample street studies of two of the new areas demonstrate no real difference of occupation or income from the Ward. The housing in the new areas was better than in the Ward, and initially there was less commercial life mixed in with residences. There is, however, some evidence that the new neighbourhoods relied more heavily on one or another *paesello's* network in attracting new settlers.

World War One marked the decline of the Ward as Toronto's main Little Italy. The exhilaration of sharing a partiotic and monarchist war effort with fellow Canadians and with compatriots in Europe gave way to difficult times and fatherless households. Some migrant males in the reserve never returned to Canada. The immigrant housing in the Ward, or the commercial and institutional frontiers of the expanding downtown, had long been a target for reformers and speculators, and the expansion of institutions like the Toronto General Hospital destroyed much of the type of housing that newcomers had depended on. Although many of the Italian communities' central institutions—the parish of Our Lady of Mt. Carmel, the two social clubs, Italian National Club and the Circolo Colombo—remained in the Ward, the younger population and the newcomers of the immediate postwar period were, by 1920, moving west to St. Agnes parish (around College and Grace streets) and to St. Clement's (St. Mary's of the Angels), the new Italian parish being built in the Dufferin area.

Toronto Italia, which had began as a patchwork of changing or multiple identities, networks and neighbourhoods, at once sub-ethnic and Italian, became a distinct Italian-Canadian entity during the years between the initial consolidation of the settlement before World War One and the total consular and Fascist effort to define the entity in the 1930s. Perhaps by mentioning some research strategies and by profiling some of the communities' institutions, we can recreate some of the ethnocultural *ambiente* of those years.

One could draw a picture of happy industrious immigrants and their childrens, playing *bocce*, organizing processions, and prospering. In the corner, a small, dark cloud threatens. Slowly and insidiously the settlement is corrupted and seized by the Italian consulate, the bourgeois *notabili*, lay and clerical, and the Fascio all'Estero. Anti-Fascist apologists draw such a portrait. In fact, the interwar Little Italies were complex and tension-filled societal entities; they were beset by contradictions in their own class structure, and by regional distrust—the dark side of sub-ethnic networks in the Depression. The Italian immigrants had been subjected to the structural violence of a culturally and bureaucratically homogeneous Ango-Celtic city. From British-born constables to Scottish health nurses to Irish priests, demons to turn one inward on the safety of the neighbourhood outnumbered multicultural "caretakers."

After 1921 immigration restrictions that seemed anti-Italian were also introduced. The growth of ethnic identity and the later sympathy for Fascism, where it did exist, sprang from the same sources—a combination of struggling against discrimination, wounded ethnic amour propre, and World War One patriotism. The amalgam showed itself in every aspect of the *ambiente*. Even the Church, dominated by unsympathetic Irish and German prelates, added to the pain.

The provincial superior of the Redemptorists had written at the turn of the century warning Toronto's archbishop that "we know that the spiritual betterment of these southern Italians is an almost impossible task."[11] Later, the Italian pastor of St. Clement's showed some of the scars that characterized the assaulted immigrant in the Little Italies and prepared the way for the Lateran Pact and Fascism to influence the community later. In his 1920 parish bulletin, he wrote:

> In the war, we have shown that we are not degenere te Latins as some wished to believe. In Peace we must also show our true colours in the matter of Religion. " ... Italians We will build our new church in this city and remove the blemish from the good name of Italians."[12]

John Diggins has characterized American Italians as being "ripe for Fascism" because of a "nascent inferiority complex, nostalgic nationalism, and a fear for family solidarity and community."[13] It should come as no surprise that each of those same feelings was also present among Toronto's Italians, and in Canada each had an immediate cutting edge. For example, the introduction of immigration quotas and restrictionism directed specifically at South Europeans in the 1920s led to "a nascent inferiority complex". The heroic memory of the "Treni degli Italiani" of 1915, which had carried Italian reservists and volunteers from across Canada back to Europe to participate in the war against the Hapsburgs, gave a precise Italian-Canadian content to the "nostalgic nationalism." And the statistics of exogamy and of conversion to Protestantism gave grounds for disquiet about the Italian immigrant family and its traditions. Perhaps the only weakness in Diggins' analysis is that it fails to mention how even before the Fascist formulas of "valorizzazione Italiani" emerged, those three feelings entwined to suggest either renewed *Italianità* or full acculturation as the only solution for the *colonia*.

By the 1920s, Toronto's Italians numbered somewhere between ten and fifteen thousand people concentrated in crowded neighbourhoods; the winter population, with sojourners filling the boardinghouses, was much higher than that of the summer when labourers dispersed to job sites in the North or along the Welland Canal. As late as 1940, over nine thousand people of Italian descent, about two-thirds of them in the city, resided in three wards. The centres of the three neighbourhoods were the three parishes, Our Lady of Mt. Carmel, St. Agnes (later St. Francis) and St. Clement's (later St. Mary of the Angels). In these neighbourhoods the Italian-Canadian residential and commercial density was such that a visible, if not always definable, *ambiente* existed. The steamship agencies, informal banks, newspaper offices, bookstores, restaurants and clubs of the community were there. (There were subtle differences among the three neighbourhoods that had less to do with class and prosperity and more with the degree to which the two newer parishes in the west had a slightly younger age pyramid, a higher ratio of first-generation Italians to immigrants and clearer patterns of sub-ethnic block settlement resulting from chain migration.)

Although other Italians lived and worked outside the Little Italies, these three neighbourhoods served as reference points. It was to the neighbourhood they came to replenish their ethnic food supply, see relatives, hear news of work or news from home, and find leisure and social activity. The neighbourhood was the portal back through *colonia* gossip or steamship agent to the hometown in Italy, and to its diaspora through the chief port of disembarkation, New York. Thus it is not at all strange that the *Guida per gl'italiani nel Canada* of 1929 listed the address of the Italian consul in New York first, of the American consul in Toronto second, and only then, that of the Italian consul in Toronto.[14]

The discussion of the social economy of the neighbourhood and of cultural/political activities which follows, skews the history of Italians in Canada somewhat. It reflects the world and world view of the articulate immigrants who used the ethnoculture as the medium of their business universe—from grocers and steamship agents ("Ai Connazionali raccomandiamo la loro cooperazione patrocinando le Ditta registrate in questa Guida perchè è chiaro che essi seno desiderose di fare affari cogli italiani"—"To our fellow Italians we recommend they patronize the businesses that advertise in this guide because it is obvious that they wish to serve the Italian community") to those who wrote the constitutions of the mutual aid societies urging members to preach and practical *fratellanza fra la colonia*, to the Fascist consular officials and their allies, the club and organization *notabili*, who wished through "energetic tutelage" to teach the community "to think and act italianamente." All of these leaders advocated an ethnic collectivity and community which was not a reality.[15]

This was true of the democratic anti-Fascists who reminded the local Fascio in the pages of *L'Emigrato* that the *colonia* had organized itself during World War One without "either Fascism or instructions from Rome but simply in response to its own conscience."[16] In other words, those whose records and remarks come to the historian from traditional sources leave a picture of Little Italy as a cultural and political entity ignoring the ragged edges of slippage (acculturation) or the underlying, and ofter controlling, role of sub-ethnic (regional) identity and network.

Permit me a note of caution here. This paper is not about Italian ethnicity in Toronto, but only about Little Italy. The census of 1941, as we have noted, shows at least one-third of the Italian population was not in the ethnically defined geographical cluster. By that time, over 80 per cent of Italians were naturalized Canadians; only British stock had a higher rate of intermarriage with other groups than the Italians did. And while 90 per cent of those over forty gave Italian as their mother tongue, the figure dropped in half for those under fifteen and only 2 per cent of the Italian-descent group spoke only Italian. So a Little Italy reflected not an Italian enclave but rather an ethnoculture in flux, and no study of the neighbourhood can ever yield up a truthful measure of the confused spectrum of loyalty—to *paese*, to Italy, to Italo-Canada, to English Canada—along which members of the group ranged.

The interwar *colonia* contained a variety of associations and organizations which influenced its attitudes. Periodically efforts were made to coordinate those associations into an umbrella organization, a *comitato intersociale* by the Italian consular officials, but such efforts rarely succeec. d. That lack of success had deeper causes than fractiousness or jealousy among leaders. If one looks at the officers of different organizations in the 1920s, one is immediately struck by the diversity and relative equality of the elite. Although the stereotype of Italian settlements usually contains *prominenti, notabili, grossi personaggi*, padroni who are seen as controlling sentiment and often business as well, Toronto Little Italies simply were not like that.[17] No Italian consul, no Franciscan or Salesian priest, no president of a benevolent society or head of a Friulan, Sicilian, Lucchese, or Basilicata *paese* club or clan group, no immigrant banker effectively dominated or controlled anyone but his own clientele. Even the notables who gravitated to the local Fascio had, in the late 1920s, little influence beyond it. It was rare for a man to be an officer of more than one organization and ascriptive status based on having many *paesani* or a good reputation clearly mattered more than business success or general political clout in being elected to organizational positions. Some men and families from Pisticci and Laurenzana clearly enjoyed great informal reputations. The president of the Societa di Mutuo Soccorso Italo-Canadese could stare down the stray Black Hander in the community with impunity, threaten to punch the Fascist consul, force the clergy to keep a youth athletic club from being infiltrated by the *Avanguardisti*, (a Fascist youth group), condone the publishing of an anti-Fascist newspaper from the society's offices and yet be willing to extend his influence beyond the early settlers from his *paese*.

A well-known doctor, one of only four of Italian descent, himself a veteran of the war and of the earliest Fascist street fighting in Italy, could not carry large numbers of patients into Fascism with him even though he appeared on the executive of the Fascio, the Ex-Combattants Association, and the Comitato Intersociale, and even though he was respected for his education and as a healer. Power was not transferable because, in a sense, despite the wishful thinking of the intelligentsia, there was no *colonia*. A list of the so-called *associazioni coloniali*—from the Giuseppe Garibaldi Orange Lodge (led by a Protestant Italian evangelist), through mutual aid societies, drama groups, lodges of the Sons of Italy, sodalities, *paese* clubs, to leisure clubs—reflects the remarkably diffuse activity and leadership in the colony.

Cross-referencing the lists of officers of associations with one another does not yield interlocking directorates or a single colonial elite. A published list of Italian businessmen and professionals in Toronto from the 1930s offers a chance to study the class base of the organizational leadership. It becomes clear that class or occupational status influenced organizational life far less than paesanism and ascriptive reputation did.

Even the contrived societies steered by the consulate and the Fascio *involved* volatile alliances of professionals and businessmen with local fanatics, veterans and *fascista di prima ora,* representing a local parallel to the Italian reality of the 1920s.

While all these opportunists insisted on the need for the *colonia* to be a single entity and viewed its inhabitants as compatriots or as a community of Italian families, the common people of the neighbourhoods had their habits of defensiveness about dialect-speaking, about humble origins, about the familialism and paesanism reinforced. They were made constantly to see themselves as failed Italians by their own intelligentsia.

In fact, they were simply who they were—immigrants and migrants in North America caught between their own startling mobility and their search for security, moving through socio-economic networks and cultural settings at once regional, Italian and Canadian.

For example, the bankruptcy files of Ontario contain proceedings that deal with two of the more devastating immigrant bank/steamship agent defaults in the city in the 1930s. From those records, the historian can build a detailed picture of a Little Italy entrepreneurial career in its relationship to family, *paese* group and the whole *colonia.* From the extant guides and almanacs of the community, one can find the number and variety of Italian professionals and businesses, and the memory culture provides information about their clientele and regional background. This sort of detail when compared with other Little Italies leads to very interesting historical differences.

The consolidation of the *colonia* into a single Italian-Canadian ethnicity never fully replaced the more natural local and familial values of the immigrants. It did however give the appearance of heightened Italian patriotism and of less factionalism. So it served as both cause and effect, and occasionally justification, for the interventionism that the Italian consular service was to practise. Lamenting the fractiousness of Little Italies—"a place of a thousand trifling, provincial, and local animosities" ... "an army without officers, commanded by corporals and sergeants"—had been a favourite pastime of the Italian consuls and upper-class visitors from Italy long before the Fascist rise to power. The slogan of the Fascists and their plan to provide the moral impetus, ("lo spirito propulsore") to the Italianizing of the Little Italies was merely the culmination of such thought.[18]

The Italian consular officials, immigrant bankers and colony intelligentsia had a virtual monopoly of contact with the homeland. When the former became agents of Fascism, the impact on the total community was inevitable. Probably a little over one-third of Toronto's Italian community were Italian-born, but most families had more precise ties with the homeland than nostalgia or a vague sense of kin. The continuous volume of flow of remittances is a better way of measuring that than pointing to the drying up of new immigration that came with restrictions in 1924.

So although Toronto had its own *fascista di prima ora,* who were veterans of the Italian war effort, and then immigrated, and although the *colonia* had certainly been prepared by the patriotic gore of World

War One and the Revisionist rhetoric of the postwar years for the coming of Fascism, when it came, it came as an intervention of the Italian government into the affairs of a Canadian ethnic group.

In return for "energetic tutelage," the protection promised "under the tricolore," North American Italians and their communities would, Mussolini hoped, be subject to a "penetrazione duraturo ed efficace" of Fascist values. They would be shaped into a powerful lobby that could put pressure on the American and Canadian governments in favour of the political interests of the Italian homeland. In fact, Bastianini, the head of the Fascio all'Estero, compared the political clout of a "few million Irish Americans" and the Jugoslav committees in the United States during World War One to the political disorganization and impotence of "Little Italies". He saw in the new Fascio a means of creating "un anima sola" in the colonies, a means of overcoming that sense of Italy pervasive among the immigrants, as "una somma di ricordi tristi e lieti o un cumulo di rancori repressi." The new effort would lead to an increased Italianization by every means in every field.[19] Italianizing of the *colonie*, of course, meant not just making the ethnic group prouder of itself and more consequential in North American politics, it also implied that with Fascist leadership, localisms and fractiousness which characterized Little Italies would be broken down and replaced with high (national) Italian politics and culture.

So through the consular service, Fascist Italy intended to "guide the lives, co-ordinate and encourage the activities, encourage initiation of our people in foreign lands." The immigrant would no longer be abandoned to his new proprietors; the regime hoped to keep him as much an Italian—with the rights and duties of the citizen—as it could. Between 1925 and 1940, the Italian consular service in Canada succeeded in some of its goals. Certainly they compounded the confusion of immigrants between the party and the homeland, and the bureaucracy; they also managed to leave the impression with the larger Anglo-Canadian society that most Italian-Canadians were involved with Fascism. Although that was not other than a respectable activity until after 1935, the later reaction to it cost the community dearly. For those who found themselves rounded up as dangerous subversives in 1940 simply because their names appeared on the guest list of the Casa d'Italia (consular offices as well), there was terrible irony in the metaphor of Mussolini's earliest speeches on the new "energetic tutelage." In 1923, the Duce had described the new cable being laid to the Americas as "un braccio gigantesco che la patria distende sui suoi figli lontani per attrarli a se e per renderli sempre più partecipi dei sui dolori delle sue gioie, del suo lavoro, della sua grandezza e della sua gloria"—("a giant arm which the nation extends to its sons far away in order to attract them to itself and to let them share in its sorrows, joys, its work, its greatness and its glory.")[20] Contact with the "giant arm" had given many Canadians of Italian descent a real taste of the old country's sorrows.

However, as late as 1934, those in the Italian community who protested against Fascist influence in Toronto were seen as a cranky leftist minority and those who supported Mussolini's regime were viewed, not incorrectly, as simply doing honour to their heritage. It was only when Great Britain herself turned against Mussolini, during the Ethiopian conflict, that the more powerful agencies of Anglo-Canadian public opinion began to attack foreign influence in Toronto. Until then Mussolini, the champion of the middle classes against Bolshevism, seemed to be winning respect and approval for Italy in the world. His solution to the problem of the "red flaggers" and later the Depression found support from part of the press in Canada, from many business-men, academics and veterans. Respectable Italian-Canadians, full of the patriotism of World War One, could, between 1922 and 1935, support Fascism with the full approval of their fellow Canadians. At last for the Anglo-Saxons, who, many Italians felt, had never understood the impor-tance of Dante or Verdi, there was an Italian and an Italy to obliterate the image of ragged street musicians and migrant track labourers. That Italian and his way of running a country was praised by everyone from the American ambassador to leading British politicians. In a debate at McGill, Knights of Columbus debaters had outpointed a visiting Oxford team which had tried to defend the proposition that Fascism was not good for Italy. A Canadian senator, not of Italian descent, had contrib-uted the money to paint Mussolini's picture on the apse of Madonna della Difesa parish in Montreal's Mile End. At the Central Neighbour-hood House in Toronto, long a centre of the Anglo-Celtic "caretakers" efforts to acculturate Italians, a little bit of Fascism was an accepted part of the Italian Ladies Club ritual.

> At tables gay with the national colours are served homemade macaroni, force-meat and salad, all the traditional dishes— the whole thing prepared by club members. Following the feast comes the dance when young and old join in the Tarantella—accompanied by the tambourine, and the eve-ning is brought to a close with the Fascisti "national an-them."[21]

So the singing of "Giovinezza" was as cute, as Italian, as normal to Anglo-Canadians as was the tarantella. Obviously there was no con-flict between admiration for Fascism and acceptance in Canadian so-ciety before 1935. That fact alone probably led many Italian-Canadians into closer contact with the regime than they might otherwise have deemed wise. And criticism of Fascism was turned aside by "respect-able" Anglo-Canadians who continued to see the critics as reds and malcontents or to see the problem as one of factions within Little Italy. For example, protest to the Separate School Board that children were being inculcated with Fascism in the Italian heritage (after hours) classes, was turned aside by the Italian priest the board consulted. He said that the protest came from a well-known CCF club member who, worse yet, was a member of the Giuseppe Garibaldi Orange Lodge. A leader of the local Fascio, defending the classes, wrote that they avoided "the teaching of any political doctrine or of any other subject other than religion, Italian languages, and elementary *notions* of Italian his-tory and geography."[22]

In general, the host society took the view, encouraged by the Fascist eidtor of *Il Bollettino*, the dominant paper in Toronto, that the enthusiasm for Fascism was a matter for the *colonia* not Canada to concern itself with, and that while some Toronto Italians "might admire fascism as it operates in Italy, they had no desire to impose such a doctrine on Canadians."[23] In effect this meant that the community was left to itself to resist the Fascist and consular initiatives.

The logic of serving as a moral impetus perhaps made the vice-consuls see their role more as vice-duce occasionally. It is certain that they, as much as many of the residents of the *colonia*, confused Fascism with their bureaucratic duties and confused the centralization of the daily liturgy of the community with the cause of Italian culture in Canada. A note from the consul in Montreal about the Italian press there (and much the same would have been said of *Il Bollettino* in Toronto) showed this conflation: "Both periodicals are Fascist—and serve the interests of Italy and of the Italian community, following with discipline the direction of this Consulate."[24] Organizing and controlling the *colonia* and using its *ambiente* in the interest of the regime and Rome seemed, then, a possibility by the early 1930s. The major institutions and the *prominente* were ready. What remained was some effort to reach out to the whole *colonia* to cement them to the regime and to confirm the absolute identification of government, Fascism and Italians abroad or more simply of the vice-consul and his colony.

The resistance to the consular/Fascist plan can be seen on two levels. On the one hand, there was organized ideological resistance from badly split leftist groups—socialist, communist, and anarchist. Toronto had its Matteotti club, an anti-Fascist Mazzini club (auxiliary to the CCF club). By the 1930s these groups, with some intervention and help from New York and international elements, had created three short-lived anti-Fascist newspapers in the city: *La Voce Operaia*, *Il Lavoratore*, and finally *La Voce Degli Italo-Canadesi*. Through front organizations like the League Against War and Fascism, they fought back against Fascist influence. This latter's greatest moment came in 1937, when they disrupted a Fascist rally in favour of Italy's intervention in Ethiopia at the Odd Fellows Hall on College Street. At the rally, one of the more articulate local Fascists, later interned, in his oration had said, one assumes by way of justifying Italian imperialism, that "Garibaldi did more to raise the negro to the level of the white man than any other man in the world's history."[25]

The organized international anti-Fascist resistance was loud and rowdy but ineffective. Much more admirable was the proud common-sensical, Italian-Canadian resistance to the consulate and to the more pompous Fascist notables. That resistance grew up around the social clubs and mutual aid societies like the Fratellanza and the Societa Italo-Canadese. Labour leaders like Lou Palermo and the societies generally resisted the various campaigns and devices of the consul and his allies. From the headquarters of the Societa Italo-Canadese appeared *L'Emigrato*, the single most effective and Toronto-based statement of anti-Fascism. *L'Emigrato* didn't lack grim humour, for when it heard that each lodge of the Fascio would be named after "quello di un morto per la causa fascista" ("one of those who have died for the Fascist cause"), it suggested the first one should be named Giacomo Matteotti. The paper insisted throughout on two simple points. First that one could be a 100 per cent Italian while not being a Fascist, and second, that "not aversion to Mussolini, not anti-fascism alone but simply the need for dignity and feeling for their land of adoption was turning the Italian colony against the Fascio and the consulate."[26]

Although overbearing, Fascist officials in Canada were generally neither fanatics nor fools. The Consul General in Ottawa, for example, continually warned Rome against becoming involved with either French-Canadian right wing manifestations or native anti-semitic and pro-Nazi groups such as the Anglo-Celtic Toronto Swastika Club, later called the Beaches Protection Association. He also hesitated to give a list of Fascio members to his German consular colleague, and often the consuls seemed to find the loyal notables on the one hand and the excombattants on the other a burden rather than a help in reaching the whole community. The better among them recognized and tolerated the umbertine and conservative quality of Italian-Canadian fascism; a quality expressed by Harry Corti, the aging editor of *La Tribuna*, who told a meeting of the Stella Alpina "that one mustn't forget that in Italy beside the government and the Duce, there is also the King and that is a good thing."[27]

From 1930 on, then, there was a natural Fascist logic to the idea of creating a viceregal palace for the consul in Toronto that would be the centre for the maintenance of the cultural and ethnic life of the community. Such a cultural centre would shelter all the organizations of the colony. In the short time allowed them between the consolidation of influence in the late 1920s and the reversal of Canadian opinion toward Fascism brought on by the Ethiopian War, the Fascio and the consul undertook a number of efforts to increase the community's *Italianità*. Some devices were inspired from Rome, and some reflected the real ethnic cultural needs of the *colonia*, either in the form of the *prominenti's* dream for status and hierarchy or the more demotic need for "fellow-feeling," a taste of high culture and ethnic pride. Through Dopolavoro, the Fascists organized sport activities and free trips to Italy for children to study the mother tongue. This program was often free of politics: and was truly popular with Italian-Canadians.

The year in which most of the effort to centralize ethnicity came to a head was 1934. In that year the campaigns for the creation of a Casa d'Italia in Toronto began. A simultaneous effort to have the Italian John Cabot recognized as official discoverer of Canada rather than Jacques Cartier, began as artifice, but inspired popular enthusiasm. The decision to create or build a Casa d'Italia was, of course, part of an effort that went on throughout Italian communities overseas, and a mark of the colonial mentality of the Toronto community then and of many of the students of it now is that they tend to see the issue as generated by local Toronto events and the machinations of vice-consuls and Fascists here.

When the decision to buy one of Toronto's more stately downtown properties, "Chudleigh," in the heart of the city at Dundas and Beverley, was made, it was a public assertion of the respectability of Fascism and the substance, taste and probity of the *colonia*. Even though the campaign to raise funds from Toronto Italians to buy the property included the usual rumours of corruption, fraud and personal gain. So despite the fact that the Casa d'Italia was to be the focus of the struggle between 1938 and 1941 and of the denouement of consular power and fascism in the *ambiente*, to understand it properly we need to assert that the colony and Anglo-Canadians found it an absolutely acceptable and patriotic idea in 1934. This description of the announcement of the plans for an Italian cultural centre from the *Globe* of 5 November, 1934 (Italian Armistice Day) shows all the themes of respectability and compatability between the loyal allies of World War One, the veterans of each nationality in between Fascism and Canada:

> The platform was a colourful spectacle, being decorated with the Union Jack and the Italian colours, in the midst of which were set pictures of King George V, King Victor Emanuele III and Mussolini. Interspersed among the chairs were numerous banners of various Italian organizations and as the Vice-Consul entered, the York Township Boys' Brass Band played the British National Anthem, and at various points during the speeches when II Duce's name was mentioned the audience rose and gave the Fascist salute while the band played "Giovinezza," the Fascist hymn. On the platform were Professor E. Goggio of the University of Toronto and Dr. P. Fontanella. All speeches were in Italian, and at the conclusion a march to the Cenotaph took place, where the Vice-Consul laid a wreath in honour of Italy's dead.[28]

It took several years for the Casa d'Italia at Beverley and Dundas to emerge. During that period *Il Bollettino*, the clergy, and most of the *prominenti* supported all of the moves of the consul even though the *colonia* itself was raising the money. As a Fascist editorial put it, "Intanto il Cav. Tiberi e soddisfatto lo sua dovere fazione e la migliore assicurazioni per noi" ("In the meantime Cavaliere Tiberi [the consul] is fulfilling his duties and that assures all is well"). The Casa d'Italia established at "Chudleigh" became the centre of government, Fascist and community activities. Italian-language classes, Dopolavoro, and many other community clubs and cultural groups met there. Government consular activities also went on there.

As Fascist foreign policy became aggression, Canadian public opinion, following that of Great Britain, grew hostile to Italy and to the overt political activity in the Toronto and Montreal Italian communities. At a time when Toronto's Italian women were sending their wedding rings to be melted down to pay for Italy's new imperialism, the Canadian press denounced Mussolini's aggression in Ethiopia. Between 1936 and 1940 Italians recognized the possibility of conflict between their primary loyalty to Canada and sympathy for the mother country and its politics. When Italy declared war against Great Britain and her allies, Italian-Canadians were confused and apprehensive. One old Italian, interned as a dangerous enemy alien at Petawawa, had to ask a fellow prisoner whether Italy had declared war on France or Germany.[29]

Non-Italians who had flirted with the varieties of Fascism over-
came their indiscretions by loyalty and sacrifice during the war. It was
not so easy for Toronto Italians. On 13 June, 1940 the Minister of Justice
announced to the House of Commons the government's policy toward
known Fascists and all those of "Italian racial origins who have become
naturalized British subjects since September 1, 1929." Mr. Lapointe
explained that "the very minute that news was received that Italy had
declared war on Great Britain and France I signed an order for the
internment of many hundreds of men whose names were on the list of
the RCMP as suspects. I cannot give the House the number; I have been
asked by the head of the Mounted Police not to do this because it might
hamper his work."[30]

One can imagine the terror and upset among the city's people of
Italian descent. The RCMP raids were directed only against potential fifth
columnists but they appeared inclusive and retrospective in their definition of Fascists. The rumour persisted in Toronto that the RCMP confiscated the guest book of the Casa d'Italia and rounded up everyone on it.
More frightening was the violence and vigilantism of the Toronto public.
It was reported in the House and in the press that at least sixteen Italian
storefronts in the city were vandalized when war broke out. Instances of
harassment and estrangement occurred with painful frequency in the
first days of the war. Then, too, while members of Parliament assured
the government that various German groups were loyal Canadian citizens, no Toronto voices there were raised on behalf of the Italians. Far
from it. The member from Broadview warned that "During the Spanish
trouble, Italian submarines found shelter on the southeast coast of that
country, and Italy has modern submarines that can cross the Atlantic
Ocean and return without refueling." Continued American neutrality
and the ties of kinship and commerce between Toronto and New York
Italians also troubled the legislators.

> This writer goes on to say that we must watch out when Italy
> enters the war, because of the number of foreigners in the
> United States, and the German-Italian-Russian spy propa-
> ganda. He also says that there are more coloured people in
> that country than there are in Africa and urges that some
> organization in the Dominions should cope with these ques-
> tions before it is too late.[31]

The member for York West congratulated the government on the absence of sabotage in his riding which was "an industrial constituency,
one in which we have a large number of foreigners." Thus the disloyalty
of the Italian population was thwarted and assumed at the same time.

The impact of internment on Toronto Italians is hard to assess. It
cannot be compared with the removal of the Japanese. No one's property was confiscated. More political and random than racial, the cost to
the community was nonetheless terrible. Men who one day held government contracts to produce war material, the next day found themselves
shipped to Camp Petawawa where they languished or wasted their
talent on road gangs. A Montreal Italian, Mario Duliani, has written a

moving account of the life at Petawawa, *La Ville Sans Femmes*. Fascists and Italian-Canadian leaders were interned at the camp, but the real hardship fell upon their dependants. Families were left with no livelihood during the difficult first months of the war. The Church and other organizations reacted carefully lest their efforts be interpreted as support for Fascist sympathizers.

The Fascist years and the difficult sifting out of loyalties and prejudice during the war years were the final writing on the palimpsest that Toronto's prewar Little Italies provided for the post-World War Two Italian settlements here. A new and vaster immigration of Italians began in the 1950s. In any single year in the decade of the 1950s, more Italian immigrants came to Toronto than the total of the city's prewar Italian-Canadian population. But the Italian-Canadians shaped the new neighbourhoods. Their locations in the city, the chains of migration that drew newcomers from certain *paesi*, and the leadership, all reflected the early settlers' influence and their own historical experience.

Notes

1. *Calendario per Gli Emigranti di Societa Umanitaria* (Milan, 1914).

2. Much of the reconstruction of historical detail about the early Italian community is drawn from the tape-recorded reminiscences of older immigrants to the city. An extensive bank of this oral testimony is held by the Multicultural History Society of Ontario.

3. On the Laurenzanesi, see the unpublished MA thesis by J. Zucchi, "Paesani in a Toronto Neighbourhood: Italian Immigrants in the Ward, 1870-1940" (The University of Toronto, 1979).

4. A. Fitzpatrick, *Handbook for New Canadians: A Reader* (Toronto, 1919), p. 49.

5. J.M. Cuddihy, *The Ordeal of Civility, Freud, Marx, Levi-Strauss and the Jewish Struggle with Modernity* (New York: Delta, 1976), p. 179.

6. A. Bernardy, *America Vissuta* (Turin, 1911), p. 323.

7. The *Globe and Mail* (Toronto), 21 December 1906, p. 10.

8. Robert F. Harney, "Chiaroscuro: Italians in Toronto, 1885-1915" in *Italian Americana* (Spring 1975).

9. Robert F. Harney, "Boarding and Belonging" in *Urban History Review* (Fall 1978).

10. Robert F. Harney, "Ambiente and Social Class in North American Little Italies" in *Canadian Review of Studies in Nationalism* (Fall 1974).

11. Correspondence of Archbishop McEvay, McEvay Papers, Toronto Diocesan Archives.

12. Parrochia di San Clemente, *Annuario 1920*.

13. John Diggins, *Mussolini and Fascism. The View from America* (Princeton, 1972), p. 80.

14. *Guida per gl'Italiani nel Canada 1929* (Toronto, 1929). Only a study of steamship passenger lists can show the true magnitude of the Italian flow through New York and Boston to Toronto.

15. Constitutions of Fratellanza and of the Societa Italo-Canadese mutual aid societies in the collection of the Multicultural History Society of Ontario. The Fascist consular view can be found in G. Bastianini, "I Fasci italiani all'estero," *Genarchia* LV: 10 (October 1925), p. 635.

16. *L'Emigrato* (Toronto) March 30, 1932, anno 11:5, p. 1. Copy in Multicultural History Society collection.

17. The following discussion of the *notabili* and Fascism depends upon extensive oral testimony as well as analysis of the leadership of the Italian community's organization as reported in various guides and the *Ente sociale* sections of *Il Bollettino Italo-Canadese* and other newspapers.

18. L. Villari, "L'Emigrazione italiana negli Stati Uniti," *Nuova Antologia* CXLIII, p. 298.

19. Bastianini, "I Fasci italiani all estero," p. 636.

20. *Opera Omnia di Benito Mussolini*, XXIII, p. 88; for the "braccio gigantesco" speech, see *Opera Omnia* XIX, p. 408.

21. Central Neighbourhood House, 1930, a pamphlet in the CNH collection of City of Toronto Archives.

22. Meeting of the Committee of Supervision, 5 May 1939, *Minutes*. Separate School Board of Toronto Archives.

23. Tommaso Mari quoted in *The Telegram*, "Italians Here Linked with Fascists." 21 October 1936, p. 7.

24. Archivio Storico Diplomatico of the Italian Ministero degli Affari Esteri in the Serie Affari Politici, 29 July 1936, Canada 3/4 telepresso #12905-283 (microfilm of these consular reports held by the Multicultural History Society of Ontario.) *Il Bollettino* of Toronto received a $60 a month subsidy.

25. The Public Archives of Canada and the Multicultural History Society of Ontario have microfilmed runs of *La Voce Operaia, Il Lavoratore*, and *La Voce degli Italo-Canadese*. An account of the meeting at the Odd Fellows Hall can be found in the *Toronto Star*, "Toronto Italians Fight in Streets Over War Issue," August 13, 1935.

26. *L'Emigrato* March 30, 1932 11: 5, pp. 3 and 1. Multicultural History Society of Ontario collection.

27. *La Favilla*, 1926.

28. The *Globe and Mail*, 20 September 1937.

29. M. Duliani, *La Ville Sans Femmes* (Montreal, 1945) p. 54.

30. Speeches of the Minister of Justice, 11 and 13 June, 1940, House of Commons (Canada) *Debates* (1940) 1: p. 637, 744-45.

31. *Manchester Guardian* article read into the parliamentary record by Tommy Church, M.P. for Broadview, House of Commons *Debates* (1940) 1: p. 717 and speech of A. R. Adamson, M.P. for York West, *Debates*, 13 June 1940, 1: p. 757.

The Italians of Montreal: From Sojourning to Settlement, 1900-1921

Bruno Ramirez and Michele Del Balzo

In the history of Italian immigration to Canada, the city of Montreal occupies a significant place. Because of its role as a leading North American centre and its position in the major rail, river and sea transportation networks, it was a necessary gateway for immigrants coming to exploit the work opportunities that Canada provided, and an important employment centre in its own right.

It was in Montreal that the first large concentration of Italians in Canada put down roots and gradually developed into a socio-economic and cultural entity deserving the name of "Little Italy." But from the time the Italian community was known to contemporaries as "the Italian colony" to the time in which their collective experiences and the related territorial physiognomy acquired the characteristics of a Little Italy there was a complex historical process—most of it still uncharted. Research in this area is still confronted with the essential task of locating essential archival sources, devising ways to gain access to them, and assembling basic statistical data.

Accepting these limitations, our aim here is necessarily a modest one.[1] Rather than choosing a period in which Montreal's Little Italy was already established, we have preferred to focus on what we consider to have been its formative period, during which the community underwent the transformation from a "colony" to a full-blown Little Italy. We shall examine that transformation in the light of the theme which to us has appeared to be its historical leitmotif —the transition from sojourning to settlement. This distinction between sojourning and settlement, between migrants and immigrants, reflects the experience of the great majority

MILE END - MONTREAL

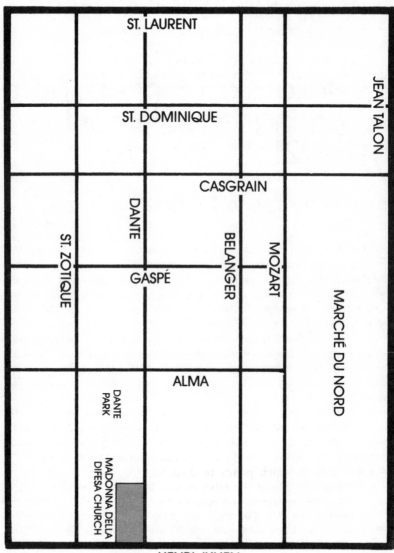

of Italians—those who passed through the city or lived in it intermittently, and those who remained and became permanent residents.[2]

The Italian community in Montreal included another group which would play a significant role in the affairs of the rapidly evolving community. Long-time residents in the city (some of them dating back many generations), by the nature of their activities had become a commercial bourgeoisie whose high degree of integration into the economy of Montreal gave them some degree of influence.[3] This group would play a crucial role as intermediaries in the commerce of migration, satisfying the demands of the Canadian economy for increasing numbers of unskilled workers and aiding the migrants in their search for employment.

Robert Harney has already described the elaborate mechanisms on which the commerce of migration rested and their function to translate the phenomenon of migration into a very important component of industrial growth.[4] What we want to stress here is the territorial dimension of the commerce of migration, the fact that an important part of this commerce consisted not only in physically moving thousands of workers from their *paesi* to the Quebec metropolis and on to their work destination, but also in servicing them while they stayed in the city. Providing food and shelter, keeping them ready and at hand for when the next request of labourers would arrive—such services could be provided in the city at low cost, and in proximity to the wider commercial infrastructures into which the commerce of migration was inserted.

At the peak of migration into Canada, when construction on the Canadian Pacific Railway called for an increasing supply of unskilled migrant labour, Italian employment agents in Montreal were placing several thousand workers every year.[5] Those who at the end of the work season did not remain in remote towns near their work sites, or did not return to their *paesi*, would spend the winter in downtown districts of Montreal, where boardinghouses, food suppliers, personal ties, and the possibility of some winter work provided the necessary incentive to wait for the following work season. According to the count made in February of 1905 by the priest of the parish serving the Italian colony, of a total Italian population of four thousand souls, half were "workers without family."[6]

It was this socio-economic cycle built into the commerce of migration which became reflected in a residential pattern marked at once by concentration and dispersion. While the members of the older Italian commercial class lived in areas spread throughout the city (denoting a residential pattern which points to their high degree of integration in the socio-economic life of the city), Italian labourers tended to congregate in areas offering cheap and easy access to the services they needed as migrant workers. St. Timothée and Ste. Agathe—two streets often referred to as the "quartier italien"—were within walking distance from the main commercial centre, where Italian employment agents, *banchieri*, travel agencies and ethnic food suppliers were mostly located. They were also part of downtown areas which showed the typical marks of urban decay, thus increasing the chances of finding low-cost dwellings and converting old commercial structures into cheap residences.

It is not easy to reconstruct in detail the precise location and degree of concentration of such a transient and mobile population, most of whose names only figure in steamship agencies' records or in employment agencies' registers. But if, as seems likely, the sojourners' residential pattern was characterized by low-cost lodging and proximity to the commercial centre, this would also explain why there was a significant degree of dispersion to areas where lodging satisfied these two basic conditions.

It may also explain the variety of lodging arrangements among sojourners, with cases of single-family boarding and extremes of up to one hundred people living in the same dwelling. Nicola Mosco, who in 1904 supplemented his earning by providing lodging to Italian migrant workers, when asked how many boarders he had, answered, "sometimes 30, 40, 60."[7] This may not represent the average capacity of boarding-houses, but it does suggest the flexible and transitory nature of sojourners' housing. Moreover, the fact that boarding charges (at least in this one case) were on a weekly basis ($2.50) may also indicate the temporary basis of the arrangements.

Overcrowding in the lodgings tended to be cyclical, coinciding with the mass arrivals of migrants in the city during the weeks and months just preceding the opening of the work season and the period following the end of the season. Such overcrowding, as well as the sanitary conditions of some of these dwellings, seems to have scandalized the local press and led the department of health to inspect some of the premises. In the case of one such dwelling on Roy Street, for instance, the reporter of *La Presse*, in an article entitled "Un foyer infect," described the men, women and children living there as "toute une colonie italienne [vivant] dans une malpropreté et une promiscuité dangereuses."[8] Even the house of refuge near Windsor Station, which had been set up under the direct auspices of the Italian consular authorities, and which housed temporarily several hundred Italian migrants, did not escape the inspection by city authorities, whose attention had been called by the complaints of neighbours who seemed to be troubled by such a concentration of Italians.[9]

What seemed to worry observers was not the overcrowding itself, but the fact that, coupled with prolonged idleness among sojourners, it tended to foster criminal behaviour. It was a worry difficult to dispel because incidents such as fights, knivings and duels were recurring items in the daily news; but the kind of coverage they were given made the sojourners more socially visible than they may have actually been in their gregarious isolation. In the case of one such incident, in which one Domenico Camino was killed during a fight among Italians, the reporter took pains to describe in detail the living quarters in which the crime had occurred, perhaps seeking to discover some association between the living conditions of Italian sojourners and their proclivity to criminal behaviour. The street where the crime had occurred, the reporter concluded, was a "ruelle infecte ou vivent des centaines d'Italiens de la classe miséreuse."[10]

It was easy for contemporary observers to view crime as a pathological manifestation of a cultural group unable to adapt to the mores and institutions of the host society. These judgments reveal a lack of understanding of the constraints that the life of sojourning imposed on Italian migrants, and were also reinforced by the creation of a cultural stereotype in the sensational coverages of *La Presse*. Italians were portrayed as being hot-tempered, uncivilized in their manners, quick to take the law into their own hands, with a proclivity for violence and the use of the knife. The description of incidents was often enriched with macabre details which probably made for very exciting reading. The suspense effect would even be increased when allegations were made that perhaps the Mafia was behind the criminal accident. Of course, the reporters may have not cared to notice that a good proportion of these incidents occurred either among Italians themselves or else were in response to discriminatory or offensive treatment the immigrants felt they had received at the hands of Canadians.

The fact is that if overcrowded living in downtown slum areas and prolonged idleness had become two inescapable features of sojourning, criminal behaviour seemed to be—at least for a sector of Montreal public opinion—its most visible social consequence.

It was an issue that also worried the members of the Italian social elite of Montreal, who may have seen in the propagation of that stereotype a threat to their own sense of social and cultural identity. There were at least two ways through which they could confront this problem. One was to try to stop the sojourning phenomenon, or at least to limit it, by controlling the sources of Italian immigration and by regulating the mechanisms of its commerce. Another one was to stress distinction in the civic qualities existing among Italians—distinctions along class lines (farmers versus peasants, skilled versus unskilled workers), or along regional lines (northerners versus southerners). According to one spokesman of this elite, the immigrants who had come "from the North of Italy ... from the Venitian province ... are good men. They are picked men, and any railway company would be glad to have these men, because they are strong and even good looking."[11]

Both ways were tried, but not without causing a series of conflicts between leaders and representatives of the Italian colony of Montreal, conflicts which, as we shall see, showed that the consequences of sojourning and its solution were much more complex than they might have appeared on the surface.

The most publicized of these conflicts was that mounting between some of the older and well-established community leaders and a new entrepreneur, Antonio Cordasco, who in the previous few years had moved from the obscure position of foreman to that of Montreal's largest employment agent. His rapid rise to power derived mainly from his position as the exclusive employment agent of Italian labour for the CPR at that time probably the largest employer of immigrant labour in Canada. Partly as a result of misleading advertising by some of the Montreal Italian employment agents, in the spring of 1904 the city was glutted with thousands of migrants who had answered the work call. Fears of unrest and of prolonged misery led to the setting up of a royal commission to investigate immigrant labour agencies' practices, and the public exposure that the inquiry gave to these practices brought this conflict to a head.[12] There are, in fact, two ways in which one can read the report and the evidence of the royal commission and evaluate its historical significance. One is to see it as an attempt to investigate and hopefully correct a business operation which by its magnitude and its susceptibility to exploitative practices justified the intervention of governmental authorities. On this level the commission's report and evidence provide important documentation on the intricate mechanism of the padrone phenomenon and of the crucial function it played in satisfying Canada's sectorial labour needs at the time.

The other way is to see the inquiry as a power struggle between two factions within the Italian *prominenti* of Montreal—factions which had progressively embarked on a collision course as the opportunities to profit from the commerce of migration increased and the social effects of the economy of sojourning became more and more explosive. On this level the royal commission presents a rare insight into the structure of notability which was shaping up during that important formative period of Montreal's Little Italy, and helps us understand the role of the *prominenti* (or at least their perception of it) as a mediating force between the wider process of migration and the more specific process of settlement in the city.

But there is another reason why this second aspect of the inquiry is being stressed here. When one considers how little public interest the inquiry generated, even in Montreal, how little direct consequence the commission's findings had on the practices it investigated, one may wonder if a royal commission would have been launched had it not been for the pressures brought about by the old Italian *notabili* and the Italian consular authorities in Montreal to undermine the rising power of Antonio Cordasco.

Unlike his rivals, Cordasco did not act through a civic association. He simply was at the head of a business mini-empire made possible by the exclusive hiring powers granted to him by Canadian Pacific, and sustained in the Italian community by a business network which included his army of foremen—small Italian entrepreneurs who, like him, fed on the economy of sojourning and maintained a network of contacts that extended to other North American Little Italies and all the way to Europe. His leadership status within the circle of Italian *notabili* may have been far from established, but on one occasion he had proved to be capable of mobilizing large crowds in his support, and even defying the claims of the established *notabili* to represent the Montreal Italian colony. The parade through downtown Montreal that took place in February of that year, followed by a much-publicized banquet and culminating with the crowning of Cordasco as "King of the Italian workers" was clearly a clever advertising operation aimed at his immediate constituency to assure them of his power and prestige just before the opening of the 1904 work season.[13] But the event must have also been perceived by the old *notabili* and the Italian consular authorities as a show of power, all the more defiant and arrogant as Cordasco used the Italian regal symbols to enhance his status with the "army of pick and shovel." That Cordasco was convinced he deserved a status commensurate to his economic power in Montreal is clear from a letter he wrote to one of his chief rivals, the Italian consul, Count Mazza. As Cordasco put it, Mazza and his Immigration Aid Society were "intrusi." Corasco himself was an English subject. Therefore he could say bluntly that the impoverished immigrants came to him and not to the Immigration Society.[14] Cordasco was convinced that it was his success with the immigrants that caused the Immigration Aid Society to make war on him on behalf of the Italian government.[5]

And war it was. The major tool deployed by his rivals against him was in fact the royal commission inquiry. There are many elements which seem to support this interpretation. First of all, let us see who were Cordasco's rivals, acting through the Immigration Aid Society, and examine the political and institutional resources they had at their disposal.

The honorary president of the Society was Count Mazza. The president was C. H. Catelli; son of a former Italian consul in Montreal, he had become the largest manufacturer of macaroni and was a member of the executive council of the Montreal Chamber of Commerce. The secretary-treasurer, Chevalier Casimiro Mariotti, had a large marble-importing business, and had previously been Italian consul in the city. The vice-president was Alberto Dini, one of the oldest employment agents and *banchieri* of the city. The Society's legal counsel was Jerome Internoscia, a successful lawyer who may have been the first Italian-Canadian to practise law in Montreal. Other prominent members-shareholders included the rector of the Italian colony, and the editor of what seemed to be at the time the leading Italian paper of Montreal, *La Patria Italiana*.[16] Clearly they represented the top stratum of the socio-economic hierarchy of the Italian community in the city. Moreover, not only could they claim the backing (moral and financial) of the Italian government, but also their Society had the prestige and recognition that similar charity organizations had in Montreal at the time. The Society had set up shortly before as a house of refuge to give food and shelter to needy Italian migrants and thus was able to get the cooperation of other charity organizations in alerting public opinion and the Montreal civic authorities to the impending crisis which the influx of large numbers of jobless migrants had provoked.[17] That they succeeded in doing so is shown by the dramatic letter that the mayor of Montreal wrote to Prime Minister Wilfrid Laurier shortly after meeting with the Society's officers:

> Persons in authority inform me that at the present time there are at least 1,200 [Italian] immigrants in the midst of our population, where of at least 600 are absolutely destitute, the other half having to depend on the kindness of friends and parents for their living . . . .
> A sentiment of fear pervades our citizens that these people who have been enticed to Montreal, may commit some excesses, because we have not sufficient employment at present to give them.[18]

A few weeks later the royal commission was set up under Judge Winchester to inquire into the circumstances that had brought so many

Italian immigrants into Montreal in the previous months, and to look into the alleged fraudulent practices of employment agencies.

It is debatable how much the pressures exerted by the *notabili* of the Society were responsible for the launching of the inquiry, but the special treatment that the Society's officers received at the hands of the commissioners cannot be disputed. First of all, the presence of Mr. Jerome Internoscia, the Society's legal counsel, among the commissioners created a sort of interlocking relationship between the commission's personnel and the Society's *notabili*. Even more important, many of the charges (in fact, the most important ones) which cost Cordasco many hours and days of interrogation and cross-examination on the witness stand could also have been laid at the door of the Society's vice-president, Alberto Dini. For instance, Dini, like his competitor, had placed an advertisement for ten thousand jobs in the Montreal paper *La Patria Italiana*, but he denied it by giving a ridiculous argument:

> QUESTION: This is an advertisement in La Patria Italiana; that is your name?
> ANSWER: I do not know who put it in.
> Q: See there is a similar advertisement put in by Mr. Cordasco?
> A: I cannot say; a man coming home, employed by La Patria Italiana say, you will see Cordasco wants about 10,000 men, and I told do what you like. I do not give number; the paper come [sic] out and I see the advertisement. . . .
> Q: How many Italians do you think you succeeded in bringing here?
> A: I did not bring any at all.
> Q: In the last ten years?
> A: I do not bring them, they come themselves.[19]

Dini also did business (importing of immigrant labour) with the notorious Societa Anonima La Svizzera of Chiasso, which operated in violation of Italian laws and whose director, a certain Mr. Ludwig, had been arrested and fined by the Italian government. And finally, when asked, Dini refused to give to the commission the names of the workers who had gotten employment through his agency, on the ground that he did not keep records (while admitting that he charged workers $1 inscription fee). On all these questions the commission did not pursue the argument, with the result that Dini was easily allowed to get off the hook.[20]

The inquiry succeeded in unravelling the intricate mechanisms of the commerce of migration and in throwing much light on the operations of the employment agencies. But it had also succeeded in putting much of the blame on Cordasco alone (and partly on the CPR) and in doing so it accomplished the objectives for which the Society's *notabili* had fought.[21]

It is not easy for the researcher to unravel the complex motivations which led to this important power struggle within the circle of Italian *prominenti*. What is clear from the evidence is that control over the commerce of migration was one of the leading factors. And this did not only involve the two leading competitors—Cordasco and Dini—but also the Society which in the past had offered to the CPR (without success) its services as supplier of Italian labourers in the attempt to bypass employment agencies.[22]

But it seems that there is another influence at work, more subtle to discern but in the long run perhaps more important historically for the understanding of the *notabili's* role in the formative period of Montreal's Italian community. And that is the claim to representativeness in the face of a fluctuating constituency. In this battle the use of symbols becomes a very important propaganda technique to mobilize support and to establish one's claim to leadership. The blow dealt Cordasco through the royal commission in his role of major competitor was not enough. He had to be dealt with also in his self-proclaimed capacity of "King" of the Italian labourers. This may explain the timing with which Count Mazza requested and got the King of Italy (the real one!) to bestow the honour of Knight of the Order of the Italian Crown on the two leading officers of the Immigration Aid Society—Catelli and Internoscia.[23]

It may also explain why during the same period a new Italian association was organized in Montreal whose founders stressed the importance of using uniforms and other patriotic symbols as a way of getting more attention in the community. Hence, it was decided to call the organization the "Military Society," and its signs and emblems had pictures of the King of Italy, King Edward VII of England, Columbus, and a high-ranking officer of the Bersaglieri Corp.

One cannot assert conclusively to what extent the decision to create this organization was prompted by the sacrilegious act of Cordasco's crowning, just a few months before. But judging from those and other similar incidents, one can suspect that the Italian community of Montreal was experiencing what one may call "a crisis of representation," and that this crisis was strictly related to the difficulty of melding the phenomenon of sojourning into a stable and permanent community.

Holding Cordasco at bay and undermining his prestige in the eyes of the community and of wider public opinion did not solve this crisis, for some basic questions still remained. What was the ultimate source of authority for a clique of *notabili* claiming to represent the community? Did it reside in their power as socio-economic actors in their immediate Montreal context, or did it ultimately reside in the chain of command which came down directly from the King of Italy?

This ambiguity, which seemed to be inherent in the very structure of notability at the time, came out into the open soon after the fight against Cordasco, prolonging and rendering more visible the crisis of representativeness. At the elections of the Immigration Aid Society in January 1905, Alberto Dini was elected president. But Count Mazza, in his capacity of honorary president, considered it in his power to disregard the decision of the members, and replaced Dini with Catelli, apparently on the basis of "instructions he had received from his government." The conflict precipitated by this act seems to have been the fiercest during this early period of the Montreal Italian community.

The issue was clearly fundamental, and thus it was fought both in the courts and in a series of highly animated public meetings. In one of these meetings, attended according to one report by about two thousand people, the insurgents led by Dini accused the consul and his allies of racist attitudes against Italian labourers, and sent a petition to the King of Italy and to the Italian Minister of External Affairs, thus hoping to bypass what they considered to be an illegal interference by the consul in the affairs of the community.[24]

This series of conflicts within the circle of Italian *prominenti* seems to have had the effect of eventually defining the place and the function of the *notabili* by making their claim to leadership more dependent on their ability to respond to the exigencies of a community in transition.

Lack of space does not permit us to discuss in detail the changes in the structure of notability and in the associational life in general produced in the course of the transition from sojourning to settlement. What we want to stress here it that the two predominant forms of mediation which had characterized the socio-economy of sojourning and which were reflected in the padrone system on the one hand, and in the Immigration Aid Society on the other, were undermined by the process of settlement.

The success of the padrone as an entrepreneur-*notabile* was closely tied to a particular industrial circumstance—strong sectorial demand of a particular type of unskilled labour power. During the period of boom in the demand of Italian unskilled labour he was able to meet the sojourners' search for a living wage and to exploit the migrant's ignorance of the language and of local conditions and institutions. But his role was a risky one, being highly vulnerable to changes in the labour market and in the immigrants' perception of their own situation.

Cordasco represents in its most extreme form this type of entrepreneur, who goes rapidly from success and prominence to a marginal position within the power hierarchy of the community. Besides the condemnation of the royal commission, he was constantly the object of harassment on the part of Italian workers who saw in him an exploiter, and thus had to undergo law suits and even threats of physical violence.[25] Finally he turned against his former employer, the CPR, accusing the company of having caused him more than $29,000 in damages, thus severing that relation which had been the key to his rapid success.[26]

Of course, the decline of *padronismo* does not mean necessarily that the men performing that function faded from the Montreal business scene. The commerce of immigration—just as much as the commerce of migration—provided ample opportunity to translate entrepreneurial skills into successful business activity. Steamship travel, the sending of remittances (and later, the selling of real estate) may have been forms of business that were interwoven with the padrone function. But these were legitimate business operations, and did not necessarily have to become subjected to the same stigma that had been attached to the employment-agency practices. Consequently, after undergoing a few years of crisis associated with his *padrone* activities, Cordasco was able to start again in banking and other related activities, and as late as 1920

La Presse refers to him as being "one of the better known Italian bankers" of Montreal. Similarly, Dini, despite his failure to take over the monopoly of the importation of Italian immigrant labour, was able to continue in his multifarious business activities "because he owns real estate and when he does not succeed in his different undertakings, sells some of his properties to continue his business."[27]

However, some of these activities, banking in particular, could quite easily become the object of fraudulent practices, and during the heyday of sojourning it afforded its practitioners good opportunities for quick profits. As late as November 1907 there were in Montreal five Italian bankers, each of them handling up to $25,000 a month in remittances, and the consular authorities were expressing serious apprehensions about their practices. But with the gradual transition from sojourning to settlement the operations of these bankers appear to have been subjected to more stringent control by governmental authorities.

At the same time, the immigrant's own sense of self-protection acted as a kind of community screen against the activities of these bank agencies. Perhaps a sojourner newly arrived in the city might not have known that years before an Italian banker had absconded with large sums of remittance money or that more recently another Italian banker with agencies in Fort William and Toronto had committed suicide leaving many Italians defrauded of more than $10,000.[28] But to Italian settlers who were gradually becoming part of a stable immigrant community such stories were common knowledge. Manzo, who arrived in Montreal in 1910, tells us that although he did not have to make regular remittances back home, when the time came to send $200 to his mother, he sent the money through a *paesano* in New Jersey because he did not trust the bankers of Montreal.[29] Similarly Monaco, who arrived a few years later and who had to send regular remittances to his wife in Abruzzi, did so through the bank office of the CPR at Windsor Station.[30]

When the first agency which also handled remittances appeared in the new Italian neighbourhood of Mile End, Italians did business with the owner because his reputation was not in question. He was not an agent of the economy of sojourning, dealing with transient persons who were at his mercy; rather, he belonged, like his customers, to the intricate socio-economic network of settlement emerging in that neighbourhood. He shopped in the same groceries as his neighbours, worshipped in the same church, and sent his children to the same school.

But if the former *padrone* had been able to convert some of his skills and resources, directing them in other lines of business, his intermediary role as merchant of Italian labour power was soon to become obsolete. The monopoly that he had held over the labour market of Italian *manovalanza*, and which for a while had made him the inevitable "narrow gate" for thousands of Italians seeking work in Canada, began to be undermined by the emerging networks of stable relationships in the community. Increasingly, newcomers were brought over by brothers, relatives or fiancés and were ensured a decent reception at their arrival. Their first step toward adjustment to the new world was greatly facilitated by the *ambiente* that their kin or *paesani* were recreating in some Montreal neighbourhood. When Monaco arrived in

Montreal soon after World War One he was not forced to live in overcrowded boardinghouses in the downtown "red light district" as had happened to his predecessors ten or twenty years before. Perhaps this is what had happened to his two brothers. Now they could act as hosts for him, procuring him a job (even if a temporary one) and lodging in their home.[31]

Similarly, the process of job-hunting was becoming a communal affair. Information on available jobs was found "within the multitude of friends, and then once we began to speak the language one could go here and there in search for work."[32]

But besides the increasing ability of newcomers to find jobs for themselves the labour market itself was undergoing a significant change. During the decade preceding World War One, Montreal experienced enormous growth. The city limits were being constantly pushed outward, and new urban infrastructures were built to respond to the needs of a growing population. Paving of city roads, construction of canals and tunnels, extension of the city's sewer system and tramway network—not to mention the building construction that accompanied such a process of urban growth—had all generated a strong demand for *manovalanza*.

Most of the work was labour-intensive and seasonal, and called for an ample supply of unskilled labourers who were willing to accept the low pay and harsh conditions imposed on them. Moreover, it was not only the seasonal nature of the work that made it precarious; this type of occupation was also subject to the vagaries of the companies' hiring and firing practices. Labourers were hired on a daily basis, and only if they were productive and submissive could they hope to be rehired the following day. The work record of Italian interviewees who arrived in Montreal during the second decade of the century resembles an occupational itinerary criss-crossing through all kinds of labouring jobs.

To them this may have been "lavoro forzato" or "lavoro da schiavi," and in some cases they would revolt against the harsh managerial practices, or would simply quit and look for better jobs. Yet this work afforded definite advantages over that which they or their predecessors had done laying railroad tracks in some remote corner of the Canadian Northwest. Access to alternative job possibilities in the urban labour market and access to the *ambiente* emerging in several neighbourhoods of Montreal could make a world of difference. And it did.

The picture emerging in the midst of this process of socio-economic transition was therefore quite different from that prevailing during the heyday of sojourning. The transformation had not only put into crisis the padrone system; it had also rendered obsolete and inoperative the seemingly more sophisticated and grandiose design that had been put forward by the Immigration Aid Society's *notabili*.[33] Their project of transforming sojourners into colonists, or more precisely of replacing the evils of sojourning with a more noble process of colonization which would have scattered thousands of Italian immigrants in available farmlands across Canada, did not quite square with the immigrants' own sense of space, territory and their need for *ambiente*. The pattern of settlement which developed among Montreal Italian immigrants, particularly during the second decade of the century, shows a collective determination to combine the advantages provided by the access to an urban labour market with those resulting from the use of free cultivable land in the city's outskirts. Although one cannot easily reconstruct the complex set of motivations which led thousands of Italians to leave the downtown areas and establish their residence north of the city, the free, productive use of the countryside could become a very important factor of territorial attraction and residential choice. Italian women could find in the bush areas north of what later became the Montreal suburb of Jean Talon all kinds of *verdura* growing wild, ready to be put on the dinner table or to be salted and conserved for the winter months. And on Sundays, or during days of unemployment, Italian men could find in the bushes wild cherries or grapes which they could turn into wine and other alcoholic beverages. But undoubtedly the most important utilization of free land by Italians was the cultivation of a small plot attached to or within walking distance of their homes, which they could turn into a vegetable garden. At a time when the cost of fresh vegetables could be prohibitive for people with modest incomes, their gardens permitted the Italians to make a productive use of their leisure time by yielding at an insignificant cost food items which were basic to their culinary tastes and habits. Any study of the Italian community in Montreal must take into account the important role the availability and use of this free land played in the immigrants' economic and cultural adaptation to the new world.

Population Trends

One of the most important indications of the gradual shift from sojourning to settlement is the changing composition of the Montreal Italian population in terms of sex ratio, age structure and living arrangements. The trend shows clearly the gradual transition from a population characterized to a significant extent by single men, to one in which the family predominates and, more specifically, in which the living arrangements (including forms of boarding and *convivenza*) are centred on the nuclear or extended family.

One of the most important challenges for the historian of Italian migration and immigration is to reconstruct the movements of a population which would spend the work season in hundreds of work sites spread throughout Canada, and would spend the winter either in Montreal, or back in their *paese*, or in one of the dozen or so of Little Italies which were already in existence in North America.[34] We know that the census figures do not accurately reflect the fluidity of such population movements. However, by supplementing the available government population statistics for Montreal with other sources for the Italian population of that city, while much still remains in the realm of hypothesis, a more complete picture emerges which seems to point toward the interpretation being argued here. These additional sources are mainly the records compiled yearly by the parish priests serving the Italian population of Montreal and formally submitted to the city's archdiocese in the form of a *Rapport Pastoral*. Starting in 1904, one year before the first Italian parish, Madonna du Mont Carmel, was established, the records show the total Italian population served by the parish, and the number of families which are part of that population. Gradually, and often intermittently, the reports show additional population information, such as the number of "individues en dehors de leur famille" (persons unattached to a family), the number of baptisms and marriages performed and the attendance in the schools provided by the parishes.

One more word of caution concerning the accuracy of these data: there is no way to verify the degree of approximation contained in these figures, and the extent to which these figures could have been inflated or deflated by the reporting priests for reasons of internal ecclesiastical politics. Moreover, in comparing some of the figures for one year with those of another, one finds some apparent inconsistencies. With all these limitations, however, these records are an important guide to long-term trends in the composition of the Montreal Italian population.

For the first year for which the family/non-family breakdown is given (1905), the parish population seems to have been made up half (2,000 persons) of people who were members of the 400 recorded families, and the other half of "workers without family."[35] In the ensuing years, the total population figures and those of the number of families fluctuate somewhat, until 1909 when we have the same total population and number of families and the same family/non-family composition as in the year 1905. For the year 1911 the figures are incomplete. This was an important year in the evolution of the process from sojourning to settlement, as the community now had a new parish (Madonna della Difesa) in the new area of Italian settlement, Mile End. The figures coming from that parish's reports show how great the need for a new church was. But one has difficulties explaining the sudden jump in the number of Italian families between the years 1909 and 1911 (from 400 to 1,200). It is very unlikely that this jump in the figures is due to a reporting error, as in the ensuing years they would show a gradual increase. Nor is the jump due to a sudden rush to the nuptial altar by Italian residents of Montreal. The explanation, then, lies partly in the fact that by 1911 at least half of the Italian population resided outside the boundaries of the Mont Carmel parish, in areas which made it impractical to be attached to the downtown parish.

Although from the years 1912 to 1920 the figures are incomplete, the ones we do have show that the few years preceding 1911 represent a turning-point in the transition from sojourning to settlement. From 1913 on, the population served by the Madonna della Difesa parish stabilizes at around 8,000, and the number of families which were part of that population also stabilizes at around 1,200. The Mont Carmel population instead experiences a gradual decline, passing from an all-time high of 7,000 in 1911 to 4,000 in 1921.

But the trend is also reflected in the number of persons unattached to a family. In the case of the Madonna della Difesa parish, they fluctuate downward—from 2,000 in 1913 to 1,000 in 1921. The most dramatic decline, however, is reflected among the Mont Carmel population, as they go from an all-time high of 3,000 in 1913 to 250 in 1921.

According to these figures, then, by 1921 the picture emerging is that of a population of which the overwhelming majority belongs to a family, and a small minority (roughly 10 per cent) is outside the family relation. This trend toward settlement and family setting seems to find further confirmation from two other indicators: the sharp decline in the sex ratio (excess of men over women), which goes from 2.2 in 1911 to 1.5 in 1921;[36] and the progressive rise in family-building functions, such as marriages and baptisms. In 1911, the total number of marriages performed was 75, but by 1921 that figure had risen to 107. Similarly, 372 baptisms took place in 1911, compared to 598 a decade later.

Institutional Presence and Social Control

A theme closely related to that of the transformation in the structure of notability and of the institutional differentiation among Italians in Montreal is the place of social control and the nature of its mechanisms as they were generated within the community itself, during its transition from sojourning to settlement. The question is to know to what extent social control was, if not imposed, managed by community leaders and ethnic institutions, and to what extent it was a more diffused phenomenon, built into the very process of settlement itself.

The institution which was probably most directly related to this function was the church, and all the evidence seems to point toward a role that will throw more light on the transition from sojourning to settlement.

It is quite clear from their annual *Pastoral Reports* that the priests responsible for the spiritual health (and consequently for the social behaviour) of the Montreal Italian population had difficulties in exerting their influence over their flock. This, however, is truer of the first part of the period under study than of the second part, when the trend was more toward settlement. The difficulties may have had little to do with the abilities of the priest, and much more with the fluctuating and extremely mobile character of the population.

Even when the work of the downtown Italian mission was formalized through the establishment of the Mont Carmel parish, the results did not seem to change much. The reports from the parish register continually complain of the indifference of the parishioners, with such lapses as poor attendance at mass and confession, and even outright neglect of their duties as Catholic parents. Parents are frequently chided for the long delay in bringing their infants to be baptized—delays consisting often of more than nine months.

However, before one passes judgment on the religious mores of those Italian parishioners, one needs to have more detailed knowledge about their life in Montreal and the extent to which the services provided by the parish were adequate to meet their needs. We know, for instance, that the seating capacity of the Mont Carmel church was 240, and its standing capacity was 150;[37] which means that less than 400 people were enough to pack the place, and this for a parish population fluctuating between 4,000 and 7,000 persons. Similarly, another important service provided by the parish, that of primary education, seems to have been most inadequate. We do not know how many school-age children made up the parish population, but clearly an attendance record fluctuating between 95 and 154 (and a teaching staff of four) shows that only a small minority of children received any form of education from the church. As the reporting priest put it in a note on the 1904 *Pastoral Report*, "A large number [of children] frequent regularly the schools of the city and escape from my control."[38]

This evidence, therefore, seems to suggest that lack of proper church facilities, inadequate educational services and, increasingly, geographical distance from the church as the population continued spreading outward, are among the main factors accounting for the limited social control the Mont Carmel parish exerted over the Italian population.

The situation seems to be somewhat different with the establishment of the Madonna della Difesa parish in Mile End. Here the church building was larger and the church personnel more numerous, and the church was well integrated into the new territorial texture which was emerging among Italian settlers. That the church fulfilled a need among a large portion of the Italian population is shown by the great degree of community participation in its erection, and by the fact that the church became the most important public reference point for the Italians of that district.[39]

More contact with the parishioners' circumstances of life and greater visibility within the neighbourhood's daily *ambiente* were in themselves important elements enhancing the function of social control of that church. Even more important, however, was the greater centrality that education took on in the parish. Two years after its establishment the parish school already counted 243 pupils, and their number would increase progressively, reaching the 770 mark by 1921.[40] Of course, a greater student population only in part presupposes greater social control. One may assume, however, that the greater the need among Italian parents, the more dependent were they on the educational services provided by the parish and on the leadership role of the priests.

One area in which this leadership was exercised throws some important light on the process of transition from sojourning to settlement. In one of the first *Pastoral Reports* of the Madonna della Difesa parish, the priest added a note saying, "We demand that the schools may be supported independently from the Church, and consequently that we be helped more by the French School Commissions who receive tax-money from the Italians, or be helped otherwise."[41] Although we do not know to what extent this feeling was shared by Italian parents at the time, this may be one of the earliest examples pointing toward a new awareness that Italian settlers in Montreal were not merely immigrants, but also taxpayers, with all the implications that this might have had. And in fact it is in this area that one of the first cases of ethnic pressure politics occurred among Montreal Italians, on the occasion of the election of the St. Edouard School Commission in 1915. Under the direction of the Italian priest and other community leaders, Italian voters helped to get two candidates in office who had pledged to fight for the absorption of the parish school into the St. Edouard School Commission, and later into the Montreal Central School Commission. This strategy proved successful, and two years later the Italian school could benefit from municipal financial support.[42]

Despite these indications of the higher degree of social control exercised through the Mile End Italian parish, one may still wonder to what extent the ecclesiastical authorities were obtaining the desired results. First of all, the larger school enrolment was not enough to satisfy the educational needs of a community whose population was increasing rapidly. Confronted with the limited facilities of their parish and discouraged by the overcrowded conditions existing in the French Catholic schools of the neighbourhood, Italian parents were forced to set up alternative schooling arrangements wherever possible. The then priest of the Madonna della Difesa parish, as well as some of the interviewed informants, have described the numerous classes set up in basements and private halls, and the efforts made in the community to provide this essential service.[43] In the long run, this state of affairs would provide an important incentive for Italian parents to enrol their children in Protestant (anglophone) schools, and make them more receptive to the proselytizing efforts of the Italian Protestant missions. In one of his reports the priest commented on what seemed to have been, at least for that year, the two major problems among his parish population: that they "assist sometimes to Protestant functions," and their "blasphemous non-observance of the Sunday."[44]

The degree to which the proliferation of Italian organizations, particularly during the 1910s, entailed new forms of social control over the immigrant community is a subject which awaits detailed study. The available evidence, however, suggests that the mechanisms of social control which had a more lasting effect were the ones generated by the process of settlement itself. They were rooted in ethnicity (used as a cultural resource), and were interwoven in the immigrants' attempt to recreate a more stable *ambiente*. They were made tangible, in particular, by the function of the neighbourhood grocery and also by the new boarding arrangements and practices.

Between 1911 and 1916 the number of Italian groceries in the Mile End district more than doubled.[45] Their proliferation parallels the significant increase of the Italian population in this neighbourhood and reflects the potential of this type of entrepreneurial venture. For grocery was first and foremost a business and as such it was subjected to the laws of the market place, to the regulations of municipal authorities, and to the ability to fulfill the material and cultural needs of the clientele. If these conditions were met, then this sector of trade could provide the opportunity to leave wage labour and pursue a less dependent type of subsistence. But doing away with one form of dependence did not prevent the grocer from finding himself or herself at the centre of a new relationship of interdependence between the collective need to recreate an *ambiente* and the specific day-to-day needs of the clientele.

The grocery business did not entail large outlays of capital. Operating costs were at a minimum, and often the grocer could reduce his expenses by combining the grocery premises with his living quarters. Of all the Italian groceries which we located for the year 1916, almost half had living quarters on the premises—normally the grocery in the front and the living quarters in the back.[46] Obviously, this arrangement encouraged the cooperation of other members of the family and gave it the character of a family business.

What made the Italian neighbourhood grocery an important ethnic institution was not simply that it catered to Italian customers, but that the business transactions which went on daily or weekly had to rest on a relationship of trust. Most Italian customers were forced to buy on credit, and the grocer in turn was forced—whether he liked it or not—to sell on credit. The customer would present a small book in which the amount of each new purchase was entered and added to the balance outstanding. The account would be settled on pay day, and often the customer would bring his pay cheque, which the grocer himself would cash (thus saving his customer a trip to the bank).

But how could the grocer be sure that after supplying a customer with groceries for fifteen days, one month (or even a whole season), the latter would pay? The extension of credit did not rest on an abstract notion of trust. Before extending credit the tradesman had to be sure that the customer was reliable, and in turn the customer who needed credit had to convince the grocer that he was a trustworthy customer. Before these conditions could be met and become translated into a permanent and stable business relationship they had to go through the informal verdict of the community where the reputation of a customer was made or unmade. A customer branded in the community as "unreliable" would have to do a lot of convincing—coupled with a strong dose of good behaviour—before the advantages of credit-purchasing would be extended to him.

Although the assertion of a contemporary settler that groceries "erano per noi la salvezza" may be a bit exaggerated, it seems that they were one of the most important reference points for the nascent Italian neighbourhood.[47] Besides the function described above, groceries served also as points of *ritrovo*, and often after business hours friends and *paesani* would gather there and spend the evening playing cards over a barrel of beer. It is no surprise that when in August 1920 policemen sought to make a search in an Italian grocery which was suspected of selling alcoholic beverages without permission, they were confronted by a crowd of armed angry Italians who forced the officers to leave the premises and return the following day.[48]

Reputation, trust and good behaviour were also at the heart of another arrangement which contributed to the daily *ambiente* of the early Montreal Italian settlements. Boarding, too, was first and foremost a business; it was a necessity for both the family who provided this service and for the *bordante*. The practice was widespread in the city, particularly in the new areas of settlement characterized by single-family housing.

Potentially, any single-house unit which had enough room space to accommodate one or more persons lent itself to a boarding arrangement. For the family, the $3 a month it received from each *bordante* (the average rent for the period from 1912 to 1916) could be a significant addition to the household budget. Besides providing a roof, the other basic services provided in the boarding arrangement were cleaning and washing, and the preparation of meals.[49] If one considers that these services were qualitatively the same as those provided by the padrona to the other members of her own family, one realizes to what extent the practice of boarding became part of the family's basic function as a social unit, and the basis of the central economic role of women in the family.

Italian immigrant men who were participants in that phase of settlement in some of Montreal's neighbourhoods recollect with some pride that their women did not have to go to work outside the home. And in fact the evidence shows that Italian women's participation in the labour market was minimal. Yet it would be interesting to multiply the $3 a month by the number of *bordanti* in any given month or year in order to see what volume of business was generated by the boarding arrangement. One can speculate that the cumulative money value was considerable, so much so as to make the practice of boarding one of the major service industries in the economy of settlement, and certainly the major, if not the only, industry "employing" Italian immigrant woman labour.

The integration of the *bordante* into the daily life of the hosting family had, however, some other implications. It made boarding a sort of *convivenza,* and therefore subject to a set of unwritten rules of behaviour and of mutual obligations. Here is where the ethnic dimension played a very important role. When the *bordante* was not a relative, he had to be known to the hosting family, and this increased the chances that he would be a *paesano,* as the social network of *paesaneria* was the surest source of information about the candidate's character and reputation.

Discipline was a quality which the padrona strove to instil in the *bordante* to render her work easier and less troublesome; but it was also a quality denoting a sense of responsibility toward a relative or a *paesano* unfortunate enough to have to work and live away from home. This is why when a *bordante* was willing to assume the obligations that the boarding arrangement involved (and to put up with the occasional annoyances that it might have caused him), he could easily regard the hosting family as a sort of substitute family.

This atmosphere of mutual respect and obligations had the advantage of making the boarding arrangement a very important place in leisure time. If one looks for what later became typical *posti di ritrovo* of Italian immigrants (for example, *paesani* bars, billiard halls, taverns), one will not find much in this early period of settlement. It seems that the function of *ritrovo* and the leisure activities which went along with it were satisfied at the communal level in the boarding arrangement. It is there that friends would most frequently meet to spend the evening together, normally playing cards over a barrel of beer. That the "padrone di casa" did not object to the *bordanti's* friends indicates not only that he and his family participated in the leisure activities going on at his house, but also that this gave him the opportunity to make a little extra profit through the sale of the beer.

In this way, therefore, the re-creation of the *ambiente* and the process of settlement were two sides of the same coin, and demonstrate the extent to which kinship and *paesaneria* ties were at the base of socio-economic practices and made for a more stable community life, while at the same time functioning as mechanisms of social control.

By the end of the second decade of the twentieth century the transition from sojourning to settlement appears to have been completed, facilitated also by the abrupt interruption in the influx of Italians caused by the war. Although the process of settlement had produced a residential pattern of both dispersion and concentration, one district displayed the marks of a typical Little Italy. It is in the Mile End area, in fact, that the largest concentration of Italians was to be found, and it is there that the trend toward home ownership had become clearly visible. Residential clustering and stable housing arrangements also explain why the Mile End district was the centre of immigrant social life represented by such organizations as ethnic patriotic associations, mutual aid societies, sport clubs and religious groups. As such, the Montreal Little Italy served not only its immediate residents but also surrounding clusterings which increasingly would take on the aspect of satellite neighbourhoods.

Further study of the residential patterns, of the associational life, of the emerging structure of community services, and of the type of *ambiente* being recreated would most likely show the extent to which the Mile End district was assuming the role of Little Italy within the wider Italian Montreal population. It would also show how the Italian community—having left behind it the sojourning and immigration stages of its development—was intent on building its own fabric of ethnicity both as a cultural need and as an ongoing contribution to the development of Québécois society.

Notes

1. The production of this paper has been made possible by the kind assistance of several friends. We wish to thank them all and, in particular, Miriana Kaludjerovic, Michael Lonardo and Sylvie Taschereau.

2. We are indebted to R. F. Harney for this important distinction which he discusses in the following articles: "Men Without Women: Italian Migrants in Canada, 1885-1930," in *The Italian Immigrant Woman in North America,* ed. B. Caroli, R. F. Harney, L. Tomasi (Toronto, 1978); "Boarding and Belonging: Thoughts on Sojourner Institutions," *Urban History Review,* No. 2 (1978); "The Padrone System and Sojourners in the Canadian North, 1885-1920," unpublished paper, Toronto, 1978.

3. The only published source which discusses these early Italian Montreal residents is G. Vangelisti, *Gli Italiani in Canada* (Montreal, 1956).

4. R. F. Harney, "The Padrone and the Immigrant," *Canadian Review of American Studies,* 5, no. 2 (Fall 1974); Harney, "The Padrone System."

5. *Royal Commission Appointed to Inquire into the Immigration of Italian Labourers to Montreal and the Alleged Fraudulent Practices of Employment Agencies* (Ottawa, Department of Labour, 1905), henceforth cited as *Royal Commission, 1904*.

6. "Rapport Pastoral de l'Eglise du Mont Carmel, 1905," Archives de la Chancellerie de l'Archevêché de Montréal, file 350.102.

7. *Royal Commission, 1904*, p. 150.

8. *La Presse*, 3 March 1905.

9. Ibid., 17 May 1904.

10. Ibid., 18 April 1904.

11. *Royal Commission, 1904*, p. 150.

12. "Report of Commissioner," *Royal Commission, 1904*, pp. xi ff.

13. *Royal Commission, 1904*, p. 102.

14. Antonio Cordasco to Count Mazza, 15 December 1904, Public Archives of Canada, *Immigration Branch Papers* RG 33/99, 1903-1904, vol. 1.

15. Ibid.

16. *Bollettino della Societa di Patronato dell' Immigrazione Italiana nel Canada*, no. 1 (October 1903); and *Royal Commission, 1904*.

17. *Royal Commission, 1904*, p. 10.

18. Letter from H. Laporte, Mayor of Montreal, to Sir Wilfrid Laurier (31 May 1904); *Royal Commission, 1904*, p. 93.

19. *Royal Commission, 1904*, p. 2.

20. Ibid.

21. "Report of Commissioner," *Royal Commission, 1904*.

22. *Royal Commission, 1904*, p. 12.

23. *La Presse*, 25 August 1904.

24. Ibid., 9 July 1904, 30 January 1905, 13 February 1905.

25. Ibid., 3 September 1904, 21 November 1904, 20 May 1905, 20 October 1905.

26. Ibid., 20 July 1905.

27. Letter (strictly reserved) from J. Internoscia, Acting Consul General for Italy, to the Solicitor General of Canada (no name given), 22 November 1907, *Immigration Branch Papers*, RG 19, Vol. 3283, file 16299A.

28. Letter from J. Internoscia.

29. Taped interview, Department of History, University of Montreal.

30. Ibid.

31. Ibid.

32. Ibid.

33. *Bollettino della Societa di Patronato dell'Immigrazione Italiana nel Canada*, No. 2 (January 1904).

34. See especially Harney, "Men without Women."

35. These data and those in the ensuing paragraphs are taken from *Rapports Pastoraux de l'Eglise du Mont Carmel* (1905-1921) *et de l'Eglise Notre Dame de la Défense* (1911-1921), Archives de la Chancellerie de l'Archevêché de Montréal, file 350.102.

36. *Fifth Census of Canada, 1911* (Ottawa, 1913), II, 426; *Sixth Census of Canada, 1921* (Ottawa, 1925), II, 352.
37. "Rapport Pastoral de l'Eglise du Mont Carmel, 1906."
38. "Rapport Pastoral de la Desserte italienne de Montréal, 1904."
39. Vangelisti, *Gli Italiani*, pp. 172 ff.
40. "Rapport Pastoral de l'Eglise Notre Dame de la Défense, 1913, 1921."
41. "Rapport Pastoral de l'Eglise Notre Dame de la Défense, 1912."
42. Vangelisti, *Gli Italiani*, pp. 204-6.
43. Ibid., p. 206.
44. "Rapport Pastoral, Notre Dame de la Défense, 1915."
45. *Montreal City Directory* (Lovell), 1911 and 1916.
46. Ibid., 1916.
47. Taped interview, Department of History, University of Montreal.
48. *La Presse*, 23 August 1920.
49. The fact that in many boarding arrangements the *bordante* was responsible for buying his own food may show a certain degree of flexibility in accommodating the *bordante*'s culinary preferences; but it may also show the unwillingness of the padrona to bother shopping according to the *bordante*'s tastes.

Bibliography

Unpublished Sources

Immigration Branch Papers. Public Archives of Canada.

Rapports Pastoraux de l'Eglise du Mont Carmel (1905-1921) *et de l'Eglise Notre Dame de la Défense* (1911-1921). Archives de la Chancellerie de l'Archevêché de Montréal.

Valuation and Assessment Roll of Immovable Property. Montreal Municipal Archives.

Bayley, Charles M. "The Social Structure of the Italian and Ukrainian Immigrant Communities in Montreal, 1935-1937." MA thesis, Sociology, McGill University, 1939.

Gibbard, Harold A. "The Means and Modes of Living of European Immigrants in Montreal." MA thesis, Sociology, McGill University, 1934.

Taped Interviews

Mr. Costanzo D'Amico
Mrs. C. D'Amico
Mr. Nicola Manzo

Mr. Antonio Monaco
Mrs. Filomena Monaco
Mr. Angelo Pompeo
Mrs. A. Pompeo

The Italian Community of Philadelphia

Richard N. Juliani

"It is better to be a poor man in South Philadelphia than a rich man somewhere else."[1] In these words, a Sicilian-born resident of Philadelphia since about 1904, expressed his attitude toward life in the city and, perhaps, suggested the feelings of thousands of other Italians who came to its neighbourhoods. Even today, in many Italian-American families who still live in South Philadelphia, this attitude has been passed down to younger generations who retain a strong sense of pride in their ethnic heritage and identification with their neighbourhood. Indeed, it is inconceivable to many Italian-Americans why or how anyone could possibly live anywhere else. The persistence of these neighbourhoods, with their strong bonds of kinship and friendship, are an important chapter in the history of Philadelphia, as well as in the Italian experience in the United States.

In the case of Philadelphia, however, the development of Italian neighbourhoods as visible physical and social communities occurred through a long and changing process. This evolution consisted of a series of phases which varied over time in terms of three main dimensions: first, the demographic, social and economic characteristics of the Italian (and Italian-American) population of the local area; second, the internal social organization of the several Italian communities of Philadelphia; and third, the relationship of the Italian experience to the larger institutional conditions of the city, region and nation. In regard to the first of these dimensions, with the passage of time the Italian population in Philadelphia changed not only in size, but also in its regional origins, motives for emigration, permanence of intentions, age and sex composi-

Areas of Italian Settlement in Philadelphia

A. South Philadelphia
B. West Philadelphia
C. North Philadelphia
D. Frankford
E. Lower Germantown-Nicetown
F. Mayfair-Tacony
G. Germantown
H. Port Richmond
I. Southwest Philadelphia
J. Manayunk
K. Chestnut Hill

PHILADELPHIA

tion, family structure, and the distribution of occupational skills. In regard to the second dimension, it is necessary to describe the locations and nature of settlement for Italian immigrants in Philadelphia; the types of institutions, whether originating within the group, or within the larger American community, which were seeking to provide services and to organize the Italian population; the patterns of interaction among the different regional groups in their newer setting; and the character and significance of leadership within the Italian community. In regard to the third dimension, over the years the Italians in Philadelphia, as elsewhere in North America, adjusted themselves to fluctuations in housing conditions, working opportunities, income, the political climate, and the attitudes and ideologies of older American groups. When these dimensions are coordinated into an analytical framework, the resulting perspective produces a sequence of six distinctive stages of Italian-American experience in Philadelphia: 1) the pre-community period (1700-1850); 2) the pioneer period (1850-1870); 3) the padrone system period (1860-1910); 4) the *paesani* system period (1890-1920); 5) the transformation period (1920-1940); and 6) the stabilization and renewal period (1950-1970).

The Pre-Community Period

Before 1820, Philadelphia had been the largest city in the United States. As a centre of power and influence, as well as of commerce and industry, Philadelphia was probably the most important city of the Americas. As a port, it had been a favourite desination for much early immigration to North America. The earliest European settlers were the Dutch, who had come in 1623, and fought against later arrivals from Sweden and England. In 1682, William Penn arrived and founded Philadelphia, a carefully developed community which corresponded to what is, today, referred to as "Center City" by area residents. The original city was bounded on the south by South Street. Below this boundary was Southwark, the city's first suburb; Moyamensing District, to the west; and extending further south, to where the Schuylkill meets the Delaware River, Passyunk District. After the consolidation of 1854, these three districts would eventually be known as South Philadelphia and, although not the only area of Italian settlement, also the hub of the Italian community and synonymous with Little Italy.

Before the American Civil War, large numbers of immigrants had already settled in Philadelphia from Great Britain, particularly from Ireland, and from Germany. In the later part of the nineteenth century, Philadelphia, along with other parts of the country, saw a substantial shift in its foreign-born population, as large numbers of the "New Immigration," as the Dillingham Commission termed it, with origins in Southern and Eastern Europe, began arriving.

The Italians were not entirely newcomers to the city. Some were in Philadelphia before the Revolutionary War.[2] A few Italians were merely visitors, stopping to give concerts or lectures. By the early nineteenth century, however, some Italians had taken up residence, work and citizenship in Philadelphia. According to one early writer, Genoesi settled in the 1830s and 1840s around Sixth to Eighth streets and Lombard Street, but had learned English quickly and had intermarried with Americans.[3] However, these Italians of the pre-community period do not appear to have established any institutions of their own, to have had much impact upon the everyday character of life in the city, and seem, for the most part, to have been absorbed without trace into the core society.

The Pioneer Period

In the early 1850s, however, the Italian population of Philadelphia manifested the earliest signs of institutional development and of the emergence of an organized community. The first concrete evidence of an Italian community is the establishment of St. Mary Magdalen de Pazzi Church in December 1853, the first Italian national parish anywhere in the United States.[4] The church, the first of twenty-three Italian national parishes in the archdiocese of Philadelphia, was founded by St. John Neumann, himself an immigrant from Bohemia, and was located in the 700 block of Montrose Street, in the old Southwark District.

The 252 baptismal entries in the records of this church, from December 1853, to January 1866, show that this early colony consisted of a large number of entire families and originated mainly in a narrow slice of Liguria, in the vicinity of Genoa. When the names of specific places within the region are provided, the province of Chiavari appears 113 times. In 1852, the chargé of the Kingdom of Piedmont had declared in a dispatch to Count Cavour that: "Almost all the natives of Chiavari were organ grinders or beggars."[5] While the occupations of fathers were given in only sixty-two cases in the baptismal records of St. Mary Magdalen de Pazzi for these years, thirty-six of them were identified as musicians, music teachers or merchants. In addition to a possible preponderance in occupations which encourage migration, these Genoesi may have also been forced to depart Italy as refugees from the political turmoil of the period. Although the same family names, such as Cuneo, Raggio, Sbarbaro and Lagomarsino, as well as similar provincial origins, appear, at a later date, in the early records of the Italian colonies of Chicago and of northern California, these families provided the historical foundation for the Italian community which would eventually emerge in Philadelphia. In addition, the same families who had participated in the founding of St. Mary Magdalen de Pazzi were conspicuously associated with the establishment of the earliest enduring business ventures among the Italians. The Italian market, the centre of retail business for the community, originally located on Eighth Street, was first organized by Genoesi merchants.

The mass immigration of Italians to the United States was closely tied to the revolution in transportation which occurred in the second half of the nineteenth century when the steamship replaced the sailing ship as the principal carrier of overseas passengers. The Inman Line inaugurated steerage service for immigrants in the early 1850s with its Liverpool to Philadelphia run.[6] In twenty years, the steamship became the only kind of vessel transporting immigrants. But Philadelphia lagged seriously behind New York City in this change,[7] and never became a major port of entry for immigration originating in the Mediterranean countries. By the 1880s, when the great competition between German and British steamship companies began, departures from Naples, Genoa, Palermo, Fiume and Trieste were landing at New York, Boston and New Orleans. Cargo ships brought only a small number of Italians. Passenger ships did come from Liverpool, Antwerp, Danzig, Hamburg, Bremen and Christiana (Oslo) on a regular basis. From 1909, when Philadelphia was directly serviced by passenger ships from the Mediterranean, until 1925, only eighty-six steamers which had touched Italian ports arrived at the city.

The limited service to Philadelphia is misleading, however, if we are interested in the growth of the Italian community. During some years, a formidable number might arrive despite the relatively small number of ships. For example, the *Philadelphia Public Ledger* reported that 19,000 Italians had disembarked at the city in the fiscal year ending on June 30, 1914. Although many of these arrivals may have gone on elsewhere to their final destinations, personal testimony provided by Italian immigrants reveals that many individuals who had Philadelphia as their destination landed at the port of New York, even when direct service to Philadelphia was available.

In the last quarter of the nineteenth century, the Italian-born population in Philadelphia increased significantly. The 1870 census had reported only 516 Italian-born residents in Philadelphia. By 1880 this figure had more than tripled to 1,656. In another ten years it was 6,799; and at the end of the century it had reached 17,829. Just after 1900 the Italians displaced the Irish as the largest foreign-born group in the Philadelphia population, reaching 45,308 in the 1910 census and 63,723 by 1920. Of the latter figure, about 44,000, or nearly 70 per cent, lived in South Philadelphia.

The actual size of the Italian-American population, including the American-born, is more difficult to determine. In 1897 John Koren, in his influential study on immigrant banks and the padrone system, claimed that the Italian colony in Philadelphia had a population of over 20,000, exceeded only by New York City and by Brooklyn.[8] Writing of the need for another parish for Italians, in the same year a church historian declared the size of the Italian population to have been almost 50,000.[9] A special publication of the leading Italian newspaper in the city in 1907 reported 80,000 in Philadelphia and 20,000 more in the surrounding suburbs, noting also that many Italians, already naturalized or with some knowledge of English, pass themselves off as Americans.[10] The U.S. Census reported that first- and second-generation Italians in Philadelphia totalled 76,734 in 1910 and 136,793 in 1920.

The Italian population of the Philadelphia area was not contained in a single colony. The first enduring settlement, consisting of almost two hundred Italians, was formed by the middle of the nineteenth century, and ran north from Carpenter Street to Christian Street, and from Seventh to Ninth Street. By the end of the century, Italians had moved further north to Catherine, Fitzwater and Bainbridge streets, just below South Street. For some time, Ninth Street to the west and Washington Avenue to the south had been risky boundaries for the Italians to cross, because of the hostility of the Irish in adjacent neighbourhoods. When Our Lady of Good Counsel Church was established in 1897, an estimated 25,000 Italians were claimed to live west of Eighth Street.

By the early twentieth century, however, numerous other colonies had emerged throughout the area. The formation of new national parishes provides a crude indication of the location of these colonies. Between 1903 and 1917, fifteen new parishes for Italians were established within the city, in Manayunk, West Philadelphia, North Philadelphia, Frankford, South Philadelphia, Nicetown and Mayfair. Outside the city, new parishes were opened in Norristown, Bristol, Strafford, Chester, Conshohocken, Coatesville and Marcus Hook. In the 1920s, additional Italian parishes were founded in Germantown, Port Richmond and Southwest Philadelphia, within the city, and Bridgeport, outside. Ironically, after 1897, despite an enormous population increase, only two more national parishes had been established for the Italians for South Philadelphia, the final one being that of Southwest Philadelphia in 1932. The massive influx of Italians, however, was transforming many territorial churches such as St. Paul's on Christian Street and the Annunciation on Tenth Street near Dickinson into de facto Italian parishes, but with smaller numbers of Irish members within the same congregations. Even some territorial parishes, opened during this period, such as St. Rita's (1907) at Broad and Ellsworth, with mixed membership, were commonly regarded as Italian churches.

During the same time span, Italian colonies also began to appear in parts of New Jersey, just across the Delaware River. In the 1870s, Giovanni Francesco Secchi de Casali, a Protestant refugee from Piacenza who had founded the first Italian-language newspaper in New York City nearly thirty years earlier, began an experimental agricultural colony. In cooperation with Charles Landis, who provided the land, Secchi de Casali organized a program by which Italians could purchase land at very liberal terms. In 1873, northern Italians began settling the pine barrens near Vineland, New Jersey. Shortly afterwards, southern Italians, including Sicilians who had lived in Philadelphia, joined the colony. After some failures, these farmers began to exploit the sandy soil of the region by planting grapes, sweet potatoes, berries, peppers, corn and forage. By 1880, the original colony had grown to six thousand members and other Italian farmers had settled Hammonton and Landisville. In addition to the farm colonies, by the early twentieth century, relatively large and distinct Italian colonies had formed in the industrial centres of South Jersey, such as Camden and Trenton. The Italian neighbourhood of South Camden, concentrated on South Third and

Fourth streets, near Our Lady of Mount Carmel Church, was a small duplication of the South Philadelphia area from which it had overflowed.

The Padrone System Period

The study of the Italian experience in urban America inevitably focuses, at some point, on the alleged role of the padrone system. The Philadelphia case is no exception, but does have its own characteristics. Moreover, the particular operation of the padrone system in Philadelphia serves to explain the pattern of immigrant settlement throughout the area.

The origins of the padrone system are customarily traced to the U.S. Contract Labor Law of 1864. In Philadelphia, the earliest indications of padrone practices involve children. An 1873 *New York Herald* article vividly reported police raids on houses on Carpenter Street and the arrest of 159 persons involved in the enslavement of Italian children to work as mendicant musicians on the streets of Philadelphia and New York.[11] Two years later, an article in the *New York Times* described an Italian boy as a slave purchased through a Philadelphia newspaper advertisement to work as an acrobat.

The most authoritative examination of the padrone system, however, came in the 1897 *Bulletin of the Department of Labor* written by John Koren.[12] In his discussion of Philadelphia, Koren linked the padrone system to the twenty-five immigrant banks located in the vicinity of South Seventh Street. Koren concluded: "Here also the bosses have intrenched themselves, but do not appear to carry things in such a high-handed manner as in New York." In his explanation for the milder padrone system in Philadelphia, Koren offered several reasons: fewer immigrant ships arrived there; most Italians had lived somewhere else and were familiar with America before coming to Philadelphia; the Italian quarter consisted mainly of owner-occupied homes and only a few large tenements; and the politicians had many Italians naturalized and organized into clubs, thus opening employment opportunities beyond the control of the bosses. Yet Koren also described how the Italians had almost exclusive control over street-cleaning in Philadelphia which depended upon membership in the Societa Operaia di Mutuo Soccorso, an organization controlled by padroni. Koren claimed that the main activity of the Philadelphia padroni was the providing of labourers for the fruit farms of neighbouring states.

Some writers have claimed that the padrone system no longer served an important function as a mechanism for the importation of immigrant labourers by the end of the nineteenth century. Nelli, for example, argues that the padroni had merely to meet immigrants at ports to recruit them as labourers for the railroads, construction companies and city departments, and that federal investigations, including the Dillingham Commission in 1907, never conclusively demonstrated that the padroni had actually induced much immigration.[13] A 1908 publication, celebrating the 225th anniversary of the founding of Philadephia, contained advertisements for seven Italian business firms which combined an interesting variety of services, including banking, currency exchange, real estate, steamship tickets, building and contracting, and the furnishing of labourers.[14] While all of these agencies were important in the Italian community, two deserve special attention: the Baldi firm for showing the evolution of the padrone system; and the DiBerardino firm for revealing the system's persistence in a more traditional pattern, after it was supposed to have been extinct.

Charles C.A. Baldi, born at Castelnuovo Cilento in Salerno, first came to the United States in 1877 at the age of fifteen, and sold fruit in Philadelphia and Atlantic City.[15] After military service in Italy, Baldi returned to Philadelphia as a fruit merchant. In 1883, called by an undertaker to serve as an interpreter among Italian labourers for the Schuylkill Valley Railroad, Baldi, joined by his brothers, secured a mining contract. Shortly afterward, the Baldi brothers opened the first coal company among the Italians of Philadelphia. Charles Baldi soon gained financial success and even some acceptance in the business community of the city, marrying Louisa E. Sobernheimer, a German-American, the sister of a noted local attorney. Baldi became, unquestionably, the most successful and powerful Italian businessman in Philadelphia, but not without arousing the hostility of his rivals. Reflecting the factionalism, the author of an early study of the Italians in America states:

> In one of our large cities there is a man of great cleverness, an outstanding example of the common type, who has graduated through all the stages of cicerone, lemon-vendor, undertaker, coal-dealer, banker, real estate agent and proprietor of an Italian newspaper, *L'Opinione*. Among the Italians he has passed for a Roman Catholic; in the American residential district where he lives, he is a member of a Protestant church. He has been able to capitalize his reputation, without holding great office, as to be the colonial boss, so that no Italian considered that he could accomplish anything without recourse to his influence. Although evidently his first thought is for himself, he himself really believes that he is giving his life for his people. It may be said that another faction, enthusiastic over Americanism, is fighting his leadership with the definite slogan, and perhaps ideal, of disinterested community service.[16]

This factionalism and the struggle for leadership in the Italian community also appears in newspaper accounts of the period which report on the meetings of Baldi's critics and opponents.[17] If any Italian in Philadelphia ever was a padrone, Charles Baldi was the man. Before his career ended, he had owned the first Italian radio station in the city and was the first Italian named to the Board of Education. He provided immigrant labourers for mines, farms and construction companies. His own son admitted that Baldi promised jobs to arriving immigrants in return for their promises that, upon naturalization, they would vote for the city Republican machine of the Vare brothers. In addition, Baldi provided a wide range of commercial services to the Italian population of Philadelphia. His son, as well as many other Italian-Americans, remember Baldi as an honest businessman and community leader. Although we may call him a padrone because of the role he played in the community, there is no evidence that he himself ever stimulated immigration. At an early point in his career, he had clearly discovered that he could achieve his economic and political goals while operating within the law.

Relatively neglected by previous research on the Italians in Philadelphia, the DiBerardino story appears to have a rather different pattern than that of the Baldi family, one which may resemble the older padrone system and which may have had far greater influence on the actual origins of much of the local population.[18] Frank DiBerardino came from Torricella Peligna in the province of Chieti, and established the bank which bore his name in 1887, later incorporating also as the Columbus Title and Trust Company. In 1908 the Frank DiBerardino Company advertised itself simply as a steamship ticket agency with offices on Christian Street in South Philadelphia, but also in West Philadelphia, where a smaller Italian community had emerged, and in Pittsburgh. DiBerardino had, apparently, received a contract from the Pennsylvania Railroad Company to furnish labourers for the extension of the railway. An interview with his son in 1939 reveals that the elder DiBerardino publicized his need for labourers in his home region, hiring them on a commission basis for the railroad. The WPA report, based on such interviews, declares:

> Agents travelled through the countryside of Abruzzi encouraging and channelizing emigration to Philadelphia with promises of immediate employment. They came as couriers of good fortune. Villagers and country dwellers alike passed on the good tidings that in Philadelphia, some place in America, there were "paesans" who not only had good jobs to give, but who also lent emigrants assistance in obtaining passage across the ocean and in becoming settled among other "paesans" and friends in a strange country. The branch office of the Philadelphia contractors, located in strategic places throughout Abruzzi, became the direct link between the hintermost hamlet in Abruzzi and adjacent regions and the Italian colony in South Philadelphia.

In order to maintain an advantage in the recruiting of labourers, Frank DiBerardino provided passage money through his agents in Abruzzi without the usual burden of interest charges.

The interview with the younger DiBerardino also provides a candid glimpse at the firm's role after the immigrants' arrival in Philadelphia:

> The bank assumed all the responsibility of the necessary busi-

ness in transporting the Italians from these regions to this country, settling them before they began working for the railroad company, and caring for their earnings and connections with the old country. Agents of the banks, including Mr. Berardini [sic] himself, used to meet the ships laden with Italian laborers at the Paulsboro breakwater for the purpose of representing these people before the customs and immigration authorities. They were recognized by authorities as responsible and accredited representatives.

The interview goes on to describe the DiBerardino role as matchmaker whenever a shipload of Italian women arrived.

The DiBerardino firm provided other services such as the writing of letters back to Italy or the distribution of incoming mail. The arrival of such mail in Italy would, eventually, have far-reaching consequences. These letters became almost the common property of the entire town and the source of general celebration:

> In Abruzzi even the most rustic villager who had probably never ventured beyond the limits of his own town became so familiar with Philadelphia as to be able to mention its streets with a specious familiarity. ... The contents of the letters were irresistible invitations to emigrants immediately. Some labor contractors, realizing the effect of such letters upon emigration, contrived to gain the permission of their immigrant friends to write their letters for them, and in these letters they wrote every description calculated to hasten expatriation and thus to swell the resevoir [sic]of common laborers in America.

The success of the DiBerardino firm in these activities is evident in an attempt by WPA workers in 1940 to construct a profile of Italian immigration to Philadelphia, based upon 36,879 case cards provided by the DiBerardino family. Despite some limitations—the absence of cases before 1900, the single firm source of these cards, and the likelihood that many of these immigrants moved elsewhere—this survey provides some impression of those who arrived in Philadelphia through the efforts of the DiBerardino firm (see table on page 95).

Of these totals, nearly one-half were from Abruzzi. In fact, the 9,463 from the province of Chieti and the 7,153 from the province of Teramo, both within Abruzzi, exceeded the totals of any other region. These figures included almost 33,000 males, over 20,000 of whom were unmarried. These cards also listed destinations beyond Philadelphia, which included twenty different states in the United States, as well as Havana, Cuba, and the province of Ontario in Canada. Of peculiar interest, fifty-eight different locations in West Virginia alone are identified as destinations. Firms such as DiBerardino supplied Italian labourers to the railroads and to the mines and, in the process, also planted the foundations of new communities in the same area. From work camps

Italian Immigration to Philadelphia through
the Help of the DiBerardino Firm

Region	1900-19	1920-29	1930-40	Totals
Abruzzi	10,321	7,179	381	17,881
Campania	1,304	2,963	178	4,445
Sicily	2,274	2,510	180	3,964
Calabria	967	1,652	114	2,733
Molise	732	1,032	63	1,827
Marche	936	692	81	1,709
Puglia	517	837	45	1,399
Lazio	823	500	40	1,363
Tuscany	129	192	15	336
Veneto	72	226	8	306
Piedmont	81	211	14	306
Emilia	61	87	4	152
Liguria	17	98	11	126
Venezia-Giulia	5	84	15	104
Sardegna	76	88	5	169
Lombardia	23	33	3	59
Totals	17,338	18,384	1,157	36,879

along Mill Creek, ironically the same area where William Penn established his first settlements of Welsh Quakers, the Italians moved into
Belmont Hills, Narberth and Ardmore on the main line of Philadelphia
to work as gardeners and in home construction. In Pottsville, Reading
and Phoenixville, they would soon abandon the railroad to become private building contractors and small shopkeepers. Whether destined for
Philadelphia itself or further out, the success of the DiBerardino Company, and others like it, in recruiting Italians, proved ultimately to be
the decisive factor in destroying the dependence of immigrants upon
such agencies. With their growing concentrations in new communities,
the lives of Italian immigrants in urban America took new directions.
With the maturation of these communities, the social history of Italians
in urban America passed into a new stage.

The Paesani Period

The tendency of padroni firms to focus their recruiting efforts created
linkages between particular villages in Italy and specific destinations in
North America. In this manner, a railroad camp could provide the basis
in later years of an Italian community in some American town with a
large portion of its members from a common origin in Italy. Urban
neighbourhoods showed the same pattern, as migration chains served,
first, to bring new residents to a particular neighbourhood and, second,
to provide a demographic and cultural basis for a new community.

As was the case in other American cities, the Philadelphia area did not have one Little Italy, but rather a number of them. The largest, of course, was in South Philadelphia, but even that area was subdivided by *campanilismo* loyalties and *paesani* solidarities. In other sections of the city, as well as in suburban areas, other Little Italies had also emerged, but in most cases reflecting a principal migration chain.[19] Each case, moreover, represented a somewhat different configuration of social institutions, which provided a distinctive character to that community and reflected its degree of autonomy as well as its relationship to the economic and political structure of the larger surrounding community. For instance, on the fringe of the Philadelphia area, in towns such as Coatesville and West Chester, Italians found themselves in relatively self-contained communities, largely out of touch and away from the influence of South Philadelphia. On the other hand, the Italians in nearby Belmont Hills, just outside the city, sometimes unwelcome in other suburban areas, still depended upon frequent trips to South Philadelphia for food and other necessities.[20] Consequently, many individuals lived in satellite colonies and maintained some dependence upon the central colony in South Philadelphia which remained the material and symbolic hub of the Italian population.

The institutional network of South Philadelphia was the broadest and most complicated in social organization, but also was the most flexible and promising as a system of opportunities for individuals. Although various writers of the period emphasized the social pathologies of the area and the times,[21] Italian immigrants and their families found another side to life in South Philadelphia in the early decades of the twentieth century. The *paesani* system was the key mechanism in bringing Italian immigrants to Philadelphia, and now it would serve as the principal device in providing the information and assistance which would integrate them into the new community. New immigrants knew upon their arrival how to find their *paesani*, whether in the many small boardinghouses or in the larger establishments. The Abruzzesi, for example, knew that restaurants such as the Corona di Ferro provided rooms for newcomers from Chieti and Pescara, and that Palumbo's did the same for immigrants from all parts of Abruzzi. For only a few cents, the immigrant could find meals and lodging among his *paesani*.

The same *paesani* could also introduce the newcomer to the boss at the workplace, whether it be in the large yards of the Pennsylvania or the Reading Railroad companies or in the rapidly expanding industries of the city. The expansion of the city had created a great need for labourers and craftsmen in the construction of new homes, streets, bridges and subways. Many other immigrants found employment in the manufacture of clothing, hats and shoes or in the finishing of wood cabinets for the radio industry. Smaller numbers of Italians found jobs in cigar factories, theatre bands, milk companies, food importing, bakeries, banks, insurance firms, dairies, street-car manufacturing, grocery stores, and the government (particularly at the U.S. Quartermaster's military uniform factory). Many Italians opened their own shops in personal services such as barbering, tailoring and shoe repair, throughout the entire city.

Many immigrants were able to shift readily through different kinds of work opportunities. General labourers learned the skills of the building trades. Similarly, the detail labour of new processes could, in a few days, make men into tailors, who could also discover that they knew enough to work on hats or shoes, because all involved the cutting and stitching of materials. Moreover, much of this work could be brought home from the factory to be placed in the hands of women and children. The shopkeeper could use his son as a boot-black. These circumstances allowed many immigrants to move easily to other jobs as one industry contracted while another expanded. Many men held two or three jobs at the same time, earning their living while learning other, more promising trades. And if some industries slowed down in the summer, many families found work opportunities on the fruit and vegetable farms nearby in South Jersey.

Despite modest incomes, the pooling of family earnings enabled Italian families to move relatively quickly from renters to home owners in the very favourable housing market found in Philadelphia. As early as 1902, two-thirds of the homes in the Italian section of South Philadelphia were reported to be owned by Italians, who were already displacing the Irish and Jews who had preceded them in the area.[22] Italian families were also moving into newly built homes on land which had still been farms in the early twentieth century in the southern end of the area, near the U.S. Navy yard. New homes and the extensive remodelling of older homes gave Italian families a far higher standard of housing than they had left in Italy.

The *paesani* period was an era of great significance for the Italian population of Philadelphia. As Warner and Burke have shown, it was during the years of the late nineteenth and early twentieth centuries that the ethnic ghettos of Southern and Eastern Europeans emerged in the larger industrial cities of the northern United States.[23] In Philadelphia, with the shift away from the padrone system to *paesani* relationships as the principal mechanism for migration and for the integration of immigrants to the social structure of a new society, the Italian-American community began to develop a comprehensive institutional order. Within the Italian colony, a full range of institutions actively solicited this population. On the public level, industries, retail businesses, churches, public and parochial schools, foreign language newspapers, fraternal aid associations, labour unions, settlement houses, and political parties all pursued the Italians—for their energies and work, for their money, or for their support. On the more private level, the family was now again intact. The peculiar age and sex ratios of the earlier stages of immigration, which saw large numbers of young males pour into the country, had been replaced in the years just before the outbreak of World War One with an increasing volume of women and children.[24] The end result was the normalization of family and communal structure.

The Italians now formed a community which contained a stratification system, with its own hierarchy of economic opportunities, political power and social prestige. It was also a community which had now become, quite visible and of growing concern to the rest of the city.

When American capitalism recognized the value of Italian immigrant workers, organized labour soon afterward discovered the necessity of including them within its membership. Similarly, the Americanization movement increased its concern over the so-called "new immigration," and the Italians of Philadelphia became a principal target for the acculturation programs of the schools, settlements, churches, industries, and the Chamber of Commerce.[25] With these developments, the several Italian colonies were connected with the larger social order of Philadelphia, and a process of transformation began which would ultimately have great consequence for everyone.

The Transformation Period

The time span from the end of World War One to the end of World War Two was a period of fundamental transformation for the Italian community of Philadelphia. The passage of the national origins quota laws of the 1920s had virtually ended any further significant increase in the population through immigration. The rewards, amenities and constraints of life in Philadelphia had begun to encourage a commitment to permanent residence for many Italians who had once intended to return to their native land. Political parties, settlement houses, schools, labour unions and churches had all sought the attention and allegiance of the Italian, sometimes with the ostensible intention of transforming him into their own image of the model American, but at other times more to advance their own organizational interests. While deliberate efforts at acculturation by these agencies met with only limited success, other aspects of everyday life, such as job experiences, home ownership and children had subtly begun to transform the Italian into an American. In addition, a series of momentous external events, which included the Great Depression of the 1930s, World War Two, and the unprecedented prosperity of the years immediately after the war ultimately created common bonds among many Americans which fostered massive assimilation, at least among white Americans, and particularly within religious groupings.

The Italians of Philadelphia, during this period from the 1920s to the late 1940s, participated in a massive process of cultural and social integration. The shared misfortunes and miseries of the Depression shattered many traditional illusions among older Americans about their social differences with groups such as the Italians. At the same time, the Depression and the Recovery program of the Roosevelt administration forced everyone, including the most recent arrivals, to become intensely concerned about the economic and political life of the nation. The rise of Mussolini fragmented Philadelphia Italians into pro-Fascist and anti-Fascist camps, sometimes with violent expression of their differences.[26] With the outbreak of World War Two, the alignment of Italy with the Axis Powers had decisive consequences for the entire community. Many Italians knew immediately the choice which had to be made. For those

individuals who lagged a bit, the onus of carrying enemy alien identification cards encouraged a final choice of political allegiance and cultural identification with the United States. By the end of this painful
period, the population was no longer Italian, but emphatically Italian-
American.

The prosperity of the postwar years confirmed the wisdom of
these decisions, particularly as second- and third-generation Italian-
Americans began to benefit from rapidly expanding economic, political
and social opportunities. In earlier periods, a middle class had emerged
by the development of institutions intended mainly to meet the special
needs of the immigrant colony. Italian physicians, pharmacists, funeral
directors, bankers, journalists and retail businessmen had achieved success within the limited confines of Little Italy. But in the period after
World War Two, an increasing number of younger Italian-Americans,
who could no longer be satisfied within the institutional network of
Little Italy, took advantage of these emerging conditions and began to
depart from the original colony and its social world. The office on South
Broad Street was abandoned for one in Center City. The home in South
Philadelphia was replaced, as for so many other Americans during these
years, by one in the suburbs. Ethnic isolation and parochialism were
rejected by these Italian-Americans who now sought success and recog-
nitionin the mainstream of the larger society.

The geographical and social assimilation of Italian-Americans into
the middle-class suburbs of Philadelphia did not necessarily represent a
total break with the past. Suburban residents continued to interact with
relatives and friends in the old neighbourhoods, particularly on holidays
and other ceremonial occasions. Aged parents who refused to leave their
homes in the city had to be visited at regular intervals. In addition, the
suburban Italian-American maintained some dependence upon particular institutions of the ethnic community, such as the stores with specialized food items, the businessman from whom a better deal could be
obtained, the nationality church which might still remain the only
conceivable place at which to be married or to baptize a child, or the
funeral parlour which had served the family as far back as anyone could
remember. However, the inconvenience of travelling back to the city
was soon overcome by the establishment of similar services in suburban
areas. For instance, Italian food markets, bakeries and other businesses
began to appear outside the city. At the same time, the Italian-American suburbanite grew gradually more satisfied with the non-Italian
stores of the suburbs. In other words, the institutional bonds between
the suburban Italian-American population and its previous urban neighbourhood were being steadily eroded.

Another indication, however, that a complete and immediate
break with the old life had not occurred was to be found in the
population composition of many new suburbs. While some Italian-
Americans had found their way into older, more established, and heterogeneous suburban communities, many families had moved into newly
developed areas in Drexel Hill, Springfield and Broomall in Delaware
County, Pennsylvania, or on the fringes of the Greater Northeast
section of the city itself, or in Pennsauken and other South Jersey

locations. These communities often contained striking clusters of Italian-American families, frequently from the same neighbourhoods of the city. Ironically, history was repeating itself in two ways. First, a new type of migration chain had begun to structure the relocation of Italian-Americans from the old neighbourhoods of Philadelphia to the new neighbourhoods of the suburbs. As *paesani* had done for earlier generations in the immigrant colonies of the city, the location of friends and relatives, already in the suburbs, now guided these newcomers in their choices of housing and community. Second, similar to the function of the urban ghettos, the concentration of Italian-Americans in the suburban enclaves appears to have eased the transition to newer ways of life.

With the growing exodus of younger generations of Italian-American families to the suburbs and the apparent dismantling of many traditional institutions, it may have appeared that the days of the Italian colony of Philadelphia were coming to an end. Indeed, to some observers, the white ethnic ghetto of the American city may have seemed to be about to become a part of the past. However, that was not quite the case. During the past thirty years, many forces have altered the lives of Italian-Americans in Philadelphia, but for individuals and for the community as a whole, the process of social change has been marked by much variation and by a broad range of outcomes. The lifestyles of many Italian-American families have been so altered as to be no longer as much a reflection of ethnic heritage as of their socio-economic positions and of their local neighbourhood. Some families have fled the old neighbourhood and have sought to break all ties with their ethnic origins, preferring to live and to see themselves simply as "Americans," indistinguishable from their neighbours. Still other families occasionally express their ethnicity, perhaps with some timidity, and seek more "dignified" ways of allowing outsiders to identify them as Italian-Americans. Yet in spite of all such changes in lifestyle, they conspicuously and proudly reveal their Italian descent. Some families have occupied the same house for three generations, and still show no inclination to abandon the neighbourhood. Their breadwinners work on occupational levels and in industries not much different from those of their grandfathers.

Stabilization and Renewal

Despite the massive outward movement of upwardly mobile families, as well as major changes within the old neighbourhoods, the Italian-American community has evolved into its most recent and, perhaps, most complicated period. The present stage has been simultaneously marked by the extinction of some Italian-American neighbourhoods, by the transformation of others, and by the persistence, stabilization and renewal of yet others. For example, the colony of railroad workers and their families which once occupied much of Haines, Rittenhouse and Price streets in the Germantown section of the city has entirely disappeared. Similarly, the community near Cambria Street in North Philadelphia, once the third-largest Italian population in the city, mainly employed in textile and hosiery mills, has also vanished. In other neighbourhoods today, such as the Haverford Avenue area in West Philadelphia, second in population size only to South Philadelphia, or the vast section of southwest Philadelphia known as Eastwick, beset by the loss of industrial jobs and by racial tensions, the future appears uncertain.

Somewhat surprisingly, the most evident signs of neighborhood persistence may be found in South Philadelphia, the first area of Italian settlement and largest area of community development. This vast section of the city, at least speciously marked by Italianita, still appears to be one enormous Italian-American colony. Along South Broad Street or Passyunk Avenue or any other major artery, the evidence of a predominance of Italian-Americans is almost startling. Broad Street is nearly saturated with the shingles of Italian-American physicians and dentists. At points, almost every other building on Broad Street seems to house a funeral home with an Italian name. The large Philadelphia banking companies provide a "Sonsitaly" office or a "Banca D'Italia" office in the area. The names of now closed immigrant banks are carved in the stone facing of some buildings. Savings and loans associations bear the names "Marconi" and "Italian Merchants." Numerous restaurants have Italian family names or the names of historical Italian figures or geographical areas, and claim to specialize in regional cuisines. Products are advertised as "imported from Italy," or by words in Italian on storefront signs. The windows display specialized Italian food products such as pasta, cheeses, wines and meats. Indeed, the area is widely known as a marketplace for authentic Italian foods and related products. In the churches, sermons are still preached in Italian, and confessions can still be heard in Italian. In the neighbouhood parks, elderly men gather throughout the day, speaking dialects to each other, playing Italian card games such as *briscola* or *scopa,* and watching the constant matches of *bocce.*

The initial impression of a nearly exclusive Italian presence in South Philadelphia is deceiving. A more careful examination of the area reveals substantial numbers of other peoples. A dwindling pocket of Jewish settlement, once quite large and at least as old as the Italian area, lies to the south, as well as an Eastern European strip to the east, along the Delaware riverfront. A sprinkling of even older residents, mainly Germans and Irish, who long preceded the Italians in the area, remains throughout South Philadelphia. After World War Two, the Black population in South Philadelphia grew tremendously and now surrounds many white blocks. In recent years, periodic outbursts of interracial violence have occurred in the area. At present, the plan for low-cost housing in the Whitman Park section, urged by the United States Department of Housing and Urban Development, has galvanized white residents into angry opposition. On a calmer scale, the Italian Market on Ninth Street also reveals the ethnic and racial transition of the area, by the growing presence of Blacks, Hispanics and Southeast Asians among the shoppers and, more recently, even among the shopkeepers. Yet, east of Broad Street and south of Tasker Avenue, the area becomes more solidly Italian-American again.

The history of South Philadelphia, only partly sketched in this paper, shows the transformation of a large section of the city into an Italian-American community which, unlike other immigrant colonies that have long ago disappeared, still provides a desirable residential climate for many families. Not without its problems, the future of the area as an Italian-American community will depend upon many factors. The residents of South Philadelphia must deal with the challenges of racial integration; the constant possibility of downgrading through zoning changes; the deterioration of municipal services; and great increases in utility costs and property taxes. Partly balancing the departure of younger people from the area today, Italian-American couples are also creating new households in the old neighbourhoods. Furthermore, since 1968, a renewed flow of immigration from Italy has injected another source of demographic growth and cultural vitality to the area. In addition to the Blacks, however, another threat to the Italian-Americans has been the encroachment of middle-class professionals, pushing the boundaries of Society Hill further toward the south into sections which were once avoided by proper Philadelphians. This trend has already disrupted the old area of Eastern European settlement known as Queen Village, just adjacent to Italian sections. The proximity of South Philadelphia to economic and cultural institutions, as well as the current energy crisis, has made the area increasingly more attractive to all kinds of potential residents. Indeed, real estate values have reportedly taken large leaps upward in recent years. Despite the problems of recent years, many different kinds of people find rational, functional advantages, as well as a powerful mystique and pride, in the neighbourhoods of South Philadelphia. Much of the attraction is inextricably tied to what immigrant groups such as the Italians found and made of the area.

Conclusion

An ethnic community such as the Italian colony of South Philadelphia, for much of its history, represented a paradoxical combination of the worst conditions of urban America and a constellation of opportunities and dreams almost beyond the imagination of most immigrants. The social reformers, in their investigations of living conditions, provided detailed descriptions of poverty, squalor, exploitation, congestion, disease, misery and despair in the ethnic ghetto. Yet even these writers, at times, allow us a glimpse of another atmosphere in the Little Italy of South Philadelphia. They also described the rag shops and macaroni factories; the outdoor life of street bands, *bocce* and *mora*; the crowds of men and boys who attended the nightly marionette theatres; and the families who watched the vaudeville shows and films at Verdi Hall, on Christian Street. Yet the real value of such neighbourhoods may be beyond the comprehension of any external observer. As Yans-

McLaughlin has written about Buffalo, and it should certainly be true about other colonies:

> ... if the inner dynamics of this community are to be fully understood, looking at it through the prism of the immigrant's social understanding proves worth while. The informal relationships within the neighborhood and day-to-day personal contacts, not formed institutional connections, dominated immigrant life. Although differing from the larger urban community, Little Italy had a social symmetry of its own.[27]

To which we can add that we probably can no longer genuinely grasp the interior life of such communities without having actually experienced it. And, perhaps, we can also better understand that the nostalgia for this past, as it is expressed today by its former inhabitants, is not all a matter of "retrospective falsification."

Foot Notes

1. Interview with Charles Porretta. Philadelphia, August 15, 1968.
2. Howard R. Marraro, "Italo-Americans in Pennsylvania in the Eighteenth Century," *Pennsylvania History* (July 1940), pp. 1-8.
3. Sister Agnes M. Gertrude, "Italian Immigration into Philadelphia," *Records of the American Catholic Historical Society of Philadelphia* (1947), p. 137.
4. Richard N. Juliani, "Church Records as Social Data: The Italians of Philadelphia in the Nineteenth Century," *Records of the American Catholic Historical Society of Philadelphia* (March-June 1974), pp. 3-16. The discussion of parish history in this section is based mainly upon an examination of the baptismal records of St. Mary Magdalen de Pazzi.
5. Howard R. Marraro, "Italians in New York in the Eighteen Fifties," *New York History* (April-July 1949), p. 198. I am indebted to George Pozzetta for bringing this quotation to my attention.
6. Maldwyn Allen Jones, *American Immigration* (Chicago: University of Chicago Press, 1960), p. 184.
7. Juliani, "The Social Organization of Immigration: The Italians in Philadelphia (Ph.D. dissertation, University of Pennsylvania, 1971), p. 111. Information from various sources shows that by 1873, only 3.2 per cent of the total shipping entering New York consisted of sailing ships, while in the case of Philadelphia, as late as 1880, almost 87 per cent of the foreign vessels which entered the port were still sailing ships. Although by 1919, even in Philadelphia, the sailing ship was all but extinct, yet a higher proportion of such ships still entered that port than had entered New York harbour forty-six years earlier.
8. John Koren, "The Padrone System and Immigrant Banks," *Bulletin of the Department of Labor*, 9 (March 1897), p. 123.

9. Joseph L.J. Kirlin, *Catholicity in Philadelphia* (Philadelphia: John J. McVey, 1909), p. 504.

10. A. Frangini, "La Colonia," *Italiani in Filadelfia* (Philadelphia, 1907), p. 5.

11. "Italian Slave Children," *New York Herald* (September 16, 1873) in the *The Ordeal of Assimilation*, Stanley Feldstein and Lawrence Costello, eds. (Garden City, New York: Anchor Books, 1974) pp. 284-89; and "Italian Children Sold into Slavery," *New York Times* (November 18, 1875) in *Wop! A Documentary History of Anti-Italian Discrimination in the United States*, Salvatore J. LaGumina ed. (San Francisco: Straight Arrow Books, 1973), pp. 42-44.

12. Koren, "The Padrone System," pp. 113-129.

13. Humbert S. Nelli, "The Italian Padrone System in the United States," *Labor History*, v (Spring 1964), pp. 153-67.

14. *Philadelphia: Its Founding and Development, 1683 to 1908*. Official Historical Souvenir (Philadelphia: Joseph and Sefton, 1908), pp. 259-61ff.

15. A. Frangini, "La Colonia," pp. 14-21.

16. Phillip M. Rose, *The Italians in America* (New York: George H. Doran Company, 1922), p. 82.

17. "Italians at Meeting Repudiate Bossism," *Philadelphia Public Ledger* (October, 5, 1917), p. 3.

18. Works Progress Administration Ethnic Survey, 1938-1941, "Italians in Philadelphia." These materials are partly based upon interviews with Frank DiBerardino, Jr. This collection is presently held by the Bureau of Archives and History, Pennsylvania Historical and Museum Commission, Commonwealth of Pennsylvania, Harrisburg, Pennsylvania.

19. John S. MacDonald and Leatrice D. MacDonald, "Chain Migration, Ethnic Neighborhood Formation and Social Networks," *Milbank Memorial Fund Quarterly*, XLII (January 1964), pp. 82-91. The work of the MacDonalds is an excellent general examination of these processes.

20. Vincent DiLella, "Hill Family Life During Depression," *Main Line Times* (January 11, 1979), p. 21.

21. Emily Dinwiddie, *Housing Conditions in Philadelphia* (Philadelphia: Octavia Hill Association, 1904). The monograph by Dinwiddie is probably the most relevant example of this writing.

22. Robert F. Foerster, *The Italian Emigration of Our Times* (Cambridge, Mass.: Harvard University Press, 1924), p. 375.

23. Sam Bass Warner, Jr. and Colin B. Burke, "Cultural Change and the Ghetto," *Journal of Contemporary History* 4 (October 1969), pp. 173-88.

24. Walter F. Willcox, *International Migrations*, II (New York: National Bureau of Economic Research, Inc., 1929), pp. 112-13; and Juliani, "The Social Organization of Immigration . . . ," pp. 156-60.

25. *Americanization in Philadelphia* (Philadelphia: Philadelphia Chamber of Commerce, 1923).

26. Hugo V. Maiale, "The Italian Vote in Philadelphia between 1928 and 1946," (Ph.D. dissertation, University of Pennsylvania, 1950).

27. Virginia Yans-McLaughlin, *Family and Community: Italian Immigrants in Buffalo, 1880-1930* (Ithaca, New York: Cornell University Press, 1977), p. 130.

Observations on an Ethnic Community: Baltimore's Little Italy

J. Vincenza Scarpaci

On 30 March, 1874 an observer looking out into the Baltimore harbour counted forty-five vessels flying the Italian tricolor. Only New York and for a while New Orleans had such regular maritime and commercial relations with Italy. Ships mainly from Genoa and the Ligurian coast made lucrative runs in a triangular trade involving American grain, English coal, and Italian fancy goods and marble. Baltimore, with its rail connections to middle western grain, its reputation as a monumental city and its proximity to the nation's capital with its many building projects, lay at the centre of that trade. So it was natural that the city's first settlers reached Baltimore from the sea.[1]

Baltimore's early Italian population served the larger community. The formation of a residential cluster with identifiable characteristics occurred over time as Italian immigrants responded to job opportunities in an expanding city. The very nature of that colony was in turn affected by the environment, both human and physical, of Baltimore. The Italian colony grew up in a low-cost housing area near the harbour close to transportation facilities, and adjacent to the centre of municipal government and downtown business districts.

Compared with other Little Italies, Baltimore ranks as a minor settlement dwarfed by Philadelphia, New York and even, at times, New Orleans. Yet the city's Italians developed a viable community by selectively accommodating to the unique local situation. In this paper I want to outline the growth of Baltimore's Little Italy and point to its variation from the general pattern of Little Italies. The important features of

BALTIMORE

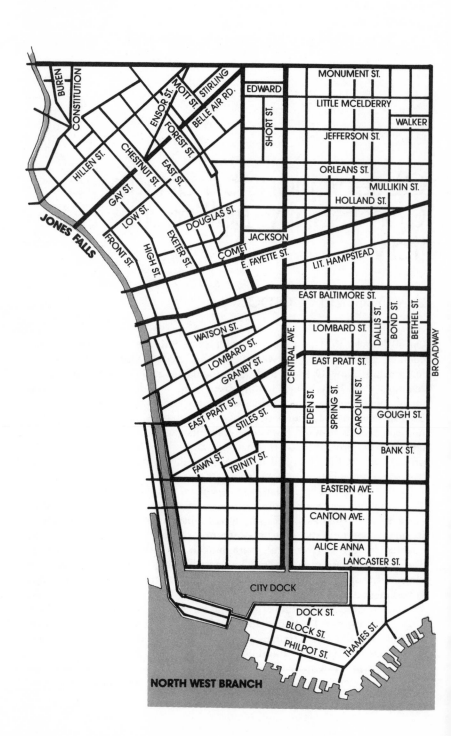

Baltimore's Italian community provide an interesting basis of comparison with other Little Italies. Taken together, these features would seem to make the community different from other Italian settlements on the eastern seaboard.

First you must picture Baltimore as the southern city it is. One might anticipate that competition from slave labour worked to repel immigrants in the Antebellum period. Yet we must also keep in mind the fact that Baltimore had the largest free black urban population in the country. Many blacks, like Frederick Douglas, learned marketable skills in that urban setting. Also we must keep in mind other important aspects of Baltimore's socioeconomic life. Throughout the nineteenth century Germans represented the largest immigrant group in the entire state. This German presence, as Kathleen Conzen tells us of Milwaukee, worked against the settlement of large numbers of Irish. German artisans, labourers, businessmen, dominated the city's economic and cultural life. During the nineteenth century every law passed in Annapolis had to be published in a German language daily, and the Baltimore city school system established free schools that instructed in German. Baltimore's direct sea connections with the North German ports established a transatlantic economy that shipped grain out to Europe and returned with passengers from Central Europe.[2] Later in the century these same transportation routes brought Poles, Czechs, Lithuanians and East European Jews directly into Baltimore, but the German artisan group created an almost impermeable phalanx against ambitious newcomers.

The presence of a German or Central European flavour to the city provided institutions that influenced all newcomers. Foremost were the building and loan associations founded by businessmen who pooled their resources to finance small loans for home purchases. When the Italians came they adopted this practice rather than the padrone bank systems used elsewhere. Another striking feature of the Italian experience in Baltimore perhaps also attributable to the German influence is the support and cooperation provided by the church hierarchy for the establishment of national parishes and the recognition of the importance of matching language and religion. Relations between the Italians and the archdiocese remained harmonious, and the life of Little Italy centred around its Italian national parish.

The occupational and entrepreneurial profile of the city's Italian population reflects the presence of a large German artisan group which dampened opportunities for the newcomers. Italians served as the railroad workers and construction workers for city projects—mainly sewage projects. Italians expanded and monopolized the city's wholesale and retail fruit business. While early Italian sculptors brought artistic interpretation to the city's monuments, later less skilled *scalpettini* provided the ornamental marble work on the public and commercial buildings of this Victorian city. Later Italian masons and bricklayers saved Baltimore from "smelling like 1,000 polecats" (Mencken's line describing the area around the Hollins Street market) as sewers were built throughout the city. Many of the residents of Little Italy commuted to jobs outside the area. Only as the Italian urban population expanded did Italians earn a living by serving their own co-nationals and the larger community with enterprise and artisan skills.

The political arena in Baltimore also faced the Italians with an atypical situation. Since Italians never constituted a large enough voting group, they depended upon the patronage support of a multi-ethnic party machine. Irish politicians inherited the Democratic machine from native American bosses in 1907. Instead of closing off participation to the Italians, the Irish groomed them as party members and then as candidates. Yet it was the 1920s eruption of internal Irish political warfare that catapulted Maryland's first elected Italian-born official from Little Italy to a federal office. Later in the 1930s factionalism rather than ethnicity permeated a primary contest between two Italians seeking the same office.[3]

In order to understand how and why these and other patterns developed, I will have to discuss the sources available to the historian of urban ethnic history, and the method of research and the type of source materials that should be used to explore the history of Baltimore's Little Italy.

Rather than follow the standard Maryland procedure of claiming English-born William Paca, a signer of the Declaration of Independence, as the founder of the Italian colony, I hope you will forgive a different kind of Mayflowerism as I describe some of the earliest contacts of Italians with Baltimore. It begins with the birth of the United States, a young country dedicated to an image of itself as unique and special, but at the same time still dependent on derivative literary and artistic modes from Europe, especially those linked to the traditions of the Roman Republic and its leaders.

In 1806 President Thomas Jefferson invited the Italian sculptors Giuseppe Franzoni and Giovanni Andrei to the United States to create the ornamental frieze on the House of Rrepresentatives chamber of the Capitol. Like most migrant workers, they looked around for extra work and found it in Baltimore, like the nation a young city determined to find its place in the sun. The sculptors did a large lunette of Ceres and Neptune for the tympanium of the Union Bank. (The piece is now on the garden wall of the Peale Museum in Baltimore.)

Shortly after, Baltimore's pretensions to elegance and city artwork lured the sculptors Enrico Causici and Antonio Capellano to the city. Causici sculpted the figure of George Washington atop the first monument erected to the Revolutionary War leader. Capellano produced the artistic rendition of Victory that crowns the Battle Monument—Baltimore's commemoration of the successful defence of Fort McHenry in 1812. An etching of the Battle Monument serves as the official seal of Baltimore city.[4]

Marble for the ornamentation of the nation's capital as well as for Baltimore's public buildings was imported from Carrara. Italian ships transported the stone to Baltimore, the nearest major sailing port which was linked in the 1840s by rail to Washington, D. C. In a 1836 painting by the Neapolitan-born artist, Nicolino Calyo, Baltimore's harbour seems a pleasant as well as vital feature of the growing city.[5]

Of course these early contacts fall far short of permanent settlement and local oral tradition maintains that gold rush adventurers from Italy and Italian seamen who got no further than the port area constituted the first wave of settlement.[6] These men arrived in a city that offered few attractions for sojourners. Baltimore's slave and free black labour force supplied many skills from shipbuilding to printing to less skilled jobs as stevedores and hucksters. In addition, the city's large German population covered the entire occupational span starting with the merchant princes who acquired fortunes from the grain trade which linked Baltimore and the old Hanseatic ports, to a whole range of German artisans listed in the city directories as barbers, butchers, shoemakers and brewers.

Yet by mid-century, Baltimore's thirst for the amenities of middle-class life and a desire to produce a grand architectural style attracted those Italians who could supply the fancy goods or skills and services now in demand. We can track the results through the census.

Joseph Passano was typical of this kind of immigrant. The 1860 census listed him as a broker in fancy goods and notions. He lived rather well in Ward Four—later the area of Baltimore's Little Italy. Both he and his wife were born in Italy; their oldest child, 31-year-old Mary, and her two younger sisters were born in Maryland. Over the years Passano accumulated $22,000 in real estate property and $6,000 in personal property. The entire family enjoyed the luxury of two live-in maids, Mary McCarthy and Mary Sullivan, who had emigrated from Ireland.

When Passano settled in Ward Four, it was home to many middle-class residents; some were Italian like a drygoods store owner from Tuscany who claimed $17,000 in personal property and an Italian-born fruit dealer married to an Irish-born woman. South of Ward Four, along the water's edge in Ward Two, there were residences containing Italians listed as musicians.[7] None of these people lived in this area in the 1870 census enumeration. A scattering of Italians lived in this region of the city during the 1870s and 1880s. To study the Italian settlement during its formative years, one must draw its perimeter broadly because there were natural boundaries and institutions that unified the area. So though certain blocks had heavy concentrations of East European Jews, they also had a significant Italian presence.

To map our Little Italy we begin at the water's edge near the wharfs that berthed the barges carrying products for rail connections and proceed northward about twenty blocks past St. Vincent de Paul Church to Orleans Street where the Belair produce market was located. On the west the Jones Falls, a stream that once ran through the city supplying power for canvas duck mills, served as a natural boundary. To the east Broadway marked the point at which Italian settlement and business is submerged in predominantly Irish, German, Polish and Czech population.

Any definition of a community or neighbourhood depends upon a variety of factors. Continuous settlement, unbroken stretches of population, or index of dissimilarity is not always the salient characteristic. I start with a holistic geographical definition of Little Italy because community life traversed the whole area. Italians worshipped at St. Vincent de Paul Church on Front and Fallsway until January 1881 when the first Italian national parish, St. Leo, was opened. The Belair produce market, where some Italians worked, created a northern boundary for this area. A sample of city directory listings shows Italians scattered and clustered throughout. In addition, the pastors of St. Leo considered the larger area part of their sphere of ecclesiastical ethnic influence.[8] They attempted to incorporate both areas in 1910 when they moved St. Leo's school to the site of the former St. Vincent's male orphange. In the final analysis it will remain the task of oral testimony to establish the validity of using this large definition. The psychic map on which people living close to each other with similar interests and occupations in this area can only be disclosed by those people. We might discover a change over time, that is, an early loose definition altered as Italian population density increased on either side of the East European Jewish corridor. We know that by World War One at least the Italians in the Belair market's fifth ward had their own political clubs and many attended St. Vincent's rather than St. Leo's.[9]

The historian's problem of neighbourhood reconstruction remains aggravated by inadequate source materials. Records of mutual benefit associations, business records, newspapers, disappear over time. Even a central institution such as the still-functioning church office does not contain any of the early parish census records. What has survived is a combination of primary sources from within the community plus the outside view from censuses, city directories, and official reports that lack the detail necessary to recreate a time or place. Only the memory culture of the community can bring order and interpretation to the fragmented, atrophied sources.

Let me list some of the available sources and describe their limitations. City directories often serve as a basic source for the reconstruction of neighbourhoods. However, the Baltimore directories until 1928 only list city residents alphabetically and not by street location. Separate listings of businesses do not include categories for day labourers, factory workers, or other kinds of occupations associated with newly arrived immigrants. One approach is to take a sampling of the names listed by location in the 1928 directory as a core group to trace backward over time in the earlier directories. This method might also establish a pattern of out-migration from Little Italy, since by 1928 other Italian colonies had developed, especially near the Lexington markets and in Highlandtown. Italian national parishes were created in these areas, St. John the Baptist in 1917, and Our Lady of Pompeii in 1922. Also, the Hanover Street market parish, Our Lady of Sorrows, was assigned an Italian-speaking priest about this time.[10]

Yet even a listing by street address provides only a surface description of an area's ethnicity. Italian names clustered on streets at certain addresses do not identify sub-ethnicities (regionalism) or specify whether people who came from different *paesi* lived in the same houses or on the same streets or if they intermarried.

Heads of household census, available as recently as 1900, offers another aid for neighbourhood reconstruction because it lists the name, age, place of birth and occupation of all persons in each household unit. Today we hear how the black and hispanic populations are undercounted in census enumeration. Imagine the problems of a white Anglo-Saxon Baltimorean enumerator trying to deal with a floating population little interested in or suspicious of being counted and of limited literacy in English or Italian. Anthony *Conney* is listed as a musician from Italy, John *Shalen* runs a boarding house, Raphel *Vannock* is a masterpainter moulder, Louis *Sanemintek* a fruit dealer. Obviously the enumerator attempted to render the names he heard. He often wrote them in illegible handwriting. Such variations of spelling create problems for linking one source with another.[11]

Church records listing marriages and baptisms should be a more accurate source. A preliminary glance at St. Leo's records from 1881 to 1905 uncovers some strengths and weaknesses. While the Turin-born pastor Father Andreis had little difficulty spelling names and providing either *paese, regione* or *provincia* origin, the forms he used did not include addresses or occupations. Again a sampling of these names traced to directories and census records ought to give some sense of settlement pattern and interrelation of *paese* or regional contact. (Once in a while Father Sullivan performed the ceremony and leaves us nothing but the names of the principals.)[12]

Baltimore had no Italian newspaper published until the 1920s, but issues of that paper, *Il Risorgimento,* are stored in the Pratt Library and can show the preoccupations of the community in that decade. An English-language newspaper, the *Italian Journal,* appeared for a short time in the early 1930s, but the Pratt has not been able to locate its holdings to date.

Many of the community's mutual benefit, religious and business associations and political organizations are no longer extant or claim to have retained no records. Fragments that surface provide a blurred view of the past. A 1915 time book of an Italian contractor, the record book of the Italian Methodist mission in Little Italy, the record book of the first treasurer of the Sons of Italy, give clues but may mislead.

Memory culture used properly can cease to be fragmentary and cement the pieces. Knowing from an interview that Pastore's first food supply store was the largest establishment on Lombard Street in the Jewish Corridor or that Stayman's coffee shop served both Italian and Jewish customers; that some of the "Neighbourhood" (for that is what Little Italy is called) women did home work for the men's clothing industry and worked in some of the canneries located near the water's edge; that some of Little Italy's residents entered the United States at Philadelphia and travelled by the Philadelphia, Wilmington and Baltimore Railroad to its President Street Station—all this builds a sense of the *ambiente* and of the colony's own perspective.

At this point, even before such a systematic search of the documents, records and oral testimony has been completed, some sense can be gained of the beginnings, characteristics and changes in Little Italy from the 1870s to 1930.

Settlement and Occupational Patterns

Baltimore's Little Italy became a magnet for settlement because of a variety of factors. In the first place, the area began to change during the 1870s. The comfortable Passano family moved out and it appears that other middle-class Italian businessmen such as J. Edward Sisco, owner of the Sisco Flag Manufacturing Company and Joseph Bolgiano, the owner of a seed company, lived away from the area. But residing far from the area did not always mean a separation or avoidance on the part of middle-class Italians. The Schiaffino-Lavarello family illustrates both the transition of the Italian presence from that of service to the larger community to that of providing goods for a growing Italian colony and the tradition of maintaining contacts with the core settlement.

Ship captain Prospero Schiaffino sailed with his family on his father's barca in 1875 to Baltimore from Camogli (near Genova). He established himself as a ship's broker and chandler handling the paper work for cargo clearance and supplying maritime provisions. In 1879 his brother Giovanni and brother-in-law Philip Lavarello came with their families. Philip Lavarello established a grocery and food supply business for ships at 702 South Broadway. Philip's three brothers came from Camogli to help him. Sometime later Giovanni Schiaffino opened a grocery store at South Eutaw Street, where Italian products were sold as well as ship provisions. Eventually he opened a branch store on Forrest Street to accommodate the Italian population settled around the Belair market.

The Schiaffino family played a role in the memorializing and ornamenting of the city. Prospero's older brother Melchiore worked on consignment, buying Carrara marble for the Evans Marble Company of Baltimore. Prospero's son Giacomo established a similar contract with the Hilgartener Company of Baltimore. The latter company supplied marble to many east coast contractors and provided the material for the construction of the Department of Commerce Building in Washington, D.C.

Neither Prospero Schiaffino nor his brother ever lived in Little Italy but both served as vice-consul for Italy and sold steamship tickets. Giovanni was on the board of directors for the Italian Orphan Asylum. Both were ex officio members of all the settlement's organizations and when Prospero's daughter married her first cousin, a Lavarello, they were married in St. Leo's. Their children were baptized there. Their *Italianita* survived living outside the neighbourhood. Prospero's grandson still speaks the Genovese dialect his grandfather taught him, and both Giovanni's and Prospero's daughters helped the Little Italy community, one working as a translator for the Family Welfare League, the other organizing fund raising projects for the Italian orphange.[13]

Church records and government reports record the deterioration of the area at the end of the century and the low incomes of its immigrant residents, mainly Jews and Italians, with some holdovers from an earlier Irish and German settlement. By 1897 the area was labelled a slum. Baltimore's slowness in providing a municipal sewage system helped to compound the decline. In a 1907 report on housing conditions in the area one case was reported of an Italian man and wife and fourteen male boarders occupying a four-room apartment.[14]

The Italian consul in 1903 documented the modest incomes of most of the immigrant population as ranging from $1.35 to $1.50 a day. The *scalpettini* engaged to do ornate work in marble earned about $15 a week. Italian tailors, cobblers and barbers averaged from $10 to 25 a week. According to oral testimony, wages for day labourers remained about the same in the prewar period. Immigrants remembered the daily shape-ups for jobs digging ditches and the frequent moving around because they lacked job security and followed new opportunities as city projects expanded.[15]

The second fact in determining the settlement pattern of Little Italy was the location of the downtown garment factories, harbour facilities and railroad lines. Residents could walk to work, much as they did in the agrotowns of Italy, or they could travel on the municipal streetcars.[16] Most of the area's residents worked close to home. A few opened small hotels and hostelries in nearby neighbourhoods (in 1875 Mrs. Mary Cherrego ran a boardinghouse at 60 President Street). Others brought in fresh produce from the port and worked as fruit merchants, peddlers and hucksters (in 1880 John Ratto was a fruit dealer at 3 North Holliday and lived at South Plowman).

The importation of fruit and its retail distribution within the city as well as across the nation was an important source of income for the Baltimore community. Here Cefaludesi and others (and this was true of New Orleans as well) figured prominently in the development of this business. Two major companies, both national in their scope, started in the 1890s. Both the G. Fava and DiGiorgio companies were founded by men from Cefalù. Fruit imports not only reflected the commercial preferences of these Sicilians but also benefited from Baltimore's position between 1914 and 1939 as the second-largest seaport in foreign commerce and first in shipments westward through the Panama Canal. The banana was the chief article imported and the Baltimore-based Lanasa Importing and Steamship Company was the third most important company in volume of business handled.

Most of the men specializing in handling fruit as peddlers, hucksters, or operators of small stalls

> visited the wholesale markets in person, shopped for bargains, and haggled over prices. Most of them paid cash, furnished their own transportation, performed their own conditioning and carried the produce to the customers' doors or sold them in the large neighborhood public market.[17]

Baltimore's produce commerce was built around a number of large markets. The fruit and vegetable stalls at most of the city's markets were dominated by Italians. A look at the 1928 directory that lists stall proprietors indicates that out of 500 stalls of every kind the 90 run by Italians, except for one florist, several confectioners, and a few produce shops, sold fruit and vegetables. Other types of stalls—butchering, confectionary, bakeries, pickled goods, poultry, cheese, etc.—were run by Germans, Poles and Jews. A number of confectioners were Greeks.

In 1928 the Belair market located in Forrest from Hillen to Orleans had 350 stalls. Again we see the concentration of type of trade. Of 40 Italian stalls more than 35 were fruit and vegetable stands. Out of the 100-odd meat men and butchers in Belair market only two are Italian. The variety of trades by stall among the Poles and Germans was much greater. Italians also worked and lived around the Hollins Street market, the Hanover Street market and the Broadway market.

Not only do certain families cluster in the fruit trade, but also one notes the proliferation of stalls belonging to the same families. An examination of market records and oral testimony might show that the practice of nuclear family entrepreneurship developed for these Sicilians in a pattern similar to the German farmer purchasing farms for each son of marriageable age.[18] While some residents supported themselves by serving co-nationals—Benedict Malatesta ran a saloon at 61 President Street, Antonio Cella a restaurant at 63 President Street and Joshua Jagmetti a grocery store at Eastern Avenue and Exeter Street—most of the immigrants had to go out of the neighbourhood to earn a living. Italians travelled to public construction projects which included digging sewers, repaving streets, laying underground electrical wires, building schools, and, after the 1904 fire, constructing the Jones Fallsway. They also worked laying tracks and as repair workmen and in tunnel work near Baltimore. Some found employment in the men's and boys' clothing factories on Baltimore Street. A few worked in the canning plants in southeastern Baltimore.[19]

The Church

If it was the combination of low rents, proximity to job sites, and transportation routes that brought Italians into Little Italy, it was the life and activity of that community which held them there. The church, St. Leo's, served as the focal point for Italian identity.

The establishment of St. Leo's as the first national church at the intersection of Exeter and Stiles streets in 1880 appeared to be a recognition of the growing community there and a policy of ethnic tolerance by the church hierarchy. The Baltimore diocese accepted ethnic pluralism. Cardinal Gibbons was extraordinarily sensitive to population shifts within parishes. As pastor of St. Bridget's in Fell's Point he had rowed across the harbour every Sunday morning to say mass for the Irish parishioners at St. Laurence O'Toole in Locust Point. Later when Germans moved into that area he assigned German-speaking clergy. Gibbons' support of national parishes did not stem from Cahaleyism, but from a firm conviction that immigrant parishes would permit a gradual acculturation for the newcomers into mainstream American life.[20]

Gibbons in fact wanted to reserve St. Leo's for Italians. It was the new pastor, Father Andreis, who argued in favour of allowing the Irish and German residents in the area to attend the church. Before coming to St. Leo's in 1881, Father Andreis had served as assistant pastor at St. Vincent de Paul, which had been attended by immigrants from Livorno, Lucca, Genoa, Rovegna and Naples.[21] The first congregation included one hundred Italians and fifteen hundred "Americans."

Undaunted by the large debt incurred from the construction of the church in 1880, Andreis established a school in 1883. By 1909 the Italian congregation had increased to two thousand, yet this did little to improve the financial status of the church, which still had a debt of $20,900.

In 1909 Gibbons assigned the Pallotine order to St. Leo's. The new pastor, Father Reidel, continued the policy of expansion established by his predecessors. He arranged to assume the interest payment on a sum of $5,000 for a property at 112 North Front Street. This raised the annual interest totals to $1,000 while the annual income in the parish averaged $3,000. Reidel was careful not to let financial issues dampen his poor parishioners' enthusiasm. When they would explain their absence from mass as embarrassment over not having good clothes or a hat, he would reply:

> Come in your everyday clothes—put your shawl or handkerchief over your head—come at any cost to mass, no matter how poor you may be. There is no "admission fee" nor any "pew rent" at St. Leo's to keep you out—all is free.

From 1915 the World War which boosted Baltimore's economy increased church revenue. With the armistice Reidel kicked off a fundraising drive and by 1922 the parish was free of debt. Reidel inspired a spirit of community cooperation during his fund-raising drive; across town in Highlandtown Father Scaldione's Italian flock helped to construct as well as financially contribute towards the new parish of Our Lady of Pompeii in Highlandtown.

During this period Reidel attempted to expand St. Leo's influence north into the St. Vincent/Belair market area when he moved St. Leo's school to the property he had purchased at 112 Front Street. Few Belair market children attended this school and the 350 St. Leo students complained that the distance was inconvenient. In 1913 Reidel established the Italian orphanage in the Front Street building.[22]

Until 1917 St. Leo remained the centre of the entire Italian urban community. Its central role in the life of the community as a symbol of ethnic identity coalesced during the crisis of the 1904 Baltimore fire and the subsequent establishment of the St. Anthony of Padova Society.[23] In 1917 Cardinal Gibbons gave the Italians living in the area around the Lexington Street market St. John the Baptist as a national parish. He assigned the Pallotines to that church and gave it to the Italians debt free. By 1930 St. John's had its own school.

In February 1904 the Baltimore fire swept through the downtown business district heading eastward. As it moved toward Little Italy during the night some Italians gathered in St. Leo's and prayed to St.

Anthony. When they emerged from the church an east wind sprang up and held back the flames. In commemoration of this miracle the grateful parishioners established the St. Anthony Society which holds an annual procession each June 13th.[24]

Father Reidel's pan-Catholicism or imperialism for St. Leo's stretched not only northward to the Belair market area but eastward to the National Catholic Community House on Broadway. In September 1921 he asked Miss Ring, the director, to organize classes for the girls of St. Leo's school. Staff member Miss Koppa offered to coach a basketball team and Miss Cook taught sewing and reading classes on Wednesday night.[25]

While the church considered itself the centre of the community, it was not willing to support all Italian-American activities. In 1928 when the Italian consul established a Balilla school for young teenage boys, church officials refused to allow them to use its field for exercises.[26]

For individuals like Frank Della Nocce and Thomas D'Alessandro Jr., participation in church-connected organizations directly aided their careers. Della Nocce, a funeral director, belonged to every church organization and mutual benefit society. D'Alessandro credited his presidency of St. Leo's Holy Name Society as placing him in a city-wide organization that enabled him to meet and make alliances among Irish politicians which led to his election as mayor.[27]

Social Organizations

In addition to church related societies, other organizations flourished among the city's Italians. In 1902 the consul reported the existence of eight mutual aid societies with a total membership of one thousand. Their names reflect some regional and occupational characteristics: for example, the Abruzzi-Molise Society, the Cefaludese S. Spinuzza Society, and for those from central Sicily, the Caltaseibettese Conte Ruggero Society, the Roma Lazio, the Francesco Crispi Society, the Society Imera Croce Bianca, and the Artistica Operaia. In 1910 the Sarti Italiani organized tailors. Many of its members joined the Italian-speaking Local 51 of the Amalgamated Clothing Workers of America. Fruit vendors gathered to form their own Frutevendolo.[28]

These mutual aid societies persisted into the 1920s. Some faced financial difficulties. For example, the Society Imera Croce Bianca collapsed in 1928 and divided its disposable fund among its members. Problems other than financial also disrupted some organizations. A split occurred in the Caltaseibettese Conte Ruggero Society which resulted in the formation of a new Caltaseibettese General Armando Dias Society. The official explanation given for the rupture was friction between "the intellectual and the illiterate." *Il Risorgimento* speculated that the cause was the increasing colonial problem of personal ambition and it counselled the intellectuals to appreciate and aid the illiterates instead of cutting them down. New mutual aid societies formed in that decade continued to have a regional orientation. The Alta Italia Mutual Society founded in 1927 included people from the Piedmont, Lombardy, Veneto, Genova, Emilia, Tuscany, Romagna and Umbria. The Calabrese Society organized in 1929 and the Duca Villarosa in 1928.[29]

During the 1920s the Sons of Italy formed their Grand Lodge in Maryland. Partially as an attempt to consolidate sentiment, some members, such as Father Luigi Arena, the pastor of the Church of the Madonna Adolorata (Our Lady of Sorrows) and grand orator of the Sons of Italy, suggested that all societies federate with the Order. Some groups did, such as the Sarti Italiani, the Artistica Operaia and the Cefaludesi. The history of the Order was a stormy one during the interwar years and its efforts to establish a social house or lodge while providing other benefits for its members threatened to undermine its solvency.[30]

Mutual benefit societies have always been an essential element in immigrant society, especially in the early years of settlement, designed to absorb some of the financial damage suffered because of illness and death. For Baltimore's Italians building and loan associations can also be seen as serving something of the same purpose.

In 1902 the Italian vice-consul noted the absence of Italian banks in Baltimore with the exception of those engaged in sending money back to Italy, which he estimated handled about $12,000 a year. He also reported that some Italians had savings deposits and also owned the homes they lived in.[31] This phenomenon of Italian building and loan associations and their relationship to home ownership and the absence of padrone bankers was a unique feature to Baltimore's Italians. Around the turn of the century the President Street Building and Loan Association started. Then in 1908 the Colombo Building and Loan Association opened its office in Little Italy. Italian adaptation of this institution appears to be a form of ethno-cultural borrowing. Germans and Central European groups introduced this economic organization to Baltimore. Polish parish churches used this economic strategy to provide an opportunity for community members to borrow enough money for home purchase. Businessmen would form a board of directors and incorporate. They then pooled their money and lent it out in small short-term amounts. Banking business was conducted one night each week to enable working people to apply. No collateral was necessary for loans, only the individual's reputation in the community. Sometimes the businessmen who served on the board of directors were also the builders who sold homes to the borrowers.[32] Although the Italians adopted the structure of the buildings and loans, their contractors tended to work on municipal projects rather than the home building trade.

By 1935 there were five building and loan organizations for the Italians.[33] An obvious link between the increased Italian home purchasing and the development of building and loan associations might become more apparent if tax assessment records and insurance maps were correlated with a list of the names or numbers of borrowers. (Loans were, by the way, only granted to people residing in the community.)

Unfortunately the records as well as the Building and Loan Association on President Street no longer exist. The Colombo Savings and

Loan's records have not yet been located. But based upon the records and oral testimony of the Garibaldi Building Association founded in 1920 on Greene Street adjacent to the Lexington markets, I can describe the salient features. Anthony Serio, one of the more successful fruit merchants in the Lexington markets frequently loaned money literally "out of his pocket" to people wanting to purchase homes. His attorney (Charles DiPaula) came to him one day and said,

> Tony, you're crazy. They come in here on Saturday night and they close their stalls and they owe you money—no books, no record. Why don't you open a savings and loan? Then you could put the loans through them and they could come in once a week and make their payments. Other fruit merchants joined. Charles Di Marco, John Aquilla, Vincent Dianna. Loans were made strictly for home purchase with a time period of eight years. No credit backing was necessary other than personal reputation.

If the Garibaldi was typical of the system, one might speculate how much it stabilized and made permanent the community. The records show that no one defaulted on a home loan even during the Depression. Individuals who were unable to make payments were "carried" until they could repay.[34]

The establishment of the Garibaldi Association in the Lexington Markets area and the designation of St. John the Baptist parish in 1917 as the second Italian national parish in Baltimore show the importance of the fruitmen and greengrocers in the community. Giovanni Schiavo observed in 1925 that few Baltimore Italians were labourers. The majority, he said, "if not in the fruit business are either barbers or shoemakers or have entered the clothing business" [as subcontractors].[35]

Politics

While Italians almost everywhere in America found opportunities in construction work, in Baltimore work for the day labourer as well as the independent contractor seemed to be on public projects. This type of construction work demanded that city employees be naturalized. The Italian vice-consul reported in 1902 that one-third of the twelve thousand Italians were naturalized.[36] Such a high naturalization rate at this early date might be understood as an economic strategy to obtain work. So the awarding of contracts might have been done as a form of political patronage. Italians had to learn the ropes of Baltimore city politics early.

The 1920s seemed to be a time of growing self-awareness for the Italian population, and a period when they began to make inroads in Maryland politics. The newspaper *Il Risorgimento* championed causes for group recognition. It argued in favour of naturalization and block voting to support Italian candidates. It criticized the city government's neglect of Italians as prospective appointees for office. The paper faulted organized groups and prominent individuals in the community for not accepting their responsibility to further group prestige. The condemnation ranged from the *prominenti* in the Italian Club who separated themselves from the masses of Italians, to Vincent Palmisano, a future congressman who ran for more than one office at the same time, thus preventing other Italian candidates from entering those races.

After a brief period of pro-Fascist editorial control, a new editor of *Il Risorgimento* followed a policy of supporting Italian Fascism but opposing its activity in the Baltimore Italian community. Especially strong was the paper's opposition to the Italian consul's attempt to introduce Fascist programs in Baltimore.[37]

Although two men, Vincent Palmisano and Anthony Dimarco, gained public office prior to 1920, it was during this decade that Baltimore's party politics enabled Italian contenders to influence candidate selection. In politics, too, Baltimore's Little Italy may be unique. Maryland politics and particularly the Baltimore scene, is dominated by one party—the Democratic, which at the turn of the century was controlled by the Irish. Italians never constituted sufficient numbers to win elections without party support. Therefore Italian political success was tied to coalitions with Irish party bosses.

In 1926 Vincent Palmisano from Little Italy won the primary as the Democratic party congressional candidate, and with the backing of one of the Irish political factions, he won. Palmisano, born in Termini Imerese, Sicily, had served in city and state office since 1914 and was the first congressman of Italian birth in the United States. He ran unopposed until 1938 when an Abruzzese insurance man, Thomas D'Alessandro, decided to challenge Palmisano in the primary. D'Alessandro used showmanship and some La Guardia multi-ethnic tactics to win the primary by a small margin.[38]

D'Alessandro was popular not only within Little Italy where he still lives, but also throughout the city. His pro-labour record gained support from his multi-ethnic working class district and he remained in Congress until 1947 when he became Baltimore's first Italian mayor. He served three terms in office and maybe not ironically he made the decision to place a largely Black public housing project in Little Italy.

Today these public housing projects cut across the northern edge of Little Italy, reducing it to twelve square blocks. Some of the Black parents in the projects send their children to St. Leo's; otherwise Pratt Street is the unspoken boundary between two ethnic worlds. Today's Little Italy is a quaint replica of an Italian neighbourhood with a few small grocery stores, about four Italian food-processing and importing companies, a funeral parlour, travel and insurance agencies, St. Leo's and many tourist restaurants. The neighbourhood survives in some way as a caricature of what it was as an immigrant quarter, but it survives.

Notes

1. "100 Years Ago week ended March 30, 1874" in "This Was Baltimore: From the files of the Sun," *Baltimore Sun*, 31 March, 1974.

2. Kathleen Neils Conzen, *Immigrant Milwaukee 1836-1860: Accommodation and Community in a Frontier City* (Cambridge, Mass.: Harvard University Press, 1976) and Dieter Cunz, *The Maryland Germans, a History* (Princeton, N.J.: Princeton University Press, 1948).

3. Sara Jean Reilly, "The Italian Immigrants 1920-1930: A Case Study in Baltimore" (M.A. thesis, Johns Hopkins University, 1962).

4. Regina Soria, "Early Italian Sculptors in the United States," *Italian Americana* II, no. 2 (Spring 1976) pp. 175-76, 181-85.

5. "A View of the Port of Baltimore, 1836" by Calyo (1799-1884) hangs in the Baltimore Museum of Art.

6. Lee McCardell, "Little Italy Remains Most Picturesque of City's Foreign Colonies," *Evening Sun*, 21 March 1938.

7. United States, Manuscript Federal Census, 1860 for Wards Two and Four in the city of Baltimore, Maryland.

8. Baltimore City Directories 1867-1880 and *Historical Sketch of St. Leo's Parish from its Organization to the Present Day 1881-1922*, and City directories.

9. Reilly, "The Italian Immigrants 1920-1930: A Case Study in Baltimore," p. 120.

10. Ibid., p. 16.

11. U.S. Federal Manuscript Census, 1860.

12. St. Leo's Parish Marriage and Baptism Records, 1881-1903.

13. Notes taken in interviews with Mr. Philip and Miss Angela and Miss Lillian Lavarella, April and May 1979, Baltimore, Maryland. Their grandfather was Prospero Schiaffino.

14. Janet Kemp, *Housing Conditions in Baltimore* (Baltimore, 1907).

15. Italy, Ministero Degli Affari Esteri, Commissariato dell'Emigrazione, *Bollettino dell'Emigrazione, Anno 1903* (Roma, 1904), #10, G. Naselli, "Stati Uniti—gli Italiani nel distretto consolare di Filadelfia," pp. 19-41. Naselli, the Royal Consul for Philadelphia, probably summarized reports sent in by the various vice-consuls, e.g., Prospero Schiaffino in Baltimore. Taped interview of Mr. John Matricianni (Mr. "Little Italy") by Deborah Batchelor, 7 May 1973, Maryland Historical Society.

    In 1902 the Italian consul estimated the Baltimore Italian population as approximately 10,000 (first and second generation). About 3,000 earned their living as merchants, hucksters, peddlers. 1,200 were manual labourers, 700 workers, 300 factory workers and 300 artist stonecutters.

    The wards constituting my larger definition of Little Italy including the Belair market (Ward 5) in 1910 contained 3,738 Italian born residents. Minus Ward 5 = 2,779. (City wide total 5,043 Italian born.) In 1920 the city wide total of 7,911 Italian born. Little Italy including Ward 5 had 3,444 people (minus Ward 5 = 2,436).

This table shows Italian foreign-born in these wards:

	1910	1920
Ward 2	69	81
Ward 3	1,581	1,809
Ward 4	506	546
Ward 5	959	1,008

Census figures from United States, Department of Commerce.

16. United States Commissioner of Labor, Seventh Special Report, "The Slums of Baltimore, Chicago, New York and Philadelphia," (Washington, 1894) and *Industrial Survey 1914-1939* (Baltimore, 1939).

17. Reilly, "The Italian Immigrants," pp. 24-30. She cites Robert Deupree, *The Wholesale Marketing of Fruits and Vegetables in Baltimore* (Baltimore, 1939).

18. City directories.

19. United States, Department of Labor, Industrial Commission Report 1902, G. Naselli's report in *Bollettino dell'Emigrazione* and *Industrial Survey*.

20. Phyllis Lynn Rogers, "The Evolution of a Parish: An Irish Chapel becomes an Americanized Parish." Undergraduate paper, Towson State University, 1974. See also Richard Linkh, *American Catholicism and European Immigrants (1900-1924)* (Center For Migration Studies, 1975).

21. St. Vincent de Paul's Parish, Marriage Records 1874-1881, Baltimore, Maryland.

22. *Historical Sketch of St. Leo's.*

23. Ibid.

24. Gilbert, *The Neighborhood: The Story of Baltimore's Little Italy* (Bondine and Associates, 1974), pp. 28-31.

25. *Historical Sketch.*

26. Reilly, "The Italian Immigrants," pp. 104, 186.

27. Ibid. cites interview with Thomas D'Alessandro, Jr., January 1961. And notes taken during interview with Genvieve and Gerald Della Nocce, November 1978, Baltimore, Maryland.

28. *Bollettino dell'Emigrazione, Anno 1902,* #11, "Gli Italiani in alcuni stati della confederazione dell'America del Nord (Maryland, Ohio, Kentucky, Louisiana and Missouri). Article on Maryland is a report from Vice-Consul Prospero Schiaffino. Reilly, "The Italian Immigrants," pp. 37-42. Also notes taken during interview with Frederico Matucci, former member of the Italian local and organizer for the Amalgamated Clothing Workers of America, May 1979, Baltimore, Maryland.

29. Reilly, "The Italian Immigrants," pp. 38, 46-47. She cites *Il Risorgimento,* May and June 1928.

30. Ibid. cites various issues of *Il Risorgimento.*

31. *Bollettino dell'Emigrazione, 1902.*

32. Barry Lanman, "Small Ethnic Credit Institutions in Baltimore: Three Interviews with Officers of Garibaldi Federal Savings and Loan Association," transcript of interview done for undergraduate course at Towson State University, 1972.

33. Reilly, "The Italian Immigrants," p. 25. She cites a 1935 survey done by Helen Garvin, director of the International Institute of the YWCA in Baltimore, Maryland.

34. Lanman, "Credit Institutions"; interview with Mr. John Serio, 10 July, 1972.

35. Giovanni Schiavo, "Italians of Baltimore Follow Varied Vocations," the *Sun*, 18 January, 1925.

36. *Bollettino dell'Emigrazione, Anno 1902.*

37. Reilly, "The Italian Immigrants." Her major source of data comes from the issues of *Il Risorgimento.*

38. Sandler, *The Neighborhood*, pp. 32-46 and Reilly, "The Italian Immigrants," pp. 123, 135 and 140.

Photo: Maryland Historical Society

An Italian grocery store, established in the 1870s at 408 President Street, Baltimore. The picture was taken in 1890, and, among those standing, are Antonio Jorio, the store owner, and his daughter.

The committee members of the 25th anniversary of the St. Anthony of Padua Festival, 1929. The festival was begun in 1904 to thank the saint for saving the Little Italy from destruction in the Baltimore fire.

DAL 1904 AL 1929
25.mo Anniversario Della Festa
DI S. ANTONIO DI PADOVA
Comitato Festa Sociale E Coloniale

Photo: Maryland Historical Society

Vincent Palimisano, a Baltimore resident, was the first person of Italian birth to be elected to the United States Congress. He became a congressman in 1926. ▼

VINCENT L. PALMISANO

CANDIDATE FOR THE

First Branch City Council

THIRD WARD

Subject to the Democratic Primaries,
Tuesday, April 6th, 1915

If you are not registered you may do so on
Monday, April 5th, 1915

Photo: Maryland Historical Society

▲ Calabrese street railway workers, Toronto, c. 1912

▼ A class in mothercraft, Central Neighbourhood House, Toronto, c. 1913

A hurdy-gurdy man, Toronto, c. 1920 ►

Houses in the Ward, Toronto, c. 1912.
Shown in the background is the Toronto
City Hall which faced on Terauley Street,
later re-named Bay Street. ▼

▲ The Casa Ravello Milk Station, also called the Baby Saving Station, Philadelphia, c. 1910

▼ A group of women and children standing outside the Baby Saving Station, Philadelphia

Men standing around a
pushcart, Philadelphia
◄

The students of Professor
R. Scocozza's school,
Tampa, 1903. The school
was at Seventh Avenue
and Eighteenth Street.
Standing beside Professor
Scocozza, top right, is
Miss Mamie Vick, an
Anglo-American who
taught English to the
Italian children.▼

St. Ambrose, St. Louis. This, the second church building, was constructed in 1926. ▲

The first St. Ambrose, built in ➤
1903. The parish supported a
school which had about 150
pupils, instructed by lay teachers.

▲ A Columbus Day celebration in Tampa, c. 1910. "Christopher Columbus" stands on the bow of the fishing smack, Dippioca, surrounded by his crew attired in U.S. Navy garb. The boat is ready to land at the rickety dock to the accompaniment of an Italian brass band.

▼ A local brass band, Oswego, c. 1920s

▲ A Saint Bartholemew procession from the old St. Joseph's Roman Catholic Church, Oswego

▼ Giovanni Battista, custodian of St. Joseph's Roman Catholic Church, Oswego

The Italian Heritage in Tampa

Anthony P. Pizzo

Early Pioneers

The first recorded page in the history of the Italians in the Tampa Bay area dates back to the dramatic days of discovery and exploration. Very little has been recorded of the participation of Italians in the early explorations of America.

During the four hundred and thirty years of Spanish rule of Southern Italy and Sicily, beginning with the reign of Ferdinand and Isabella, many Italians were living in Spain. They occupied important positions in Spanish life as bankers, clerics, traders, engineers, navigators, technicians, printers, mariners and soldiers. Some Italians held political power in Spain and even more numerous were the Italians who took part in the conquest and settlement of the new world. The relationship between the Spaniards and Italians was amicable. The Spanish government treated the Italian subjects on an equal footing with Spanish citizens. There was a popular saying in those days, "No hay hombre bajo el sol como el Italiano y el Español" ("There is no man under the sun like the Italian and the Spaniard.")

It is little wonder that the Italian historic connection with Tampa should start with the Spaniard Juan Ponce de Leon and the discovery of Florida. On his voyage of discovery de Leon sailed his small fleet of three vessels into the Gulf of Mexico. On 24 May, 1513, the expedition entered the mouth of Tampa Bay. The explorers tarried here for nine days. The flagship of the fleet was named *Santa Maria de la Consola-*

LITTLE ITALY IN YBOR CITY, TAMPA'S LATIN QUARTER

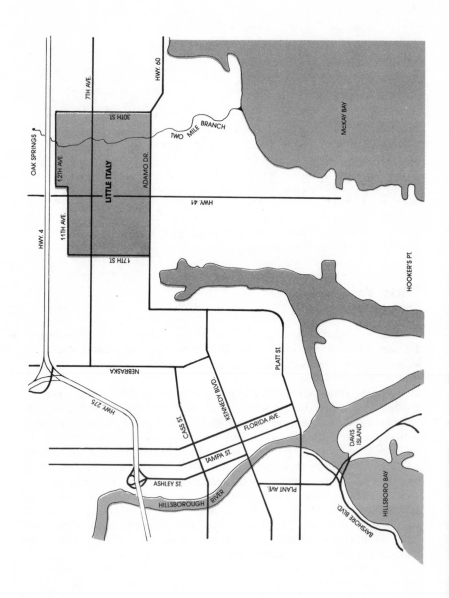

cion, and its master was an Italian named Juan Bonno.[1] With typical Italian zest for la dolce vita, it comes as no surprise that an Italian should have been with Ponce de Leon on his famous quest for the illusive Fountain of Youth!

When the great but ill-starred conquistador, the Adelantado Hernando De Soto and his six hundred men landed at Tampa Bay on 30 May, 1539, four Italians formed an important part of his expedition. One of them was Captain Micer Espindola, a native of Genoa, who was in charge of sixty halberdiers of De Soto's guard. Another was Maestro Francisco Aceituono, a Genoese engineer, and a great craftsman in carpentry and shipbuilding. The other two were calkers. Their names have been lost to history.

Maestro Francisco, "whom God had been pleased to spare," proved to be the lifesaver of the expedition. He was the only one among the explorers who knew how to construct the seven brigantines which took the 311 survivors of the ill-fated expedition down the Mississippi River and back to civilization.[2]

For three centuries after the glittering cavalcade of De Soto's expedition had faded into history, Tampa Bay remained a remote and forgotten harbour. Only the seagulls and Indian canoes were seen upon the lonely waters. Through the long and silent years, an occasional Cuban trader or fisherman, and pirates, contrabandists and slave traders from the Caribbean ventured into the secluded bay. There is no record of a settlement on the shores of Tampa Bay until Fort Brooke was established at the mouth of the Hillsborough River by the Americans in 1824. Soon after, settlers began to squat on the northern fringe of the fort, and the little community became known as Tampa.

The quiet fort on Tampa Bay was startled into action on December 28, 1835, when the Seminoles took to the war path, and commenced the Second Seminole War. Fort Brooke became the chief depot of supplies, and the centre of military operations. During the bloody seven-year struggle two names of Italian origin became linked with Tampa history. On March 26, 1836, a Major Lawrence Taliaferro[3] is reported to have repelled a band of Indians concealed behind a hummock within the present-day city limits of Tampa. Administering to the sick and wounded was a surgeon with the name of Dr. L. J. Trotti.[4] It is believed that Trotti was from Florida, and a descendant of Gaspar Trotti who is listed as residing in Saint Augustine in 1773. In 1830, James F. Trotti, a bank examiner, and most likely a relative of Dr. Trotti, signed a petition to President Andrew Jackson asking statehood for the Territory of Florida.

After the devastating hurricane of 1848 that all but wiped out the fort and village, a number of inhabitants from Saint Augustine were attracted to Tampa by the rebuilding boom that followed. By 1850, the town of Tampa boasted of a population of 185 souls. Among the newcomers were descendants of the 110 Italian colonists who had come to Florida to settle New Smyrna in 1768. They became a part of the pioneer fibre of the spunky little village, and provided the heritage of Italian participation for the immigrants who would arrive in Tampa a few decades later. These colourful people brought their musical names such as Leonardi, Pacetti, Maestre, Papi and Canova to the little Anglo-Saxon community.[5]

In 1853, civilization began to make its mark on the geography of the area which thirty-five years later would be known as Ybor City, Tampa's colourful Latin Quarter. Helping as a chainman for a survey team was a young man named Andrew Pacetti, a third-generation immigrant from Trapani, Sicily. He did not stay on this job very long. When the little town of Tampa held its first civic election in February 1856, Pacetti was elected town marshall. It is likely that Pacetti is the first Italian elected as town marshall in the United States.[6]

Another Pacetti made the Tampa scene in 1857, when the Billy Bowlegs War was at its height. He was Captain A. N. Pacetti, commander of the boat companies which scouted the "big lake" (Okeechobee) for forty-two days. To prove that he had been in the wild and dangerous region of the Everglades, Pacetti carved deep into a cypress trunk, "Captain A. N. Pacetti 10 September 1857." About one hundred years later, the trunk of the tree with the inscription was discovered, and it is now in the possession of the Florida Historical Society.[7]

Another Italian who earned a prominent niche in history during the Billy Bowlegs War was Andrew P. Canova, one of the crew of Captain Jacob E. Mickler's Boat Company. Canova recorded his colourful life as an Indian fighter of Florida in his book, *Life and Adventure in South Florida*. This invaluable account is the only description we have of the Billy Bowlegs War from a soldier's point of view.

The year 1849 saw the arrival of Captain Dominico Ghira, a native of Ravenna, Italy. He was the first native-born Italian to come to Tampa and remain permanently. In 1850, at the age of twenty-four, he married Domenica (Masters) Maestre, a young lady of Italian parentage. They made their home on what is now the site of the present Exchange National Bank Building.

In early life Captain Ghira engaged in seafaring pursuits, and later conducted a mercantile business. In 1864, he was appointed by the county commissioners to run the Tampa Ferry on the Hillsborough River for a period of four years. During the last Indian war, with Captain James McKay and Robert Bolesta he patrolled along the waterways of the west coast of Florida. On occasions he joined John P. Leonardi on night guard duty on the outskirts of Tampa watching for possible Indian raids.

Domenico Ghira was a leader in the early development of the downtown district. Through the years he acquired valuable pieces of real estate, and became a wealthy man. He died, admired and respected, on 22 May, 1897, at the age of eight-one. Ghira is remembered as one of the pioneers who contributed greatly to the physical, cultural and religious development of Tampa.

During the Civil War, the Italians of Tampa aided the cause of the South,[8] serving as home guards, supplying cattle to the rebels fighting in the North, and tending salt works. Although the town itself was pretty well bottled up by the Federal blockade, Tampa blockade-runners, men of great daring, risked running the blockade.

When Henry B. Plant, the railroad tycoon, made Tampa a railhead in 1883, connecting the budding community with the outside world, the first enterprise attracted to the seaport town was the fishing industry. Three large fishing companies moved to Tampa, one of which was owned by Captain John Savarese, a friend of Henry B. Plant. This young Italian, a native of Naples, came to America at the age of ten in 1872. Captain Savarese developed his wholesale fishing business into one of the most important enterprises seen in Tampa up to that time. By 1895, his operations employed 550 men. His fishing fleet consisted of fifteen sailing vessels, 150 small craft and a large steamer, the *Mistletoe*. Savarese was shipping more than 1,700 barrels of fish per month to all parts of the country, and Tampa became the most important fish-shipping centre in the South.[9]

Savarese was one of the first captains of industry of modern Tampa. Endowed with forceful leadership qualities, he had a strong influence on the economic and social progress of the community. He served as the first Italian consul of Tampa, was elected to two terms on the Tampa city council, and served on boards of business firms and financial institutions. Savarese was one of the founders and the first commodore of the Tampa Yacht and Country Club. As a crowning point in his career, he was decorated by King Victor Emmanuel III with the Cross of Cavalier of the Crown of Italy for his eminent service to the Italian government, and for his exemplary achievements in America.

The Coming of the Sicilians

The coming of the railroad brought Tampa into the modern era. Numerous lumber mills were attracted to the Bay area. Fish companies expanded their operations, citrus growers began shipping their fruit to the lucrative northern markets, and cattle barons turned away from the Cuban market to the ready beef markets of the mid-west. Plant, the railroad magnate, had become the patron saint of a very appreciative community.

During the month of March 1886, another momentuous event occurred in Tampa that would have a long-lasting influence and vitally affect its destiny. About two miles into the wilderness, east of Tampa, three Spaniards and a Cuban began the establishment of a company town for the manufacture of hand-made cigars.[10] They were Vicente Martinez Ybor and his Cuban associate Edward Manrara; Ignacio Haya and his associate Serafin Sanchez. The little village was predominantly Cuban, and christened Ybor City, but the Crackers in the immediate area called it Cuba City. With community pride these Crackers began switching from corncob pipes and chewing tobacco to Havana cigars!

At about the same time at the St. Cloud Sugar Plantation, near Kissimmee, some seventy-five miles away, a handful of Italians were barely ekeing out a living earning 75 cents a day cutting sugar cane.[11] Rumours of a Cuban boom town near Tampa began to spread through the state. Exciting stories were also told of Cubans and Spaniards coming in large numbers, of tobacco workers and construction men earning unheard of wages. Mr. Plant was said to be offering $1.25 a day for hands needed in the extension of his railroad to Port Tampa, and the construction of a Byzantine palace, his Tampa Bay Hotel! These exciting reports fired the imagination of the humble Italian immigrants at St. Cloud. They envisioned Ybor City as their "pot of gold" at the end of the rainbow.

These Italians had originally come from the bleak hills of central Sicily. Although the island had been under Spanish rule for more than four centuries, Spaniards were rarely treated as enemies or considered as foreign by the Sicilian population. Intermarriage was common, and through the years the official language of administration and social life was Catalan and Castilian. The impact of *spagnolismo* on the mould of Sicilian culture had been extensive. The Sicilian dialect is enriched with many Spanish words. Among the Sicilians arriving in Tampa from St. Cloud in the early days were some bearing such Spanish names as Reina, Pardo, Miranda, Marcello, Castellano and Barcellona. For these people, living in a Spanish environment would not be a totally new experience. Gradually, they trickled into Ybor City, where a familiar environment existed. These Italians were a kindred culture coming to renew old bonds.

The first trail-blazers from St. Cloud to Ybor City were from Santo Stefano Quisquina, Province of Agrigento, Sicily, a hilltop village dating back to the Middle Ages. In the vanguard were three Cacciatore brothers, Antonio, Salvatore and Angelo, and other *paesani* named Pietro Martino, Ignazio Comparetto, Francisco di Bona and Salvatore Reina.[12]

The trickle soon became a torrent. Glowing reports from the new Americans, often exaggerated and fuelled by steamship companies and others who would profit from their coming, began to spread through central Sicily. The flames of propaganda broadcast the fame of Tampa and Ybor City where workers were paid in solid gold coins, and one could live a life *da cristiana* (a life of Christians—a life worthy of human beings). The people of the neighbouring villages of Alessandria della Rocca (the second largest number of Italians in Tampa came from this village), Bivona, Cianciana, and Contessa Entellina were most affected by those tales, and all these villages experienced a virtual exodus.

Contessa Entellina differs from the other villages in that it was settled by Albanians fleeing from the Turkish occupation of the Balkans in the fifteenth century. The people are Greek Orthodox, and after five centuries retain a distinct identity, with their own dialect, Greco-Albanian national costume, and folklore. The Albanians who migrated to Sicily created nine new villages of which Piani degli Albanesi is the most famous. The late Frank Falsone, a descendant of this group and a highly respected citizen of Florida, once stated, "These are the most industrious people on earth. You will never see one in a bread line." This defiant work ethic was vividly illustrated in an 1896 letter to the *Tampa Tribune* stating the city's Italian community had never and would never accept a handout.

Today the Italian population of Tampa is mainly composed of descendants from these five villages, with only small numbers coming from other sections.

The first Italians settled on the eastern fringe of the small settlement of cigar-makers. Tampa's Little Italy in the 1890s extended from Seventeenth Street on the west to about Twenty-Sixth Street on the east. The southern boundary was Fourth Avenue, and at Twenty-Second Street the boundary line veered south and included Second and Third Avenues. The northern boundary was Michigan Avenue—today's Columbus Drive. In the beginning, their small wood-frame houses barely dotted this large area of wilderness. A few Italian immigrants, fearing alligators, built their cottages on stilts.

Within the Italian area there was a scattering of Spanish and Cuban families. In the heart of this section was a Spanish settlement known as La Pegueña Asturias. It stretched along Twelfth Avenue between Seventeenth Street and Twenty-First Street. Some of the Italians moved into rental cottages while others made purchases from Mr. Ybor on the instalment plan. The Italian quarters became known as La Pachata after a Cuban rent collector.[13]

The early beginnings for the Italians in Ybor City was obviously not all vino and pasta. One of the first arrivals was Giovanni Cacciatore. In 1935, at the age of seventy-five, he related his first impressions of Tampa upon his arrival in 1887.

I was born in Santo Stefano Quisiquina, Sicily, on May 12, 1860...In 1885, I decided to come to New Orleans where many Italians were living at that time. There I was employed as a foreman of a banana importing company for some two years.

Several friends described Tampa to me with such glowing colors that I soon became enthused, and decided to come here, and try for my fortune. Accordingly, in 1887, leaving my wife in New Orleans, I took the train to Mobile. At Mobile I took the boat that brought me here. We disembarked at La Fayette Street. I was then 27 years of age.

I had expected to see a flourishing city, but my expectations were too high, for what I saw before me almost brought me to tears. There was nothing! What one may truthfully say, nothing! Franklin was a long sandy street. There were very few houses, and those were far apart with tall pine trees surrounding them. The Hillsborough County Court House was a small wooden building. Some men were beginning to work on the foundation of the Tampa Bay Hotel.

Ybor City was not connected to Tampa as it is today. There was a wilderness between the two cities, and a distance of more than one mile between the two places. All of Ybor City was not worth more than one cent to me. At different places in Ybor City a tall species of grass grew (saw grass), proper of swampy places. This grass grew from five to six feet high. I was completely disillusioned with what I saw. There was a stagnant water hole where Centro Espanõl Society is today located. [This is the pioneer Spanish Mutual Aid Society which is still at the original site of 7th Avenue and 16th Street.] A small wooden bridge spanned this pond. I remember that I was afraid to cross that bridge, and especially so at night, because of the alligators that lived there. They would often crawl onto the bridge and bask there in the sun all day long.

Cacciatore also describes early conditions in the cigar industry; he was undoubtedly one of the first Italians to become a cigar-maker in an industry which was, at the time, dominated by Spanish and Cuban Workers.

The factory of Martinez Ybor had some twenty cigar-makers; Sanchez y Haya had some fifteen; while Pendas had about ten. I worked for a time at the factory of Modesto Monne as a stripper [one who removes the centre stem from the tobacco leaf] and made 35¢ for my first day's work. Of course, I was then only learning the cigar business, and could not expect to make more. When I became more skilled in my work as a stripper, I would make from $1.00 to $1.25 a day.

While still at this work, I gradually began learning the cigar-maker's trade as I saw that they were making a much more comfortable income. When I had become somewhat proficient as a cigar-maker, I was earning from $14.00 to $15.00 a week.

By 1901, according to the *Tampa Tribune*, Italians occupied 424 positions out of a total number of 1,872 cigar workers.

When I had been in Tampa some two years, I sent for my wife. When she arrived in Tampa she burst out crying at what she saw: wilderness, swamps, alligators, mosquitos, and open closets [out-houses]. The only thing she would say when she arrived was: "Why have you brought me to such a place?"

At about this time Mr. Ybor was offering homes for sale at very low prices. I went to him, and purchased a house on Eighth Avenue and Eighteenth Street for the price of $725.00. I paid $100.00 in cash and the rest in monthly terms. In all I worked twenty-eight years in the cigar factories.[14]

With the passing of time and by dint of hard work Cacciatore amassed important land holdings. The people who in the old country had lived for centuries in villages perched on hilltops for protection from marauding bands, and spent endless hours each day walking to and from the fields, now faced a new and strange life on the flats of Ybor

City. With all the virtues of tillers of the soil, and possessed with powerful loyalties and traditions, they became a people between two worlds. With raw courage and high hopes they would face the new life.

In most cases the men came to Ybor City ahead of their families. As soon as they felt they were established they would send for their loved ones. On December 14, 1892, the *Tampa Tribune* recorded for posterity, "A party of twenty-eight Italian immigrants arrived here this morning via the Florida Central and Peninsular Railway direct from Italy. Most of them were women and children of men in the Italian Colony in East Ybor."

Upon venturing into La Pachata, or the Italian area, one would immediately become aware of their sense of self-sufficiency and frugality—indeed, frugality was their overwhelming passion. Each family had a bread oven in their backyard. The oven, shaped like an igloo, was made of concrete and fire-bricks, resting on four sturdy wooden pilings. In their neat vegetable gardens were to be found new and exotic varieties of vegetables which had not been seen before by Florida natives. For example they introduced *escalore,* or endive; *cardone,* a thistle-like plant often called carder's comb; *carciofo,* artichoke, and eggplant. They also brought a species of cactus which thrives throughout Sicily called *ficco d' India.* Its delicious prickly pears with blood-red pulp are highly prized by Sicilians.

In cages they kept rabbits and pigeons; chickens roamed in the backyards along with a few guinea-hens. Their cows and goats were scattered throughout the area in vacant lots. Like all Mediterranean people, they had a penchant for *capretto arrosto,* roasted goat meat. It is interesting to note that by 1902 goat-raising had become a lucrative business. The *Tampa Tribune* reported: "One hundred head of goats were shipped from Ocala to Tampa. This is becoming quite a business. The Italians are very fond of kid, and it is relished and commands almost as high a price as mutton. The farmer does not want anything easier to grow rich on than a flock of goats."

Many social traditions died hard in Ybor City. Until the passing of the first arrivals, it was a common scene to see Italian mothers happily and proudly rocking on their front porches, humming a Sicilian lullaby to their bambinos sucking on their bare breast.[15]

Funerals were occasions of high solemnity, and were attended by virtually the entire Italian colony. They were a closely knit community. If they weren't related, they were *paesani* and in those days being a *paesano* was tantamount to family. The Italian cemetery located on Twenty-Second Avenue and Twenty-Sixth Street dates back to those days. The funeral procession left from the home where the body laid in state. The cortège was led by a black baroque hearse pulled by two white horses covered with black mesh. Families who could afford a band hired the only band available at that time—a group of Cuban cigar-makers. The band led the cortège playing funeral dirges, while small groups, wearing vestments of fraternal orders, carried banners and standards. Following on foot, trudging through the sandy streets, the seemingly endless line of Italian mourners solemnly accompanied their compatriot to the cemetery where they paid their last respects. The more extravagant ones rented a horse and carriage for one dollar. Four or five would share the rental cost, demonstrating frugality even in their extravagance.

The last funeral procession led by an Italian band was that of my maternal grandfather, Pietro Pizzolato, who died during the Spanish flu epidemic in 1918. Pizzolato was a native of Contessa Entellina who had migrated to Scorro, New Mexico, in 1879, where most of his children were born. He came to Tampa in 1892, and established a grocery store and a horse-trading enterprise on Eighth Avenue and Eighteenth Street. The family continues the grocery business at the same location today.

Building the Community

Many Sicilians at the outset found work laying out tracks for the Plant System, in the construction of the Tampa Bay Hotel, as porters in the cigar factories, and in the construction of residential and commercial buildings of the budding community. Others became engaged in truck and dairy farming, opened grocery stores, confectionary stores, fruit stands, saloons and fish markets. Some pursued their trades as cobblers, tailors and stonemasons, and some of the housewives were able to better the family lot by sewing and embroidery. The art of *pundina* or crocheting attained its highest art form at the hands of the Sicilian women.

Most of the Sicilian immigrants were farm workers, and it is little wonder that impressive vegetable farms began to appear in the Italian section. Antonio Capitano made use of a stream known as the Two Mile Branch to cultivate excellent watercress, a vegetable highly prized by Italians. One of the finest farms was located south of Adamo Drive between Twenty-Second Street and the Estuary. The rich black soil produced the finest celery and other vegetables. Its owner, Vicenzo Zambito, better known by his nickname Maraune, was a first-class agriculturalist who gave a lifetime to farming. In later years the land became too valuable for farming, and the heirs were compelled to sell it for industrial use.

The early farmers who converted the palmetto flats of Ybor City into lush and profitable farm lands were the Lazzaras, Mastinos, Valentis, Scolaros and Capitanos. Today the descendants of the Valentis, Geracis and Lazzaras are engaged in nation-wide produce enterprises which include the operation of farm lands in California, Mexico, New York State and South Florida. Others who have been prominent in the fruit and produce business are the Schiros, Pupellos, Fillipellos, Rizzos, Ippolitos, Lalas, Diecidues, Manalis, Barones, Napolis, Ferlitas and the Macalusos.

A vital part of Sicilian life is the love of wine. It was therefore inevitable that as early as 1887 Italians would be engaged in the cultivation of grapes in this area. Vincent De Leo, who was manager of the City Barber Shop located on Franklin and La Fayette streets, established a twenty-acre vineyard of malaga and scuppernong grape varieties on the Hillsborough River. In May 1891, the *Tribune* reported that "a number of Cubans and Italians have bought sixty acres, and will go into grape culture this fall—near Tampa." Bartolo Filogamo, a young immigrant from Trapani, and a very capable accountant, with Y.M. Alvarez, a cigar manufacturer, went into grape culture near Lake Bilows. If wine was ever made from these vineyards it must have been on a non-commercial basis as no later records of sales are known. Nearly three-quarters of a century later (1973) Joe D. Midulla, Sr., a member of a prominent family of wine merchants, established the first winery in the history of Tampa.

Many went into business as soon as they learned about fifty words in English; this was more to cope with the Anglo-Saxon salesmen than with their clientele, who were predominantly Cubans. If an Italian opened a grocery store, the sign went up in Italo-English, "Grosseria-Italiana." In some cases the journey was from push-cart to wagon-peddler, then to the privilege of a fruit stand and then a grocery store. Enticing displays of luscious fruits exemplified the pride with which they advertised their wares and artisitic abilities.

By 1910 there were fifty-four Italian grocery stores in Tampa. From this humble group of merchants emerged one of the miracle stories of American business. From meagre beginnings Salvatore Greco parlayed his small grocery store located at 2705 East Columbus Drive into a multi-million-dollar grocery chain known as Kash 'n Karry. In 1946, Greco pooled the resources of his family and launched into his great enterprise. He was ably assisted by his sons, Joe, John and Mac, and by his sons-in-law Frank Giunta and Joe Dominguez.

The fame of Tampa Bay as a great fishing ground, and the coming of many Italians, attracted fishermen who soon made Tampa a major Italian fishing community. Their names are well known to Tampans today as Mirabella, Felicione, Matassini, Boromei, La Bruzza and Agli-ano. Their success has been of long duration. For many years they owned large fishing fleets, and distributed their catch by refrigerated trucks throughout the southeast. In recent years some of them have gone into the seafood restaurant business with much success.

The ever-enterprising Italians soon established the first macaroni factories in Ybor City. Onofrio Mortellaro and Filippo Lodato established their factory at 1908 Seventh Avenue, and a little later Antonio Cacciatore opened his factory at 1806 Eighth Avenue. In the 1920s Greco and Ginex bought the firm from Cacciatore and continued into the years of the depression.

The early Italian dairies were quite numerous with twelve operations being reported in 1910, and all were doing good business. One of the first dairies was owned by Castenzio Ferlita and Salvatore N. Reina. In 1894, they established a milk dairy which they operated until 1916. From the profits from the dairy the Cosmopolitan Ice Co. and the Tropical Ice Cream Company were created.

From these pioneer dairies emerged Florida Dairy, one of the largest dairy enterprises in the state. The founder was Giuseppe Guagliardo, a Stefanese. He started business in the most humble circumstances, with only two milk cows and a horse and buggy to make his deliveries. At the beginning his daily house deliveries totalled seven quarts and two pints. Today, the herd exceeds eight hundred head of cattle. This Cinderella story became a reality through sheer sacrifice and dedicated industry. In 1934 Giuseppe was joined by his sons Sam, Paul, Nelson and James to form the present corporation. Sam, the oldest son, served as president of the firm until his death in April 1976. The Guagliardos are one of the most respected families in the Latin Colony. Their altruistic and humanitarian qualities are well known among the people of Ybor City. Through the Depression and cigar-makers' strikes, when many families could not pay for their weekly milk bills, the Guagliardos never stopped leaving milk at their doorsteps. Not a child would be deprived as long as there was a cow giving milk in the Guagliardo herd. A few months before Sam died, he was honored as Ybor City's outstanding citizen. The people, after so many years, still remembered.

Italians in the Cigar Industry

The great majority of the Italians who were attracted to Ybor City came with the aspiration of becoming cigar-makers. The earnings were excellent and the cigar industry offered them an opportunity to quickly improve their economic status. At the beginning they were looked upon by the Cuban cigar-makers as interlopers and a serious menace to their own employment. Therefore the Spanish manufacturers were adverse to employing Italians at the beginning for fear of alienating the Cuban cigar-makers. A strike call *para la calle* from one of the workers in a *galera* or work-bench could easily empty the factories as fast as one can say *boliche*!

In time, with their charm and goodwill, the Italians began to break the inner sanctum of the cigar factories. They started in the stripping rooms, stripping the centre stem from the tobacco leaf, and in time were given the chance to learn how to roll cigars. The strict system of apprenticeship usually required a minimum period of two years to become a master cigar-maker.

At the beginning the Italians had a rough time obtaining jobs making high-grade cigars (*vitolas*). Most of them had to accept work in the cheroot factories. Cheroots are the cheapest cigars made; they are made with *picadura* (left-over scraps of a cheap domestic leaf), instead of the highly regarded long filler Havana leaf. Since these cigars were very cheap, the Italians earned very little. The friendly Cubans, with their ever charming wit, humorously called these cheap cigars (in respectful jest, naturally) Italian Regalias or Royal Italian cigars.[16]

Cigar-making is an art form, demanding practice, aptitude and a natural gift. It did not take the Spanish manufacturers long to discover that the Italians were naturally gifted in making cigars. The Italians soon became recognized as dedicated workers, and masters at their work. The cheroot factories had to look elsewhere for hands, as the Italians graduated to making brevas, corona-coronas and regalias. The Italian women were especially signalled out as being "very good bunch-makers and rollers." The Italians gradually achieved a prosperous position due to their perseverance and thrift.

In the course of a few years, six cigar factories with Italian affiliations emerged on the scene. They were: George F. Borrotto, La Vatiata, Leonardi-Hayman, Filogamo and Alvarez, V.M. (Val) Antuono, and Andrea Re.

Of these factories, the one owned by Val Antuono marketing the C.H.S. label (Clear Havana Segars) became a fabulous success. His brand was famous from coast to coast. Antuono came to Tampa in 1886, at the age of twelve and soon began making cigars and dreaming of the day he would have his own factory. He married Jennie Geraci, and soon after the young couple commenced making cigars in their home on Twelfth Street between Seventh and Eighth avenues. In time he was able to employ three cigar-makers and moved to La Fayette and Tampa streets. The site became known as Val's Corner until the First National Bank acquired the property. Subsequently he built a large cigar factory and amassed large real estate holdings. For many years he served as consular agent of Italy.

Today the V. Guerrieri Cigar Company is the only large cigar factory owned by an Italian in Tampa. This firm was established in 1937, and has become one of the major plants in the city.

The reader (*lector*) in the cigar factories held a position of high esteem. It was required that he possess a resonant, clear voice that could be heard throughout the loft. His diction had to be perfect and the reading was always in Spanish. Italians held varied positions in the cigar industry—from night-watchmen to the exalted position of being *un fabricante*, but an Italian as a *lector?*—that would seem to be far fetched. Nevertheless, in the entire history of cigar-making an Ybor City one Italian, and only one, attained such a distinction. His name was Onofrio Palermo, a Stefanese, of high intellectual powers, and possessed with an excellent command of the Castilian language. He excelled in his vocal delivery and for years he was a favourite at the Villazon factory.[17]

During the Cuban Revolution against the Spanish the Tampa Italians gave their share in funds on *el dia de la patria* (the day of the fatherland). A few went to Cuba to fight and die.

One of the most colourful Italians to live in Ybor City was Orestes Ferrara. Standing on a soap-box on the corner of Seventh Avenue and Seventeenth Street in his red Garibaldi shirt, Ferrara fired the Cubans into frenzy for the cause of liberty. Before leaving with his Italian friends, Federico Falco and Guglielmo Petriccione, to join General Maximo Gomez in the wilderness of interior Cuba, Ferrara promised his sweetheart, Maria Luisa Sanchez, a resident of Ybor City and a daughter of General Serafin Sanchez, that if he came through the war alive he would return and marry her. In 1902, when Cuba became a republic, he kept his promise and they lived happily together for some seventy years.

Ferrara went back to Cuba and became a very wealthy man. He

served as president of the Cuban Congress and later as Cuban ambassador to the United States. He wrote several cultural and historical books. This author corresponded with him while he lived in Rome. He died a few years ago in his nineties.[18]

The Sicilians, a people with a turbulent past, were endowed with a fervent love for personal liberty. Their heritage was one of three thousand years of conquests and domination by sixteen foreign powers, which had left its mark on their variegated culture. Deeply engrained in the Sicilian mentality is the bitter hatred against oppression. It was very natural for Italian sympathies to lie on the side of the Cuban cause. It is of little surprise, therefore, to find Jose Marti, the great Cuban patriot, commenting on the Tampa Italians in *Patria*, the official organ of the Cuban Revolutionary Party, on September 3, 1892:

> Patria renders a deserving tribute to the memory of that brave Italian Natalio Argenta, who shed his blood for us, and under whose name the Italians of Tampa, lovers of liberty, offer their assistance to the grandiose task of liberating the Antilles.[19]

The Italians of Tampa, always for the underdog, like everyone who heard the classical oratory of Jose Marti, fell under its spell. It must have been an exhilarating experience for these former *contadini* to help others win their independence.

The Italian Community Matures

As time passed, the Italians, no longer bewildered by the new life, began to adjust and enjoy the ways of American society. Their new economic status gave them a comfortable feeling of security they had not known in the old country. They took part in community affairs. The children that were not attending one of the various Italian schools were going to "the free school," or American public school. The Americanization process was on its way. The offspring spoke American-English with the unshakable Italo-Spanish accent, and later their accent took on a trace of the Cracker influence, with a charming southern twang. The children were discarding the ways of the old world. Old habits and predispositions, inherited from a long and ancient ancestry, were being outgrown. Euphonic names changed, as if by magic; Marietta became Molly, Giovannina became Jenny, Domenica, Minnie; while Guido became Guy, Ignazio became Nelson, and Giuseppe, luckily, became Joe.

The early Italians of Tampa, a proud people, strongly believed in self-help. Their antipathy to outside charities and the belief of helping their own led to the establishment of the Italian Club of Tampa— L'Unione Italiana. This mutual aid society was organized 4 April 1894 with 127 members. Bartolio Filogamo, a *prominente* of Tampa, the first Italian cigar manufacturer (Filogamo y Alvarez Cigar Factory), was elected as the first president.

The club provided its members with sick and death benefits. Its comprehensive health insurance program is one of the oldest examples of cooperative social medicine in the United States. The Italian Club of Tampa is considered the fore-runner of the more than fourteen hundred mutual aid societies that flourished in Italian neighbourhoods throughout the United States.

The first clubhouse was located near the northwest corner of Seventh Avenue and Eighteenth Street. It was erected during the administration of Philip F. Licata, a notable pioneer leader who served on the city council and as Italian consular agent. One day in May 1914, the club headquarters was completely destroyed by fire. A new and impressive neo-classic, three-storey building was inaugurated in 1918 across the street from the original clubhouse. The magnificent new building became the centre for social, cultural and educational functions. Through the years it has been a symbol of pride, and a memorial to the glorious past of Italian civilization.

The club became an important gathering place. In the evenings Italian cigar-makers would meet to swap stories with their cronies, while others played card games of *scopa, briscola* and *ziceinetta* for small stakes.

Small groups of men, to while away their time, used to take a *spasseggiata* or promenade in the evenings from the Italian Club to Nebraska Avenue and return. They strolled along Seventh Avenue, at a leisurely pace, with dignity, hands clasped behind their backs *à la Napoleon* in a supreme gesture of sovereignty.

By 1910, the first generation of Tampa-born Italians were growing up, and in a polite manner asserting their views, which reflected modern and Americanized ideas. A few of the old timers decided to form a new club. On 1 September, 1910, the new club was born with the impressive name of Societa di Mutuo Soccorso Italia with Giuseppe Antonio Falsone as its first president. The clubhouse, a two-storey wooden structure, was located on the northwest corner of Eighth Avenue and Nineteenth Street. People referred to the club simply as Societa Italia, but it was generally known as *La Societa di li Vecchi*, or the old timers' club. The building was razed to make way for urban renewal, but the club remains very much alive with 150 members and substantial funds. The club was headed by banker Anthony J. Grimaldi for twenty-seven years. John Accurso is now president.

In 1923 my father, Paul Pizzo, a 34-year-old native American, proud of his heritage and seeking to strengthen the position of Italians in America, founded the first Florida chapter of the prestigious Order of the Sons of Italy. The Tampa chapter was named La Nuova Sicilia. Pizzo served as founding president for two terms. The Order was started in New York in 1905 by Dr. Vincent Sellaro, and has branched out into more than three thousand lodges. Today Tampa has three lodges, and in Florida there are twenty-six. For more than fifty years La Nuova Sicilia has rendered meritorious services to its members, and has contributed immensely to the preservation of Italian culture in Tampa. In 1960 Paul Pizzo was lauded by *Il Volto D'Italia*, which stated that although he was born in America, he "speaks of Italy with all the passion of a man in love. He is the true standard bearer of our language, our traditions, our culture, our way of life, and dignity." He did not want America to be the graveyard of Italian heritage, but fertile soil where this heritage could grow.

It was inevitable that the Italians would enter politics. Their gregarious nature and desire to better serve the social needs of their people prompted their initial entry into public life. The first Ybor City Italian elected to public office was Nunzio DiMaggio who was elected to the city council in 1911. He possessed shrewd common sense, and a burning desire to get ahead. This gave the Italians an aura of civic pride. "It is true," many exclaimed, "in a democracy everyone is equal." There were many obstacles ahead, but the mental block had been breached.

One of the most important Italian families in the political life of Tampa are the Spicolas, who have been politically active since the early thirties. The family dates to the pioneer days of Ybor City, and many of its members have given devoted service over many years. Charles, Sr. Angelo, A.G., Jr., and G.C. (Tommy, Jr.) have supported many worthwhile community projects through the Rotary and Lions Clubs. G.C. Spicola, Sr., the first of the family to settle in Tampa, established a hardware store at 1815 Seventh Avenue which eventually developed into the present Spicola Hardware Company. Judge Joseph G. Spicola served on the Justice of the Peace Court, his son, Joseph, Jr., served as state attorney. In Tampa there are forty-nine attorneys with Italian names, five of which are Spicolas.

It took seventy years for an Italian to achieve the highest political office in Tampa. Nick Nuccio, a third-generation Tampan, entered politics in 1929. He served two terms on the city council and eight terms on the County Commission. He was a politician who meant what he said, but he let his actions speak for him. Nick Nuccio became the first mayor of Tampa of Italian heritage and served the city most diligently through two terms. The boy from Eighth Avenue and Seventh Street became a legend in his own time, and is admired as being "a friend of all of the people." Nuccio was succeeded by Dick Greco, Jr., who, was thirty-four, at the time, making him the youngest mayor of a major city in the nation. Dick, called the young lion by the press, brought a Latin charisma never before seen in Tampa politics. He served with great capacity and gusto into a second term, when he resigned to take an executive position with a national company.

Conclusion

The story of the Tampa Italians is a long and colourful one. We can look back with profound admiration to those courageous pioneers who came, making the difficult break with an old way of life, to graft themselves to new and strange mores in an alien world. All came with their aspirations fixed on a happier and abundant life.

As we look at our past, a sense of immediate awareness tells us we must not lose sight of the struggles these early arrivals faced in creating roots in a seemingly arid environment, to achieve a better life for themselves and those who were to follow. These people who came to Tampa were not "birds of passage," but like eagles that came and stayed, to give us the priceless legacy of Americanism.

Notes

1. Vivente Murga Sanz, *Juan Ponce De Leon* (San Juan: Ediciones De La Universidad De Puerto Rico, 1959), p. 59.

2. Garcilaso de la Vega, *The Florida of the Inca.* Translated and edited by John Varner (Austin: University of Texas Press, 1951), pp. 537-39.

3. Anthony Pizzo, *Tampa Town—The Cracker Village with a Latin Accent* (Miami: Hurricane House Publishers, 1968), p. 6.

4. M. M. Cohen, *Notices of Florida and the Campaigns.* A facsimile reproduction of the 1836 edition (Gainsville: University of Florida Press, 1964), p. 159.

5. E. P. Panagopoulos, *New Smyrna, An Eighteenth Century Greek Odyssey* (Gainsville: University of Florida Press, 1966), p. 191.

6. In small communities during the nineteenth century there was usually only one law enforcement officer. It was customary to call him town marshall.

7. Lawrence Will, *Cracker History of Okeechobee* (St. Petersburg, Fla.: Great Outdoors, 1964), pp. 102-3.

8. D. B. McKay, *Pioneer Florida* (Tampa: The Southern Publishing Co., 1959), pp. 177-211.

9. Pizzo, *Tampa Town*, p. 82.

10. Karl Grismer, *Tampa.* Edited by D. B. McKay (St. Petersburg: The St. Petersburg Publishing Co., 1950), p. 183.

11. Angelo Massari, *La Comunita italina di Tampa* (New York: American Press, 1964), p. 706.

12. Ibid.

13. WPA, Federal Writers' Project, "History of Hillsborough County" (unpublished manuscript).

14. Ibid.

15. Wen Galvez, *Tampa, impressiones de emigrado* (Ybor City: Establecimento Tipografico Cuba, 1897), p. 95.

16. *Dedication Souvenir—Our Lady of Perpetual Help Church* (Ybor City, 1937).

17. Interview with José Vega, 15 Dec., 1975.
18. Interview with Dr. Vincent Spoto, 21 June, 1977.
19. Angelo Massari, *La Comunita italiana di Tampa*, p. 721.
20. *Tampa Tribune*, 10 Feb., 1908.

Bibliography

Canova, Andrew P. *Life and Adventures in South Florida*. Palatka, Fla., 1885.

Cohen, M. M. *Notices of Florida and the Campaigns*. A Facsimile of the 1836 edition. Gainsville: University of Florida Press, 1964.

Ferrera, Orestes. Letters to the author from Rome, 1965, 1966.

Galvez, Wen. *Tampa, impressiones de emigrado*. Ybor City: Establecimento Tipografico Cuba, 1897.

Grismer, Karl. *Tampa*. Edited by D. B. McKay. St. Petersburg, Fla.: St. Petersburg Publishing Co., 1950.

Harrison, Charles E. *Genealogical Records of the Pioneers of Tampa*, 1914.

Hazen, Pauline Brown. *The Tampa Blue Book and the History of Pioneers*. Tampa: The Tribune Publishing Co., 1914.

Marti, Jose. *Obras completas*. Vol. II. Habana, Cuba: Editorial Lex, 1946.

Massari, Angelo. *La Comunità italiana di Tampa*. New York: Europe-America Press, 1964.

Massari, Angelo. *The Wonderful World of Angelo Massari: An Autobiography*. Translated by Arthur Massolo. New York: Exposition Press, 1965.

McKay, D. B., *Pioneer Florida*. Tampa: The Southern Publishing Co., 1959.

Our Lady of Perpetual Help Church—Souvenir Program. Tampa-Ybor City: 1937.

Panagopoulos, E. P., *New Smyrna, An Eighteenth Century Greek Odyssey*. Gainsville: University of Florida Press, 1964.

Pizzo, Anthony. *Tampa Town, The Cracker Village with a Latin Accent*. Miami: Hurricane House Publishers, 1968.

Roselli, Bruno. *The Italians in Colonial Florida*. Jacksonville: The Drew Press, 1940.

Sanz, Vicente Murga. *Juan Ponce de Leon*. San Juan: Ediciones de la Universidad de Puerto Rico, 1959.

Schiavo, Giovanni. *Italian American History*. Vol. I. New York: The Vigo Press, 1947.

WPA, Federal Writers' Project.

The Hill upon a City: The Evolution of an Italian–American Community in St. Louis, 1882–1950

Gary Mormino

"First in shoes, first in Booze and last in the American League," St. Louis boosters chanted not too many years ago. Alas, the twentieth century has left the Gateway City in the starting gates. Today, St. Louis ranks neither first in shoes (the city imports slippers from Rome); nor first in beer (displaced by upstart Milwaukee); and the beloved Browns callously departed for the greener grass of Baltimore's astroturf. And people have joined the athletic franchises in fleeing St. Louis; during the decade from 1960 to 1970, the city's population fell 17 per cent.

But there was a time when St. Louis basked in the urban spotlight, a time when German beer barons sneered at Milwaukee brewmasters and sternwheelers crowded the city's bustling docks. A frontier heritage, river-boat culture, and graceful neighbourhoods imbued the Gateway City with a "touch of catfish and crystal."[1]

St. Louis had already flourished for half a century when American dragoons arrived in 1804 to assay Jefferson's monumental purchase. By 1850, census takers found cosmopolitan St. Louis the most ethnic of any American city. Nearly 60 per cent of the city's inhabitants were foreign-born, and like Gaul, St. Louis was divided into three parts: German, Irish and African. Magyars and Slavs, Latins and Jews, had displaced Celts and Teutons by 1904 when St. Louis hosted the World's Fair. St. Louis had also grown to the nation's fourth-largest city, and contained numerous ethnic enclaves. The sidewalks of "Little Italy" and "the Ghetto," located near the river, beckoned journalists and bohemian elements, but far away from the open-air markets and cramped tenements existed an Italian colony, destined to become one of the most

THE HILL

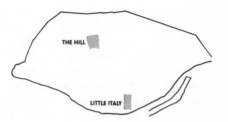

famous in America.[2]

The site chosen by Italians in southwest St. Louis had already witnessed an extraordinary amount of history in just a century. Originally claimed by a French nobleman, Charles Gratiot, the highlands located along the River des Peres were sold in the 1830s to Solomon Sublette, the famed mountain man and fur trapper. In turn, the prickly Sublette grew tired of beaver pelts and sold the land to an Englishman, who named the area Cheltenham, in honor of the famous British spa. Cheltenham opened its doors in the 1850s to a group of French communists, colonists under the red banner of Etienne Cabet who sought refuge there after ill-fated utopian experiments in Texas and Illinois. Factionalism in general and geography in particular doomed Cheltenham as a utopian dream. But ironically, geography also insured the area's economic promise.[3]

Glacial drifts and paleozoic formations had created valuable loessial clay and shale deposits in southwest St. Louis. The Cheltenham seam was discovered in the 1850s by an English labourer who, while drilling a well, penetrated a vein which resembled the famous Stourbridge fire clay of England. Urban America's insatiable demand for new building materials brought about a rapid expansion of the Cheltenham works, including factories and the construction of a Missouri Pacific Railroad terminus in 1852.[4]

An expert geologist once remarked that Cheltenham clay could easily be used in the manufacture of world-class pottery. But local capitalists preferred sewer pipe and fire brick which, rather than attracting master potters, lured thousands of unskilled labourers. In consequence, the population shifted from French aristocrats, trappers, Icarian communists, German miners and Negro muleskinners to its latest inhabitants, Lombards and Sicilians. Today the mines are used as dumping grounds and the tile factories have long since changed tenants, but the last of Cheltenham's occupants, third- and fourth-generation Italian-Americans, have defiantly refused to leave the neighbourhood.

What historical circumstances had joined together to bring about this flight of people to an industrial site in southwest St. Louis? And how does one explain the dogged persistence of these people to build a community, their own city upon a hill?

The year was 1882. In a remote village in Lombardy, a handful of pioneers began their trek to the unfathomable country of America. Originally, they intended to labour in the lead mines of Missouri but found more agreeable work in the brickyards and clay mines of St. Louis. Local inhabitants of the sparsely settled outpost of Cheltenham reluctantly approached the new workers. Hugo Schoessel, who grew up in the area, recalled the coming of the "Eye-talians." "I was about five years old," he reminisced:

> And the first Eye-talians came over here.... About half a dozen men got together and batched it.... The Germans who were here—they mistreated the first Eye-talians.... I remember in the evenings, the Eye-talians had an accordion ...and us kids used to hang on the fence listenen' to 'em.

> And then after a while they send for their friends, and their
> brothers . . . and that's how they got started here![5]

And send for their friends and brothers they did. Immigrants visualized Cheltenham as something more than just a collection of mines and factories. By the mid-1890s, several hundred Lombards and a sprinkling of Sicilians infused a degree of stability to the colony, already called by local natives "Dago Hill." Italians dubbed their new home "La Montagna."

It is all too easy to romaticize immigrant folkways, but one must not forget that these first pioneers paid a heavy price for clearing the urban wilderness. Loneliness, privation and sheer sacrifice characterized their spartan lifestyle. An 1888 inventory of the immigrants' assets included ten dilapidated wooden shacks, several dozen workers and three women. "Tomasso lived very frugally," wrote a reporter in 1907, describing one of these first pioneers. "Bologna, garlic and black bread is ordinarily what may be found at his table during the noon hour and supper."[6] The reporter also noted that Tomasso had not missed a day's work in the mines in twenty-five years. The first wave of immigrants consisted mainly of young men such as Tomasso, who often extended their meagre income through cooperative boarding arrangements. As many as ten men crowded into makeshift shanties and typically groups of ten men shared rooms in twelve-hour shifts. A handful of women worked tirelessly for the care of the boarders.

A beachhead was secured. Lombard foot-soldiers navigated the urban wilderness and their experiences in the uncharted waters of economics, travel, housing and ethnic survival would become wellspring lessons for the next generation of travellers. These pioneers forged the first link in the great chain migrations that evolved into the largest settlement of Milanese outside Lombardy.[7] Other Lombards were soon chain-riveted to the new world. Cuggiono and its neighbouring villages of Inveruno, Malvaglio, Robbechetto, Marcallo and Ossona sent their strongest and most ambitious sons, eager to escape a devastated agrarian ecosystem. If a reeling Lombard economy pushed Cuggiono to the brink of rebellion, the promises of the Hill pulled them over the brink of emigration.

The message from St. Louis forcefully brought home the promise of America. "Here I eat meat three times a day, not three times a year!" exclaimed Allesandro Ranciglio. An unsuccessful blacksmith, Ranciglio set sail for America in hopes of recouping his business and then returning to Lombardy. No bird of passage was he. "I'm not going to come back there [Lombardy]," he later wrote his wife. He added laconic instructions:

> I want you to take Tony and come here on the Hill. There's
> abundance, a lot of work and I'd like to live here. . . . If you
> don't come here, I don't come back.[8]

Americamania of epidemic proportions had struck the stagnant backwaters of Cuggiono. The air wafted optimism with stories of fabulous wealth to be had on a mountain in Missouri; the only known antidote was emigration. While it may have seemed that infectious America-mania had touched all of Italy, as a matter of fact the phenomenon was endemic, striking villages and regions with varying degrees of intensity. In 1882, Cuggiono contained 6,105 Milanese, a rise of 1,138 from the 1861 census. By 1931, Cuggiono's population had fallen to 4,475, a 25 per cent decline, and this in an era of spiralling birth rates.[9]

"Whosoever forsakes the old for the new, knows what he is losing, but not what he will find," an Italian proverb warned prospective immigrants. Not so for the Cuggionesi. Old-world kinship bonds not only survived but thrived during the transoceanic transplantation. *Paesani* needed advice, encouragement, money for passage and Beatrician guides for the arduous odyssey. New arrivals at the turn of the century emerged from well-defined currents, not alien waters, and settlers were shuffled into the colony's mainstream with astonishing swiftness. Upon arrival, the greenhorns sought jobs, housing, protection. Most of all, the three thousand Italian immigrants on the Hill came for *pane e lavore*.

It was an enticing fable, wistfully believed by the desperate emigrants, that the streets of the new world were paved with gold. Once shuffled through Ellis Island, they quickly learned the trinity of truths: first, that the streets were not paved with gold; second, the streets were not paved at all; and third, that they were expected to pave them. Italians arriving on the Hill were taught a fourth lesson: they were expected to mine the clay and fashion the bricks that lined the roads of a growing country.

From the turn of the century until the Depression, the Cheltenham mines and factories dominated the local economy, and at certain plants, Lombards and Sicilians commanded nearly all the lower-paid positions. As the precious clay deposits were exploited, the economic slack was taken up by new industries and an expanding economy. During the period after 1910, heavy and light industries were attracted to the area, including the Carondolet Foundry, the Banner Iron Works, the Quick Meal Stove Company, the McQuay-Norris Company and the National Bearing Metals Corporation.[10]

While capitalists found the Hill attractive, immigrant labourers enjoyed few of the economic benefits from the system. In 1912, unskilled labourers still earned only $1.50 for ten hours of work, prompting a social worker to declare the area as one of the least desirable industrial sectors of St. Louis. In 1917, Hill brickmakers continued to toil ten hours a day for only $2.10, while elsewhere St. Louis union labourers were paid $3.25 to $4.50 for only eight hours' work.[11]

Journalists lyricized Dago Hill as "provincial," "old-world," and "village-like," but no phrase captured the neighbourhood ethos better than "blue collar." From 1900 to the Second World War, the enclave remained the most working-class district in the city. Fashions changed very slowly in this small community. Blue collars were still very stylish in 1940. Italian-Americans were drastically over-represented in jobs at the bottom of the occupational ladder; nearly four times as many workers were classified as "unskilled laborers" (35 per cent) as in the city (9 per cent). In 1934, only six Italians in the community (.05 per cent) had achieved professional status.[12]

One of the cruellest ironies of Italian-American history may be that the very strength and cohesiveness of the ethnic ghetto arrested the occupational prospects of many of its sons. Sociologist Raymond Breton has suggested there may be an inverse relationship between the "institutional completeness" of an ethnic community and the upward mobility of its members. The greater the degree to which an ethnic organization fulfills the social requirements of its congregation, the Breton paradigm holds, the lesser the needs and opportunities for geographic and economic mobility.[13]

Once on the Hill, Lombards and Sicilians sank deep, healthy roots in the urban soil. The neighbourhood offered limited occupational mobility but, more important, the colony evolved into a community, offering residents the continuity and commonality of language, heritage, residential cohesion, entertainment, rituals, mutual aid and, most importantly, a future. But what constitutes a community? The evolution of the Hill from 1890 to 1925, the era which witnessed the dramatic change from mining camp to community, occurred because of a cluster of factors, no one of which entirely explains the later success of the ethnic colony. Clearly, the steady but restrained growth of the enclave, the urban-geographical relationships, and the remarkable homogeneity buttressed the underpinnings of community structure.

The influx of settlers after 1900 greatly changed the social complexion of the Hill. The 1907 St. Ambrose parish census revealed a community of 3,145 at a crossroads. The enclave, once the exclusive haven for Lombards, was quickly becoming an asylum for Sicilians. Northern Italians still outnumbered their southern brethren two to one but the staccato Lombard dialect soon had fierce linguistic competition. Parents unconcerned with the middle-class exigencies of birth control, coupled with the influx of newcomers, added to the burgeoning colony. Census takers counted 2,651 foreign-born Italians and 1,410 second-generation members in 1920; a decade later the number of first-generation Italians declined to 2,264 but their offspring increased to 2,983.[14]

More affluent and populous in 1930 than at the turn of the century, the Hill's intrinsic values—its cultural independence, geographic isolation and ethnic homogeneity—never changed. The colony prided itself as a Little Italy, an island to itself. The lack of transportation and communication reinforced the walled isolation, since the colony gained intra-city bus and streetcar terminals only in the late 1920s. The bus ride to Sportsmans Park widened the social vistas of a Joe Garagiola, but his parents clung desperately to their geographic blinders. "Downtown," the ex-athlete, broadcaster and raconteur reminisced, "as far as Hill mothers and fathers were concerned, was the place you went to take your citizenship test. Otherwise, downtown was as far away as the Duomo in Milan."[15] Nor had the neighbourhood tuned in to "The Shadow" and modern America. In 1930, over 50 per cent of the homes in metropolitan St. Louis owned a radio, but on the Hill, just 18 per cent of the occupants had followed the consumer fad.[16] Newspapers fared little better than the electronics medium. Only one Italian paper, *Il Pensiero* has survived the vicissitudes of publishing, and it must be classified at best a marginal influence. One must remember that as late as 1930, 35 per cent of the colony's foreign-born were classified by the government as illiterate. Moreover, on the eve of Pearl Harbor, only eleven residents claimed a high school diploma out of a total male cohort of 1,600.[17]

The keystones of the Hill's insularity were its ethnic homogeneity and its blessed geographic emplacement. Migration to the community flowed from familiar streams; more than 90 per cent of the residents hailed from a handful of Lombard and Sicilian villages and towns. There were no strangers on the Hill. The colony was anything but cosmopolitan. Between 1900 and 1930, the 32 block area bounded by factories, foundations and highways became saturated with Italians. Every source available—U.S. censuses, city directories and voting registration lists—confirm the obvious: the Hill was exclusive home of vowel-sounding sons of Italy.[18] "The Hill is strictly an Italian neighbourhood," Lawrence "Yogi" Berra professed to a writer, "except I can remember one German family that lived on the same block with us."[19]

The Hill has exuded Italian culture and character for nearly a century. But red, green and white fire hydrants and garlic reflect the exterior of the community. The heart of the Hill exists in its people-oriented institutions. Through its institutions, the clan, the village and the region were progressively transcended to meet the demands of a pluralistic, urban society. The community survived.

In the turbulent decades since the New Deal, the American neighbourhood has suffered grievously; drained by suburbia and devoured by urban renewal, ghettos pockmark the landscape. Amid the destinction of kindred neighbourhoods such as the Valley in Chicago or the West End in Boston, the Hill has emerged as a model community, united and armed for city strife. In his classic twelve-volume masterpiece, *A Study of History*, Arnold Toynbee contends that empires, civilizations, even immigrant neighbourhoods, rise or fall, flourish or decay, as a result of the adequacy or inadequacy of their responses to great challenges. In perspective, four local organizations provided institutional dynamism and leadership: the mutual aid societies, the athletic clubs, the Democratic Party and the parish Catholic Church.

Mutual Aid Societies

Immigrants came to St. Louis, not as Italians but as Cuggionesi and Catanesi. Communal attachments mattered far more than the weak tug of nationalism. Thrust into a competitive urban environment, village loyalties were quickly superseded by regional alliances: Cuggionesi and Catanesi became Lombards and Sicilians out of necessity. In the early years, ethnocentric Lombards and Sicilians got along on the Hill just about as well as they did in the old country. "The people from Toscana," Rosa Casettari whispered to a friend, "they're not good like the people from Lombardia. But they're not bad like the people from Sicilia

—I should say not. Lombardia is the last in the world to do wrong things." Sam Russo recalled his baptism to local race relations. An emigrant from Catania, Russo found employment at a terra-cotta factory. "Oh, the Lombards there treat Sicilians lousy," he exclaimed:

> The Lombards hate us—they hate us. These guys all the time
> call us, "*terra bruciate!*" You come from burned ground!
> They say, "Sicilian no good—Black Hand."[20]

Immigrants such as Russo, cognizant of the factious ethnic rivalries, were aware of their myriad needs in a new environment, and organized a number of mutual aid societies. Lombards rallied around the Nord Italia America Societa (anglicized to the North Italy America Club, or NIAC). Founded in 1897, this institution dominated the community's social life during the formative decades from 1890 to 1920. Indicative of the organizational talents of the NIAC was the Nord Italia America Mercantile, a cooperative grocery and meat market. Sicilians, while never displaying such cooperative bent as the NIAC, nevertheless organized a half-dozen voluntary societies. Both Lombards and Sicilians offered *paesani* security and protection in their fraternal societies. Petrified of being exiled at the Poor Farm or buried unnoticed at Potter's Field, clansmen were guaranteed sickness benefits and a meaningful funeral.[21]

During this period, mutual aid societies helped their members relate to the new world while at the same time functioning as private welfare agencies. But these societies and the community had reached a crossroads by 1925. Many first-generation immigrants had died and a new generation was maturing, more American than Italian, and more Italian than Lombard or Sicilian. To the young, the Nord Italia America Societa or the Megara Augusta seemed irrelevant to problems of work and play. Declining membership rosters, financial insolvency, the proliferation of private insurance firms and the Depression all weakened the hold of the mutual aid society. The NIAC dwindled from 1,400 members in 1913 to 475 *paesani* in 1927.[22]

Marriage patterns provide an even better weathervane of the era. Before 1925, a Sicilian-Lombard marriage threatened a race war. By the late 1920s that marital Rubicon had been crossed without a whiff of gunshot. "Today, Lombards and Sicilians understand each other much better," wrote Giovanni Schiavo in 1929. "Their children . . . marry into each other's families and harmony seems to be prevailing."[23] To the community's growing second-generation, new and revived institutions attracted their attention.

The Parish Church

Today, visitors to the Hill cannot escape the omnipresence of the parish church; physically, the St. Ambrose Catholic Church dwarfs the quaint,

Noah's Ark working-class homes; politically and socially, the Church commands more neighbourhood clout than a Saul Alinsky ever imagined. But power must be cultivated, and St. Ambrose acquired leverage only as the community willed it; for the Church was, after all, only a reflection of the urban immigrant and a mirror of the complex forces within the colony and city.

In 1903, to rectify a religious void on the Hill, Msgr. Cesare Spigardi, a northern Italian cleric who performed yeoman work in St. Louis, established the parish of St. Ambrose. The selection of St. Ambrose, the first Bishop of Milan, as patron saint of the parish demonstrated Spigardi's political shrewdness. However, such showmanship did not guarantee a healthy parish, and St. Ambrose's first decade disappointed St. Louis prelates. A shortage of Italian priests, impoverished parishioners, and skeptical parishioners meant that the Church was without sufficient financial support.[24]

The community's religious direction was tested in January 1921 when the wooden-framed St. Ambrose caught fire (many residents still insist a vat of moonshine exploded!) and burned down. The ominous firebell tolled haunting questions: should St. Ambrose be rebuilt, and if so, would the decision promote concord or discord among the colony's factions? If the church were to be refashioned, would the chapel be in the some-distant future inhabited solely by wrinkled immigrants, clutching their old-world rosaries and new world disappointments? Or even worse, would the parish streets be surrendered to the newest wave of urban dweller as second-generation Italian-Americans swiftly left the colony? Ironically, the very afternoon that flames scorched St. Ambrose, the editor of *La Lega Italiana* castigated the ethnic bickering. "The spirit of *campanilismo* on the Hill is deplorable," thundered the ethnic weekly. "If a Sicilian comes up with an idea, then the Lombard will reject it. This disunity and discord is our ruin and we ought to combat it."[25] The very future of St. Ambrose, the colony and future generations hung in a delicate balance between ethnic tension and institutional development.

The decision to rebuild St. Ambrose marked a milestone in the community's brief history. The challenge to not only build, but build with distinction, galvanized the colony and captivated the community's imagination. Timing was critical. The period of the early twenties seethed with change and many factors underscore the consensus to fashion the church into a community focal point. Prohibition, for instance, proved to be popular and profitable among enterprising Italian-Americans and vast amounts of revenue from bootlegging were sanctified by the collection plate. The closing of the immigrant gates in 1921 and 1924 forced the Hill to look inward and build from within. The rebuilding of St. Ambrose was helped by the enthusiasm of the younger generation on the Hill, which St. Ambrose imaginatively embraced with the recruitment of dedicated men of the cloth.

During the years from 1921 to 1926, the walls of St. Ambrose, moulded from the local red clay which burned to an enchanting red, arched skyward. The sight of such a monumental undertaking was dizzying, a stunning example of cultural transference. The old world's

Sant Ambrogio, where German emperors were canonized, was now joined by a new world namesake, which entertained less exalted guests, but nevertheless preserved the integrity of Lombard-Romanesque architecture.[26]

The new St. Ambrose Church embodied the will of its people. It is impossible to distinguish between the church and the Hill; after 1926 the two were intertwined in a symbiotic relationship. And the church lived up to its great expectations. By the eve of the Depression, St. Ambrose had become the linchpin of the community, an institution of incalculable influence. "The center for all activities ... is St. Ambrose," Giovanni Schiavo observed in 1929.

> "The priest indeed directs most of the activities in this section. ... A religious event ... assumes the importance of a national event."[27]

The church on the Hill was envisioned as something more than just an expensive ($250,000) brick and stained glass edifice, more than a sanitary shrine; it was to be a settlement house, social centre and employment agency. "We priests were the sparkplugs of the community," confessed Bishop Charles Koester, who served at St. Ambrose from 1942 to 1946. "We spoke to more people than any other person on the Hill."[28]

Upon the dedication of St. Ambrose in 1926, one of the more conspicuous gifts adorning the chapel were two angels nestling a band of holy water. The generous donor? The Fairmount Democratic Club. To Hill Republicans, the present smacked of an avenging angel. But after all, who knew better the virtues of unity and the value of compromise?

The Fairmount Democratic Club

"If you wanna get anywhere, you got to unite." Thus spake Louis Jean Gualdoni, founder of the Fairmount Democratic Club. The son of Carlo Gualdoni, who had arrived in St. Louis in 1886, Jean Gualdoni was born on the Hill in 1893. To Carlo Gualdoni's generation, politics represented a bothersome distraction from incessant work demands. But Jean Gualdoni, like his spiritual peers in the Catholic Church, recognized the changes taking place in the colony in the 1920s and acted to harness the untapped potential into a creative force.

Jean Gualdoni received his education in the mines. Quitting school at the age of thirteen to mine clay, he soon graduated to a more lucrative and political position, as grocery clerk for the North Italy America Club. After brief stints as soldier and butcher, Gualdoni returned to the Hill in 1919. In 1921, he was nominated for the sensitive position of Internal Revenue Agent by south St. Louis political boss, John Dolan. The germ of the Hill's political machine was born during that interview. "Jean," the veteran wardheeler advised, "You build that Italian vote out there and you'll have every Democratic politician after you. They'll want your friendship and support and they'll do everything they can for you."[29] Gualdoni often recollected that conversation during his three-year career as prohibition agent. It has been hinted by many local residents, and not denied by the ex-agent, that Jean was known to exercise perceptive indiscretion when patrolling Hill stills. In 1923 Gualdoni refused a transfer to Minneapolis, quit his job, and one year later was herding moonshine operators into a formidable political machine.

The Fairmount Democratic Club opened its doors in 1924. Gualdoni's keen political sense told him that the future of Hill politics lay with the large number of young men and women and the tremendous block of potential voters. Gualdoni was to organized politics what parish priests were to organized religion and what Joe Causino would be to organized sports. "Jean came down to give us a pep talk," recalled Lou Berra, who was eighteen in 1924."'Look,' Jean told us, 'I'll pay your rent, I'll buy your coal, and all you got to do is talk Democrat. Just build it up. Come election time, work for the Democratic Party.'"[30] "Jean," Berra mused, "was the first Democrat":

> He started the Fairmount Democratic Club. I believe that everybody on the Hill my age, even anyone over forty-five, at one time or another belonged to the Fairmount Democratic Club. I mean, if you didn't belong, something was wrong with you. He converted the whole damn neighborhood!

Lou Cerutti was also a charter member of the Fairmount Democrats. "Jean took teenagers like myself, figuring in a few years they'll vote!" Cerutti reminisced.

> "The club was real social. It was a place to keep off the streets... there were two, three pool tables. Every Saturday night he'd take us out to the soccer games, no matter how cold."[31]

Soccer offered more appeal to Hill Italian-Americans than discussion of tariff reform or good government. Philosophically, Gualdoni disdained ideological platforms and offered instead to his grateful constituents the politics of the personal favour. "I'll tell you something," whispered Gualdoni with a twinkle in his eye—the mark of a man of experience:

> It's only human nature that a person, whether he's Italian or not, he goes along with the guy who does the most things for him. And that's what the Italians did... and what I did. I put myself out, you know, to help these people, and I spent quite a lot of my own money! I never took a dime from 'em either. I took their votes though!... whenever I've promised to do something, I did it... That was the secret of my political activities... [32]

Gualdoni's not-so-secret ingredient for success involved his recruitment of talented and dedicated political lieutenants. In 1925 he tapped a young brickmaker, Lou "Midge" Berra. From 1926 until his death in 1964, which characteristically came while making a fiery speech, Midge Berra devoted his life to Hill politics.

When Gualdoni and Berra sat down to evaluate the Hill's political present and future, they both recognized a critical problem which had hamstrung previous efforts to build a powerhouse. Until sufficient numbers of native Italian-Americans became of voting age, the Hill's political voting bloc would of necessity be composed of naturalized immigrants. Only seventy-nine foreign-born Italians had become naturalized citizens during the period 1906 to 1920.[33] The message and mission was clear. Promptly, a clerk was hired from the Immigration Bureau to teach citizenship classes. Others became citizens through less formal means. "My Dad became a citizen," reminisced Roland De Gregorio:

He became a citizen, like other . . . because they studied their questions and answers like "Our Fathers." In other words, if you would say to him, "Who was the first President of the United States?" he knew not only the answer to that question but also the next question. . . . Now if—and it happened —if the judge asked the question and then skipped one, he would give the wrong answer. They learned their lessons like prayers.[34]

In cases where unsympathetic judges deviated from custom, Berra and Gualdoni personally accompanied the applicants to serve as their "witnesses." "One of my duties as leader of the Hill was to help with citizenship papers," Midge Berra told a reporter in 1962:

The federal government investigated me once because there were 1800 people with my name on their citizenship papers! The government thought maybe I was selling papers, but I wasn't. It was just part of the services we gave.[35]

The results paid immediate dividends. By 1940, fully 48 per cent of the Hill's immigrants claimed citizenship and another 11 per cent had taken out their first papers. The pumps were primed.[36]

The Fairmount Democratic Club quickly became a force to be reckoned with in St. Louis politics. For the machine's 24-hour, year-round services, the electorate richly rewarded the Democrats on election day. The *Globe-Democrat* speculated that the Hill maintained the most consistent delivery ward in St. Louis during the last half-century. Party brass delighted in trumpeting the fact that in 1950 the Hill contained more registered Democrats than the entire state of New Mexico. "It's not the percentage that counts so much," lectured the political patriarch Gualdoni. "Rather it is where there is a certain group that stands as a bloc, a bloc that votes together. That's what made the Italians,"[37] he deftly explained, a smile of satisfaction springing to his face. As Kerry Patch and traditional voting blocs dissolved, the Hill's political stability amplified in importance. Mayor Raymond Tucker once confessed that Midge Berra's support was worth a three to four thousand vote lead in a city-wide election.[38]

Clout begat clout. Residents were reminded by wardheelers that their vote spelled power, and as a further inducement, patronage jobs were lavishly distributed among the Democratic faithful. Gualdoni funnelled patronage through his position as Street Commissioner, 1936-41; Ward Committeeman, 1936-44 and Manager of Kiel Auditorium, 1951-63. Berra held the most powerful patronage job in the city, from 1939 to 1962 as Revenue Collector. Many residents laud Berra and Gualdoni for their political influence in the local economy. "It was hard for Italians to get jobs at Quick Meal and McQuay-Norris [local factories]," contended a local mailman:

> Up to that time, it was mainly Germans working there. Finally Midge broke the ice somehow, and if you wanted a job before and after the war, he got you a job. See? These men would try and get their people jobs. They worked for their people. I remember going to Midge Berra, and he got me a job at Quick Meal after the war in '45.[39]

While patronage greased the machine's political gears, personal service ensured a smooth and successful operation. The Gualdoni-Berra machine was foremost a community-based affair. Politics of the personal favour was no mere campaign rhetoric. "Most politicians when elected forget about the people," sneered saloon-keeper Charles Pozza, "but not these!"[40] Tales of the machine's helping hand are as common as wardheelers frequenting funeral parlours. "Midge worked in politics twenty-four hours a day," exclaimed Paul Berra, a friend and today St. Louis City Treasurer. "Midge would do anything and everything for anyone in his ward," he marvelled.[41]

The machine above all provided services which immigrants needed: physical support, jobs, food, help in securing citizenship; a buffer against an unfamiliar and imposing urban bureaucracy; and the intangibles of social friendship and sympathy. In both a manifest and latent sense, the local machine got things done. "You know, in a community like this, you gotta have somebody to keep control of things," explained eighty-year-old Caterina Borghi. "A lot of us old timers didn't know what the score was till Midge and Jean told us."[42]

"Engine" Charley Wilson once proclaimed that what was good for General Motors was good for the U.S. of A. The same could be said about the Fairmount Democratic Club and the Hill. Local political institutions, like recreational, clerical and criminal organizations, mirrored community values, and political triumphs were achievements shared by the entire ethnic colony. "Politics was a great unifying factor for the Hill," said Bishop Charles Koester:

> The relationship between the party headquarters and the church was a very close one. Anything that the community needed, as we priests saw it, all we had to do was call up

Jean Gualdoni or Midge Berra. They stood by their people ... [43]

The Catholic Church worked closely with Democratic leaders in the
implementation of policy. "There was a constant interchange between
us," remembered Bishop Koester:

> I would say that without *any* exaggeration, I could run into
> Midge Berra seven to ten times a week. ... They were in-
> volved in it and so were you. And you ran to see them about
> something rather than call them up. Just down the street. Or
> you just stopped by to see what was going on. Your whole
> life on the Hill revolved around a succession of meetings and
> people.[44]

Politics, like organized athletics and religion, both retarded and
reinforced ethnic identity. Had it not been for the Fairmount Democratic Club, hundreds of immigrants would never have become American citizens. The machine also obtained employment for many of its
residents, thus introducing them to a new work environment and social
atmosphere. Moreover, political success guaranteed cooperation, and
fifty years of electioneering brought Hill Italians into contact with a
wide range of state and local officials.

Yet party leaders were eager to use the ethnic issue as a campaign
issue. In 1938, for example, Gualdoni spearheaded the renaming of
Cooper Avenue to Marconi Avenue. Gualdoni's close friend, Mayor
Dickman, personally cut the ribbon at the dedication ceremonies.

Athletic Enterprises

Italian-American schoolchildren, like immigrants preparing for a citizenship exam, knew their holy trinity by heart. Few local observers would
not have known the organizational trinity as well, dominating the Hill
since the 1930s; precisely at the moment Lombards and Sicilians were
transforming St. Ambrose II into an activist church and Hill Democrats
were flocking to the standard of the Fairmount Democratic Club,
neighbourhood youths were being forged into an athletic alliance. Historians who ignore sports as a serious topic of study would do well to
examine the role of organized recreation at the local level. Recreational
enterprise represents a microcosm of America; the role men attribute to
sports can tell us as much about their society as can their intellectual
and political endeavors. Just as Wellington insisted the battle of Water-
loo was won on the playing fields of Eton, so the battle to win the Hill's
youth was won on the playing fields of the sandlot.

The roots of the colony's youth movement originated during the
seedbed of the 1920s. In an immediate sense, the greatest obstacle to

organizing local youths was the very pervasive gang system; in a broader sense, the gangs threatened the future of the colony. A product of many factors, such as demography, acculturation, schooling, prohibition and the leisure revolution, the Italian-American gang was not unique but part of a national phenomenon.[45] Locally, the high birth rate generated large numbers of young men for gang membership; more than seven hundred men aged fifteen to thirty matured during the twenties, followed by a thousand more in the thirties.[46] More important than the onset of collective puberty, these young men, second-generation Italian-Americans, prided themselves as being aggressively new world in social outlook. Young boys were rebelling against the patriarchal domination of their fathers, reported a local social worker. Many, he noted, "were ashamed of their parents."[47]

Another powerful Americanizing force, the neighbourhood school, existed as both a laboratory for democracy and a cauldron for socio-ethnic conflict. Italian parents looked upon the public schools with suspicion and distrust. Compounded by the growing needs of the family economy and the desire to purchase homes, Italian-Americans achieved little educational progress. "A fourteenth birthday means a work certificate and a farewell to studies," lamented Ruth Crawford in 1916.[48] Little had changed two decades later when school officials complained that few Hill students finished the eighth grade and even fewer high school. Students and ex-students usually graduated to the gang.

Inside Public School 101, for example, children were taught world geography; outside the cloistered halls they quickly learned the lessons of ethno-physical geography. "Well, let's give you a little geography," chuckled Lou Berra:

> Kingshighway . . . the creek . . . the railroad tracks . . . that was *our* boundary! . . . Up the hill we had the Blue Ridge Gang–Irish. To the northwest we had the Cheltenham Gang–a mixture of Germans and more or less natives. East of Kingshighway was the Tower Grove Gang, what most of us refer to as Hoosiers . . . then there was the Dog Town Gang . . . You go beyond that and you get your ass kicked . . . [49]

Like urban teenagers across the country, Hill Italian-Americans clustered into their street-corner societies. "Every kid on the Hill belonged to a gang or club," remembered Joe Garagiola. "You either belonged or were out of the action."[50] Called the Hawks, Falcons, Ravens, Little Caesars, and Stags, gangs proliferated throughout the twenties and thirties, climaxing in 1941 when nearly fifty neighbourhood clubs boasted a thousand neighbourhood members. Internally, Hill Italian-Americans divided into gangs on the basis of geography, a kind of urban *campanilismo*. "All the kids around my age who lived on Elizabeth Avenue made up a sports club," reminisced Yogi Berra.[51] The Hill thus faced external and internal threats in the early 1920s.

If young Italian-Americans were unable to relate to civic lessons and schoolmates, they found outside the classroom a world suddenly relevant to the adventurous. The 1920s brought, among other things, prohibition to the Hill. Disdainful of the Volstead Act, Italians saw the puritanical law as an easy and exciting way to supplement one's income. Bootleggers, like good businessmen, utilized a natural resource to maximize their operations—the gang. Undeterred by police, indeed often assisted by lawmen, gang members laboured for local suppliers in a variety of ways, from running moonshine to distilling white lightning. "Young kids, old men," crackled one old timer, "they were all there making moonshine. There was a lot of money made in this neighborhood!"[52] "What young chap would attend school when such money was available?" pondered a social worker.[53]

Finally, the younger generation were beneficiaries of the 1920s leisure revolution. The first waves of Italian immigrants had neither the time nor the inclination to play stickball or join athletic clubs. By the mid-twenties, industrial labourers were receiving one-and-a-half days' rest per week and some had paid holidays. Moreover, the young, compared to their immigrant fathers, remained in school longer and began work at a later age. Social workers, increasingly aware of the importance of environment, became concerned with the leisure activities of urban youth.

In sports, as in life, there exists a fine edge between a keen and healthy rivalry and rancorous, self-destructive competition. Sports had polarized the clubs by the early 1920s. "We had soccer teams nobody could beat," insisted a proud Roland De Gregorio. "But then," he said, his voice slipping noticeably, "we used to fight among ourselves."[54] The man who would change all that swaggered down Cooper Avenue in 1925, eager to proselytize the gospel of sports and brotherhood. By the time his work was completed in the 1950s, Cooper Avenue had been changed to Marconi Avenue, and his recruits had kicked and battled the Italian colony to international fame.

The man was Joseph Causino, representing the St. Louis Southside YMCA. His arrival, coinciding with the completion of St. Ambrose Church in 1926, signalled a seminal event in the Hill's history. A Father Flanagan in gym shoes, he was described as "carrying a Bible in one hand and a wallop in the other."[55] The enthusiastic Causino, part of the new breed of social worker, accepted the gauntlet thrown by Hill toughs. "He kept us out of jail," volunteered one of the many Italian gang members:

> Because, like I said, we had cousins and big brothers who were gangsters, with knives and guns. It took a guy like Joe Causino to see that we were headed for trouble.... We let off steam that way [with sports]. And that's why a lot of guys will tell you, that by the grace of God and Uncle Joe Causino, we were all clean-cut kids![56]

Mused a former gang member: "It finally got to the point where Uncle Joe got us working together. One of the things that welded us together was sports."[57]

Causino hawked pride, character, unity, and the strenuous life through the appealing packaging of baseball and soccer. He had personally witnessed the vicious wounds that gang warfare had wrought upon the downtown colony, Little Italy, and was determined that the Hill youth would avoid such fratricidal conflict. Causino's techniques and programs worked. His recreational programs, dovetailed with the extensive St. Ambrose youth movement, created an effective, all-encompassing pincer movement on the colony's young, leaving little room or inclination for deviation. Sports brought pride to the Hill, and the community, in turn, brought recognition and fame to the Gateway City. Soccer and baseball offered antidotes for the Depression-strapped Hill.

The blistering competitiveness, channelled into a community-wide spirit, proved unbeatable on diamond and turf. The Hill's athletic *prowess* upset the balance of power in St. Louis soccer, hitherto dominated by the German Sports Club, the Spanish Society and the Irish Catholic League.[58] Trouncing Micks, Krauts and Latinos added a new dimension to ethnic rivalries and became far more popular and desirable than belting the *paesano* next door. Sports offered a safety valve, an acceptable outlet for the free-spirited Italian-Americans. Given youth's predilection toward violence and crime, soccer collisions exercised a mild form of cathartic release, a social safety valve.[59]

The Hill completed a remarkable athletic transformation in a span of less than twenty years. When Jean Gualdoni founded the Fairmount Democratic Club in the early 1920s and attempted to organize a soccer team, the frustrated politician could find no qualified Italians with which to stock the team and thereby attract Democratic voters. By 1929, the first organized Hill soccer team had won the divisional championship, and by 1940 St. Ambrose climaxed the prewar successes by winning the Missouri Ozark Amateur Championship. The fiery centre from that team, Joe Numi, would return after the war to lead area soccer teams to new heights. Coach Numi was guaranteed quality players, since his farm team, St. Ambrose, won the Sublette Park Parish School League title for eleven consecutive years, from 1934 to 1945.[60]

Sports had a galvanic impact upon the Hill, an effect measured far beyond tarnished trophies. Potentially the greatest threat to community stability, solidarity and image had been the gang, for if the Hill could not win the affections of its young, it was doomed to the ethnic graveyard. Organized recreation wiped out more than hard feelings. Sports became a handmaiden for solidarity, a vehicle which helped transform factional conflict into creative competition. The Hill had by 1941 become, partly through the medium of sports, an ethnic phalanx. Young and old, Lombard and Sicilian, old-world mustachioed Petes and new-world Yogis passionately identified themselves with the Hill, with St. Ambrose, with neighbourhood teams. "What impressed me the most about the kids from the Hill," insisted Fr. Anthony Palumbo, priest and soccer coach at St. Ambrose from 1932 to 1948, "was that they were willing to make a lot of sacrifices to play on the team ... they were willing to sacrifice for the Hill."[61]

The camaraderie and fiery athletic spirit helped solidify the community and prepare the neighbourhood for the ultimate opponent: World War Two. It should be no coincidence that it was a young priest who doubled as soccer coach and editor of a rag-tag newspaper (named after a parish athletic club) that forged the unity which enabled Dago Hill to withstand yet another crisis.

World War Two and After

Life on the Hill entered a new era on a cold December afternoon in 1941. America's soft underbelly was penetrated that Sunday with news that Japanese forces had attacked Pearl Harbor. Shock, disbelief and fear swept the once-insular neighbourhood, for Pearl Harbor, like the Hill, was once an island to itself.

War would mean different things to different people. To hundreds of thousands of hyphenated Americans living in Little Italy and Hunky Hollow, the war forced a denouement, a choice between an old way of life and a new. To fifteen hundred sons eligible for the draft on the Hill, the future seemed unclear. What would happen to a colony suddenly shorn of its youth? The greatest plague to a city, Plato noted in *The Laws*, was "not faction but distraction." Piqued, excited, impassioned and perhaps bored by the parochial environment, Hill Italian-Americans stampeded to induction centres in herds. For the first time in the colony's history, large numbers took the Vandeventer bus, not to Dollar Day at Famous-Barr, but to the more exotic confines of basic training camps. Over 1,100 men enlisted in the services, twenty-four of whom never returned.[62]

Few battles were fought with more intensity and pride than the Hill's homefront campaign to win the war, Unlike 1917, when immigrants were cajoled and coerced into demonstrations of 100 per cent Americanism. Perhaps mainly to show their fellow Americans their hostility to the Fascist regime in Italy, the Hill led the charge into this conflict.[63] This involved more than a fight to win the war; more importantly, this was a battle for community.

Ironically, the man who spearheaded the homefront campaign was not Italian. Charles Koester was a 24-year-old German-American priest in 1939 at the American College in Rome when the European apocalypse drove him into exile. In 1942 Koester received his first assignment —the parish of St. Ambrose. Koester's youthful appearance, sincerity and fluent Italian immediately endeared him to the skeptical congregation. In his first weeks on the Hill, Koester received several vivid impressions: first, "the tremendous enthusiasm of the school children"; and secondly, "the desperate need to supply local servicemen with news from the home front."[64] The *Crusader Clarion* was born—a neighbourhood paper to reach the soldiers. The priest had simply figured out what political scientists call the flow chart. By starting a local newspaper, Koester had tapped into the power structure: the Fairmount Democratic Club bankrolled the venture, schoolchildren supplied muscle and energy; and the entire operation was assembled in the community cockpit at St. Ambrose Church. The first edition of the *Crusader Clarion* rolled off a crude mimeograph machine in November 1942. Never was a medium hotter. "It was a great contribution to many parents," explained Editor Koester. "You see, many of the parents couldn't write a letter... and simply could not supply the information we could."[65] Accounting procedures were disregarded; copies were mailed gratis to servicemen.

Lonely soldiers, hopelessly homesick for the things they "ain't got," reacted emotionally to the *Crusader Clarion*. "As I read the paper my heart overflowed with happiness," exulted Charlie Ferrario, recalling receipt of the first issue.[66] The tabloid offered men a sense of continuity. "That paper is what really kept us together," mused one resident-soldier. "You go back and ask, 'What kept the Hill together?' That paper is what kept us together. It was like a letter from your buddy. In that paper was letters, names, everybody knew where and what your friends were doing... "[67]

When the boys finally returned, the community was braced for the homecoming. VJ day was collectively the happiest day in the colony's history. But memories of the the Battle of the Bulge and New Caledonia quickly faded as local residents grasped the magnitude of the postwar challenges. The colony's very future rested with its ability to respond to the complex changes wrought by war, demanded by big government and sought by the young. War, while unquestionably broadening the social horizons of the Hill, also manifested an intense, reintegrating force which strengthened the community.[68]

"The momentum was really here on the Hill," reminisced Bishop Koester, reflecting back on the local scene in 1945. "There is no question about it. Those were stirring events... especially the great enthusiasm and unity that existed among these people. Such a strong, wholesome unity. The momentum was really there... "[69]

Local leaders sought to harness this impetus into socially meaningful projects which appealed to younger Italian-Americans. In 1949, for instance, the new St. Ambrose School was erected, the culmination of a long-needed drive to meet the colony's educational needs.[70] Dramatically, education became suddenly relevant to Hill parents, students and ex-students, as the war, with its attractive G. I. Bill, enabled many veterans to finish or further their limited schooling. Not unrelated, the number of male professions on the Hill rose impressively after the war; the percentage of professionals/managers in the local work force grew from 1 per cent to 16 per cent during the period from 1940 to 1960.[71]

The drive to improve the community's educational standards proved an easier struggle than the fight to upgrade neighbourhood housing. No index better illustrates the Hill's character than housing. In 1900, census takers found no Italian homeowners in the hardscrabble colony. But if, during the community's formative period from 1890 to 1920, the neighbourhood offended aesthetic tastes because of its open sewers and gaunt shacks, its dilapidation evoked the squalor of hope, not the squalor of resignation. On the eve of Pearl Harbor, an extraordinary 53 per cent of the homes on the Hill were occupied by their owner, a rate double that of the rest of the city of St. Louis and a percentage unrivalled by any ethnic group in the city, and few in the United States.[72]

But the percentage of homeownership belied the serious problems confronting returning veterans in 1945. Crowded and antiquated at worst, clean and dignified at best, housing, or the lack of it, posed a serious obstacle to the postwar enclave. Moreover, nearly three-quarters of the residential structures had been contructed before 1919, and only 66 per cent of these homes had both a flush toilet and a private bath.[73]

An earlier generation had prided itself on the Hill's single-minded ability to lift itself up by its own collective bootstraps without assistance from a far-away government. "I am now convinced that much of the uniqueness of this settlement was due to a sense of common purpose present in most of the Hill family units," reflected Elmer Shorb Wood, a social worker in the area in the 1930s:

> Perhaps even more so was the depth of emotional commitment given to this common purpose. Because of several factors and certain amplifying events in the early 1930s, it was unusual to find a member living on the Hill who did not support the common cause—to establish a home—an Italian-American home and maintain it in this country of their adoption.[74]

But by 1945, New Deal and Fair Deal agencies hindered older neighbourhood's efforts to compete against newer suburbs by discouraging the renovation of older homes in favour of the purchase of newer properties.[75] The road to an America of Los Angeleses was further paved by the appeal of the postwar automobile culture, the construction of high-speed freeways (often through immigrant neighbourhoods), and the relocation of jobs. Remarkably, the Hill withstood these challenges and the community held together, building from within. A brick bungalow had become emblematic of an immigrant group who had come to America to make bricks, and a brick façade added after the war added an emphatic endorsement to the future of the neighbourhood.

The postwar Hill witnessed not only an internal building renaissance, but also a movement to the contiguous neighbourhoods. By the 1950s, the area southwest of the colony, known as Blue Ridge Heights, became a geographical extension of the Hill, as Italian-American families spilled into previously built homes. The Hill was no shrinking ghetto, but rather an expanding colony.

The Catholic archdiocese charted residential patterns closer than real estate sharks. Consequently, two of the more popular pastors at St. Ambrose, Fathers Koester and Palumbo, were reassigned to contiguous parishes. Indicative of these residential-demographic changes, St. Ambrose was recategorized in 1955 from an Italian national parish to a regular diocesan territorial one.

Since the 1920s, St. Ambrose had orchestrated an intensive movement among parish youth. Area athletic teams had scored impressive victories since the Depression, but none more spectacular than those during the recreational *risorgimento* of the postwar period. "All is not spaghetti, macaroni and choice wine on the Hill, that famed neighborhood in Southwest St. Louis," ballyhooed a columnist in 1949:

The principal occupation is sports and the main export is known athletes. Many people think it is baseball because of Berra, Garagiola, and Restelli. But almost every sport has produced a similar quota of great stars.[76]

City power-brokers, like athletic recruiters, swarmed to the postwar Hill to nurture political support. Buttressed by patronage and stirred by the enemy-alien crisis of 1941-42, voting became not only one's political duty, but also one's patriotic obligation, and nothing touched party hearts like an electorate loyal to the Democrats. The crushing political victories engineered by the machine, in the decade after the war forcefully impressed city fathers, resulting in the dedication of Macklind (later renamed Berra) Park.

Increasingly after VJ Day, the Hill stood out as the Great White Hope, the last St. Louis immigrant colony to elude the vicious circle of urban decay and out-migration. The Hill's census tracts easily contained the highest percentage of immigrants in the city. While mandolins and Caruso arias may have deferred to Sinatra discs and television, few outsiders mistook the community as anything but Italian. "The best way to describe the Hill is to call it a village," gushed a journalist, "an Italian village separate from the rest of the city."[77]

Notes

1. Ernest Kirschten, *Catfish and Crystal* (Garden City: Doubleday, 1965).

2. St. Louis *Star*, 21 Jan. 1912; St. Louis *Republic*, 20 May, 1905; St. Louis *Post-Dispatch*, 18 May, 1912; St. Louis *Globe-Democrat*, 7 Oct. 1900. St. Louis newspapers hereafter referred to as *Star, Republic, Post-Dispatch* and *Globe-Democrat*.

3. George Brooks, "Some Views of Old Cheltenham," Missouri Historical Society *Bulletin*, XXII (Oct. 1965), pp. 32-35; Lewis Thomas, "The Sequence of Areal Occupation in a Section of St. Louis," *Annals of the Association of American Geographers*, XXI (March, 1931), pp. 75-90; Doris Blick and H. Roger Grant, "French Icarians in St. Louis," Missouri Historical Society *Bulletin*, XXX (Oct. 1973), pp. 3-28.

4. Henry Reis and Henry Leighton, *History of the Clayworking Industry in the United States* (New York: John Wiley and Sons, 1909); Esther Louise Aschemeyer, "The Urban Geography of the Clay Products Industry of Metropolitan St. Louis." (Master's Thesis, Washington University, 1943); *Brick and Clay Record*, 1898-1910.

5. Interview with Hugo Schoessel, 10 July, 1973.

6. "Toilers of the Dark," *Globe-Democrat*, 9 June, 1907.

7. Letter from Angelo Sala to Gary Mormino, 18 Aug. 1975; *Post-Dispatch*, 23 Jan. 1898; Frank Thistlewaite, "Migration from Europe Overseas in the

Nineteenth and Twentieth Centuries," in *Population Movements in Modern European History*. John MacDonald, "Chain Migration," in *Milbank Memorial Fund Quarterly*, 42 (1964), pp. 82-97.

8. Interview with Antonio Ranciglio, 29 May, 1975.

9. Instituto centrale di statistica popolazione residente dei communi al censimenti: dal 1861 al 1961 (Roma: 1961).

10. Thirteenth Census of The United States: 1910, Vol. IV, *Population and Occupational Statistics* (Washington D. C.: U. S. Government Printing Office, 1914); Aschemeyer, "The Urban Geography of the Clay Products Industry," pp. 50-60; Interviews; Grace Keating, "A Study of Americanization of the Italian Immigrant in that District Known as 'The Hill,'" (Master's Thesis, St. Louis University, 1935).

11. Twelfth Census of the United States: 1900, *Statistics of Occupations* (Washington D. C.: U. S. Government Printing Office, 1903), pp. 708-9; *Federal Census for Metropolitan St. Louis, 1930* (St. Louis); *Post-Dispatch*, May 26, 1901; *Post-Dispatch*, April 30, 1912; Irving Crossland, "Immigrants in Industry," (St. Louis: Studies in Social Economy, 1915), pp. 17-18; Grace Foster, "The Hill: A Survey," (St. Louis: International Association, 1934). Hill precincts 13B and 13C coincide exactly with the colony's boundaries, hence the danger of ecological fallacy is minimal.

12. Ibid.

13. Raymond Breton, "Institutional Completeness of Ethnic Communities and the Personal Relations of Immigrants," *American Journal of Sociology*, 70 (1964), pp. 193-205.

14. U.S. Bureau of the Census, Twelfth Census, 1900, National Archives, Washington, D.C.; St. Ambrose Archives, St. Ambrose Church; U.S. Bureau of the Census, Fourteenth Census, 1920; *Population II; Federal Census for Metropolitan St. Louis, 1930.*

15. Joe Garagiola, *Baseball is a Funny Game,* (Boston: J.P. Lippincott, 1960), p. 3.

16. *Federal Census for Metropolitan St. Louis, 1930,* pp. 120-21.

17. Sixteenth Census of the United States: 1940, *Population and Housing,* Vol.VI.

18. *Gould's St. Louis Red-Blue Book,* 1900-1940; Voting Registration Lists, Municipal Archives, City Hall, St. Louis, Mo.

19. Yogi Berra with Ed Fitzgerald, *Yogi: The Autobiography of a Professional Baseball Player* (Garden City: Doubleday, 1961), p. 33.

20. Marie Hall Ets, *Rosa: The Life of an Italian Immigrant* (Minneapolis: University of Minnesota Press, 1970), p. 209.

21. *Post-Dispatch*, 26 May, 1901; *Republic*, 1 Sept. 1907; Interviews.

22. *Il Pensiero*, 17 Aug., 1929; Silvio Pucci, "My Memoirs of the Hill," unpublished autobiography.

23. Giovanni Schiavo, *The Italians in Missouri* (Chicago: Italian Publishing Co., 1929), p. 59.

24. John Walter Galus, "The History of the Catholic Italians in St. Louis," (Master's Thesis, St. Louis University, 1936); Francesco Zabogolio to Bishop Scalabrin, 1889, St. Louis, Archives, Congregation of Saint Charles (Rome), Missionari Di S. Carlo Scalabriniani; Rev. John Rothensteiner, *History of the Archdiocese of St. Louis* (St. Louis: Blackwell-Wielandy, 1928); Interviews.

25. *La Lega Italiana*, 21 Jan. 1921.
26. Bruce Alsopp, *Romanesque Architecture*.
27. Schiavo, *The Italians in Missouri*, p. 60.
28. Interview with Bishop Charles Koester, 9 July, 1973 and 16 Feb. 1976.
29. Interview with Louis Jean Gualdoni, 19 Aug. 1973.
30. Interview with Lou Berra, 11 July, 1973.
31. Interview with Lou Cerutti, 7 Aug. 1975.
32. Interview with Gualdoni.
33. Naturalization Papers, 1906-1936, Immigration Bureau, U.S. District Court, St. Louis.
34. Interview with Roland De Gregorio, 18 Aug. 1973.
35. *Globe-Democrat*, 22 April, 1963.
36. Naturalization Petitions; U.S. Census Bureau, Sixteenth Census of the United States: 1940, *Population and Housing*, Vol. VI, Table 3.
37. Interview with Gualdoni; Globe-Democrat, 12 Dec. 1970; Interview with Lou Berra Jr., 17 Aug. 1973.
38. *Globe-Democrat*, 22 April, 1963; *Post-Dispatch*, 19 May, 1964.
39. Interview with De Gregorio.
40. Interview with Charles Pozza, 6 Aug. 1975.
41. Interview with Paul Berra, 31 July, 1973.
42. Interview with Caterina Borghi, 29 July, 1975.
43. Interview with Koester.
44. Ibid.
45. Frederic Thrasher, *The Gang* (Chicago: University of Chicago Press, 1927); William Foote Whyte, *Street Corner Society* (Chicago: University of Chicago Press, 1943); Harvey Warren Zorbaugh, *The Gold Coast and the Slum* (Chicago: University of Chicago Press, 1929).
46. *Federal Census for Metropolitan St. Louis*. pp. 85-87.
47. Elmer Shorb Wood, "Fairmount Heights: An Italian Colony in St. Louis," (Master's Thesis, Washington University, 1936), p. 45.
48. Ruth Crawford, *The Immigrant in St. Louis* (St. Louis: n.p. 1916), p. 54.
49. Interview with Berra.
50. Garagiola, *Baseball is a Funny Game*, p. 15.
51. Berra, *Yogi*, p. 35.
52. Interview, participant preferred to remain anonymous.
53. Wood, "Fairmount Heights," p. 24.
54. Interview with De Gregorio.
55. *Post-Dispatch*, 9 May, 1941.
56. Interview with De Gregorio.
57. Interview with Lou Berra.
58. James Francis Robinson, "The History of Soccer in the City of St. Louis," (Ph.D. Dissertation, St. Louis University, 1966).
59. Eugen Weber, "Gymnastics and Sports in *Fin-de-Siecle*, France: Opium of the Classes?" *American Historical Review*, 76 (1971), pp. 70-98; Frederic Paxson, "The Rise of Sport," *Mississippi Valley Historical Review*, IV (1917), pp. 142-68.

60. *Post-Dispatch,* 9 May, 1941; Interview with Joe Correnti, 30 April, 1976; *Post-Dispatch,* 1 March, 1953 interview with Bill Kerch, 28 April, 1976; Joe Correnti, "History of Correnti's Soccer Team, 1946-47," (unpublished manuscript).

61. Interview with Fr. Anthony Palumbo, 23 Aug. 1973.

62. Interviews; American Legion records.

63. Gary Mormino, "Over Here: St. Louis Italo-Americans and the First World War," Missouri Historical Society *Bulletin,* XXX (Oct. 1973); John Higham, *Strangers in the Land* (Boston: Atheneum, 1970).

64. Interview with Koester.

65. Ibid.

66. *Crusader Clarion,* 11 Jan. 1943.

67. Interview with De Gregorio.

68. Richard Polenberg, *War and Society: The United States, 1941-45* (Philadelphia: Lippincott, 1972).

69. Interview with Koester.

70. St. Ambrose Archives; *Historical Review of St. Ambrose Church.*

71. Seventeenth Census of the United States: 1950, *Population and Housing Statistics* (Washington: U.S. Government Printing Office, 1952), pp. 199-201.

72. Sixteenth Census of the United States: 1940, *Population and Housing,* Table 2.

73. Letter, Elmer Wood to author, 22 Aug. 1973.

74. Ibid.

75. "Urban Decay in St. Louis," The Institute for Urban and Regional Studies, Washington University, Working Paper Number Ten, March, 1972; Barbara Williams, *St. Louis: A City and its Suburbs* (Santa Monica: The Rand Corporation, 1973).

76. *Star-Times,* 8 Aug. 1949.

77. Mark Geers, "Ethnics Alive and Well on the Hill," *St. Louisan,* V (Sept. 1974), p. 38.

The Italians of Oswego

Luciano Iorizzo

Introduction

As the twentieth century approached, Oswego was being transformed from a commercial into an industrial city. Reflecting deep economic and social changes, its busy port and mills were giving way to light and heavy industry. Oswegonians during these unsettling times were seldom willing to take up the rough, hard labour required to keep pace with the industrial growth. The Irish, German and French-Canadian immigrants provided many willing labourers, but hardly enough to meet the enormous demands of Oswego's burgeoning economy. Accordingly, the door was thrown open to the masses from Southern and Eastern Europe. They came by the thousands and both complemented and competed with the local workforce. Sometimes they accepted lower wages; frequently they struck for equality in higher wages and better working conditions. On occasion they were used as strikebreakers; at other times they themselves were the strikers. Hungry for work, the newcomers gladly filled the bottom rungs of the economic ladder and pushed the earlier immigrants up into positions of economic security and social respectability.

After 1900 industrial expansion proceeded at a frenzied pace. By 1905 local manufacturers were complaining that full capacity operations were being hampered by a shortage of boardinghouses, which discouraged the movement to Oswego of a plentiful and cheap labour supply. Though a large number of houses were subsequently built, the pressure of overcrowding was only partially relieved. The mill and factory managers continued to complain that they could not get enough people to work for them and began a search for independent agents to go outside the community to bring in desirable labour.[1]

Through the ups and downs of the business cycle, industrial growth was maintained. New companies located in the city: Ontario Industrial Company, Howard Thermostat Company, Benson Paper Box Company, Barnes Gear Company, to name a few. The railroads added new freight terminals, yards and other improvements. Some of the old plants such as Ames Iron Works, and even some of the new ones such as Diamond Match, modernized old factories and added new ones. First National Bank built a new facility; City Savings Bank and the Second National Bank remodelled. The city erected a lower bridge, a water plant and a new high school. It also undertook an extensive street-paving and sewer construction program.

In brief, the transformation of Oswego had taken place by 1910. The riverfront, with its flourishing flour mills and majestically standing grain elevators, had once been the economic centre of the community. Sailing and steam vessels had carried salt, lumber, grain and railroad iron, which passed daily through the port. Now Oswegonians were finding employment away from the waterfront. The lots located toward the eastern and western limits of the city were being taken over by manufacturing companies and newer immigrants.

Early Years of the Italian Community

When Antonio Russo settled in Oswego in 1874 with his wife, Rosalia, and their three children, Joseph, Rosalia, and Sarah, only a handful of Italians were living in the city. Joseph became active in the Oswego Business Men's Association and emerged as one of the first interpreters for the vanguard of Italians who appeared in Oswego in the early 1890s. Later in that decade he moved to Syracuse, where he became acquainted with Thomas Marnell, the outstanding leader of the Italians in central New York. A number of Oswego's early Italian settlers came via Syracuse, and Russo and Marnell provided the most important links between the Italians in those communities.

Sarah Russo won a reputation in Oswego as an organist, teacher and public-spirited citizen who volunteered much of her time to civic causes. She teamed with her husband, Rosario D'Angelo, to provide middleman services to the masses of Italians who began streaming into Oswego in the 1890s. The D'Angelos ran an importing store in the heart of the main Italian neighbourhood on the west side of the city. They helped to get people jobs and housing. Sometimes they would take in boarders themselves. They arranged for agricultural workers in season and handled steamship tickets and remittances.

These services were appreciated by Italian and American alike. They helped to provide the labourers so sorely needed in Oswego and smoothed the transition from Italian to American. Rosario worked especially hard to Americanize the Italians. Wooed first by the Democrats and later the Republicans, he joined the latter and exhorted his countrymen to do the same. He encouraged Italians to learn English and to become educated. He preached non-violence before that word became a modern shibboleth. He counselled the Italians to avoid carrying concealed weapons and to place their protection in the hands of the law. He urged his countrymen in the mills and factories to pay no heed to the numerous annoyances to which they were subjected daily. Instead, he suggested that they work hard for the success which would mitigate the prejudice against them.

And prejudice there certainly was. The beginning of the mass migration of Italians to Oswego coincided with the bad press coming out of an incident in New Orleans, when the chief of police was gunned down as he was about to expose *mafiosi* in the city. The emerging consensus on Italians in Oswego was probably summed up in one headline to the story: "Down with the Dagoes." Other national incidents which drew local attention were the murder of a Denver priest and the assassination of Detective Joseph Petrosino. It is no wonder that when two of Oswego's earliest Italian settlers came in the early 1890s they were missed at the railroad station by a local attorney who was charged to meet them. It seems that he was looking for two "strange, foreign, very different-looking men, perhaps a species of human never before seen in Oswego." He was surprised to learn that he could not pick them out of the passengers disembarking at the station.

This, then, was the Oswego to which the masses came. It was a city coming of age in the industrial era. And it had a small colony of Southern Italians who were ready, willing and able to assist the newcomers as they pondered how and where they would fit in.

By 1890 over forty Italians had settled in Oswego. Their numbers rose to 339 in the next decade, then to 809 in 1910, before peaking out in 1915 at 1,229. On the eve of America's restrictionist legislation in the 1920s, the number fell to 900 and dropped each decade thereafter. I have examined the origins of 339 Italian families in Oswego. The majority, 60 per cent, came from the region of Sicily, especially the province of Messina. Of the 203 Sicilian families identified, 108, or 53 per cent, were Messinese. Over half of these came from two areas in the province, the Lipari Islands (43) and Casalvecchio (23), a small community on the sea, south of the city of Messina. The province of Palermo (41) accounted for most of the other Sicilians.[2]

Two regions from the mainland accounted for over half of the remaining 40 per cent: Lazio (45) and Campania (29). Sgurgolo and Morolo, communities in the province of Frosinone, accounted for most of the migration from Lazio; Cilento and Mattonti in the province of Salerno were the main sources of the emigrants from Campania. Lightly represented were the regions of Calabria (Oriolo and Siderno), Basilicata (Potenza), Puglie (Bari and Taranto), Abruzzi and Molise (Campobasso), and Marche (Ancona).

The Italians settled essentially in five of the eight wards of the city, which was separated into the east side and the west side by the

Oswego River. The second ward located on the east side consistently attracted the most Italians; they were mostly from the province of Messina, specifically the Lipari Islands and Casalvecchio. Their neighbourhood, known as the Lakeshore settlement because of its closeness to Lake Ontario, was split in two by the New York, Ontario and Western Railroad, whose trains rumbled daily by the houses of Italians who lived within thirty feet of the tracks. Houses in this area are small frame dwellings which the immigrants were able to purchase in the earlier part of this century for under $1,000. The Lakeshore neighbourhood was not among the most desirable in the city because of the industrial complexes, either in or adjoining it. Mainland Italians, especially, avoided settling there because of that and because of their aversion for mingling with Sicilians. A minimum goal of the Sicilian residents in the area was to move to a better section on the east side, for example, into the adjoining fourth ward, or, better yet, to move to the west side where lived some Sicilian groups and virtually all the mainland Italians.

Lakeshore residents were infinitely better off than the crews of migrant day labourers who would periodically work in Oswego. Forced to live in shanties and shacks on the river or beside the construction sites at which they worked, the migrants were an especially sorry lot. Newspaper descriptions of these locations pictured them as dirty, dangerous places inhabited by Italians who were ready to fight at the drop of a hat, especially when pay call was late in coming. It is virtually impossible to tell where they came from in Italy or where they eventually settled. They simply disappeared without a trace.

The Lakeshore area was marked by a number of neighbourhood saloons, restaurants, grocery and drygoods stores, run by and catering to Italian immigrants. By 1916 there were eighteen Italian grocers throughout the city listed in the City Directory. About a dozen Italian saloons were located near the groceries. All of them on the east side were within a three-block radius of each other. Like the ones on the west side, they served as centres of immigrant activity. The customers played cards, hustled for jobs, made business deals, sought out interpreters, inquired of the last news from the old country and, in good weather, went out back to play *bocce* where space was available. The east side also had a lumber yard and a bakery run by Italians.[3]

Away from the centre of town and its commercial activity, the Lakeshore was in the midst of factories which produced woollen and yarn goods and heavy boiler products. Most of the Italians worked at day labour, and the industrial aura of the neighbourhood was a constant reminder to them of their lot in life. For some, it was an omen of their rise up to factory employment. For others, it served as a constant spur to upward social and economic mobility. A saving grace in the area was the availability of tillable land. Among the last sections of the city to be developed, it had much to offer the prospective gardener. Houses were not built touching each other as was the custom in larger cities. Large lots were vacant. Thus, there were available open fields or backyards which Italians would work before going to their jobs in the morning and again on their return at night. Over the years the Lakeshore community developed into a clean, modest, attractive settlement though it has never completely lost its industrial flavour.

On the west side, a small group of Sicilians from San Fratello and Cacamo lived in the first ward near the Diamond Match Company which opened a factory there in the 1890s. Many Italians worked for the company. But most of the mainland Italians lived in the third and fifth wards. Following the example of the first group, they settled near the railroad round house which was a source of employment and a rallying point for social events.[4] It was nearby that Sereno's Bar was located. James Sereno was one of the few early Sicilians who, marrying a Roman, settled among the Romans and Neapolitans. Taking over a bar which had operated earlier, he began catering to railroad workers from 1912 on. He helped Italians get jobs, served as an interpreter, became involved in politics as a Democrat, and was generally well respected as one of the influential and trustworthy Italian leaders in town. Though he made a good profit from his bar business, his reputation as a go-between was not marked by the usual indictment of overcharging for his services.[5]

Italians in the Labour Force

Italians who settled in Oswego in the early part of this century went overwhelmingly into railroad and day labouring jobs. The state census in 1905 revealed that in the City of Oswego more than 250 Italian-born were employed, 80 per cent of whom were railroad and day labourers. Most of the others worked at the Diamond Match factory or in the various knitting and yarn mills. A few were self-employed craftsmen and shopkeepers. There was one music teacher, but no other professionals.[6]

The jobs held by Italians reflected the need in Oswego for manual labourers who could help the city make the transition from a commercial to an industrial community. As new factories were attracted to the area, the city went ahead with an ambitious and much-needed sewer program. Railroads maintained their tracks and added spur lines to feed the new industries. Roads were built to accommodate the emerging automobile and trucking industries. In 1901 the Delaware, Lackawanna and Western Railroad built a new engine house and laid track at West Ninth and Utica streets in what became the largest Italian section in the city. In this first decade of the twentieth century Italians did much bull work such as shovelling coal at the port, maintaining railway tracks and building and maintaining the New York State Barge Canal.

Until 1909 Italians worked almost exclusively for non-Italians. It was in that year that the first Italian contractor, Anthony Sposato, from nearby Syracuse, shows up as a low bidder for a new sewer system, appropriately enough in the heart of the east side Italian neighbourhood. Sposato was awarded the contract. Within a few years Italian contractors utilizing Italian labourers became common, figuring largely in public works projects, mostly sewer construction, in the city.

The Italian labour employed was not always drawn from those

who settled in the area. Transient padrone labour often came on the scene and sometimes presented problems for area contractors. The builders of the highway from Oswego to Fulton complained that it was difficult to keep such labourers on the job since padrones sought to move their crews when another job came along so as to earn another brokerage fee. Nonetheless, a preference developed for Italians since they were the most plentiful labourers to be had for that kind of work.

In the early years of the twentieth century, with the exception of the barbering trade, Italians had little opportunity to develop skills and break into craft unions. Plumbers, electricians, carpenters and masons are conspicuous by their absence in Oswego's Italian workforce.

Education

The Italian community soon realized that their hope of advancement in their adopted country, for their children if not for themselves, lay through the education system. Although there may have been very few Italian children attending public school at the turn of the century, as the years progressed an increasing percentage of Italians were enrolled in the public school system.

By 1913 Italian students began to get some favourable press, a number of them being cited for perfect attendance and punctuality by the *Daily Palladium*. The conditions under which they struggled to get their educations came out in an unusual story reported by the newspaper. Charges were brought that forty school children were sent home because of the failure of the Education Department in Oswego to appoint a teacher for them. The superintendent, C. W. Richards, denied the accusations. He claimed that only nineteen pupils were sent home of whom six were under five-and-a-half years old, the minimum age set by board policy for school attendance. Some were too young to talk, and others could not speak English, claimed Richards. He continued:

> If a school is to be maintained for them it must be with a special teacher who can devote her entire time to teaching them to speak and understand English. It wouldn't be fair to the pupils of English speaking parents to compel the teacher in a mixed class to give the greater part of her time to the others; that's why I say if they are to receive training in our schools a special teacher ... [is needed].[7]

Apparently the fault for the inability of the school system to provide education for foreign children rests with the parents, for Richards concluded:

> If the children are permitted to play with others they will learn to speak English in that way and when five and a half years old will go to school with a knowledge of English.[8]

Even the Italian children born and raised in Oswego experienced difficulties in school, and it is certain that scores of Italian children felt "uncomfortable" in Oswego's schools. By virtue of their dress, their manner of speech, their unfamiliarity with local custom, they found it difficult to be accepted as "one of the group." Only those with unusual ability, determination and perseverance could hope to survive the social and psychological pressures they were forced to undergo in Oswego's schools. If a child came from poor circumstances, the problem was exacerbated. Initially, very few made it to high school.

A special problem in the grade schools was what to do with older children and young adults who needed or wanted to learn English. Often they would be placed in the elementary schools, a painfully embarrassing situation which no foreigner could long endure. An alternative seemed to be the night school.

In October 1907 the City of Oswego began a night school operation mainly at the request of Italians. For men only, it was open four nights a week, with an initial enrolment of over sixty. The curriculum consisted of the three Rs, the rudiments of mechanical drawing being considered too complex. Since most of the Italians could neither read nor write and spoke little English, Rosario D'Angelo, one of the promoters of the night school movement, served as an interpreter.

One immigrant who attended night school in these early years has described his educational experiences. Encouraged by Mrs. D'Angelo, Albert Canale was eighteen years old and working for a yarn mill in town when he decided to go to public day school. He was tested from a grade one reader and placed in the sixth grade. While attending school he tried to find a part-time job but was unable to do so. When his money ran out after three months he was forced to leave. He then went to work for the Diamond Match Company and dug ditches for the railroad. Desirous of continuing his education he attended night school, but confessed that after ten hours of hard labour he was just too tired to get much out of it.[8]

Canale's story probably reflects the attitude of the majority of Italians toward night school. Many wanted to learn basic English in order to read the newspapers and get along better on their jobs. Filled with good intentions, their energy and interest flagged after a few months as their English became passable and the pressure of working all day and going to school at night began to catch up with them. Complicating the matter in Oswego was the winter weather which more often than not encouraged Oswegonians to remain indoors at night unless compelled to venture out.

Apparently the night school movement faded quickly since little is written of it from 1908 until 1914 when the Chamber of Commerce decided to do something about educating foreigners. Alarmed by labour troubles in Paterson, New Jersey, and in nearby Auburn, New York, the Chamber pushed for better treatment of foreigners which would enable them to become better citizens. In this way it hoped to reduce the threat of dissatisfied workers bringing "injury" to the city.

By 1916, the plan to reinstitute night schools for immigrants was still only in the talking stage. Education authorities voiced the opinion that "there is no other way to educate residents of foreign birth than through the night schools." It was estimated that about $3,000 was needed to operate the night school. The Oswego *Weekly Palladium* came out in support of education for immigrants:

> The quickest, the best and most effective way to make good citizens out of the foreigners who come among us is to educate them in the English language so they can become acquainted with our purposes and our form of government. . . .
>
> Whatever it may cost to conduct a night school will be a good investment for the city of Oswego; it will come back to us a hundred fold.
>
> There are many foreigners in this city who are anxious to attend such a school and secure all the benefits possible from it.[9]

Amid strong newspaper support, appeals from the pulpits in Oswego, and the urgings of the Chamber of Commerce, the question of raising $3,400 for night schools was put to the people. They promptly defeated it. Speaking to students at the Oswego Normal School on Columbus Day, 1917, District Attorney Francis D. Culkin commented:

> To the everlasting shame of Oswego the proposition to appropriate a miserable two thousand dollars . . . was defeated last year. When this matter comes up again, I trust that every pulpit in Oswego, every influence for decency will speak in thunder tones in its favor so that the Americanization of these aliens may be speedily achieved.
>
> Let us do our duty in connection with this problem intelligently and sympathetically so that this race [Italians] will be speedily assimilated, without danger to American institutions.[10]

Culkin was obviously not in the majority in Oswego. Taxpayers refused to support the night school. Immigrants would have to wait for more propitious times to obtain a formal education after work.

More than a few Italian-Americans are extremely bitter over their educational experiences, expecially the women. One says she regularly got a 90 + average through grade school and high school, but her teachers consistently steered her away from professional preparatory courses and into the commercial program. They convinced her that Italians, in particular Italian women, were not capable enough for college and the professions. She insists that hers was no isolated case. Other women have confirmed her assessment. It is impossible to determine how devastatingly demoralizing on Italian-American students were the effects of such negative stereotyping.

Social Organizations

Faced with the indifference, if not downright hostility, of the host society, it was natural that the Italian community should turn inward for support. Mutual aid societies and fraternal/social groups sprang up to make use of whatever power they could muster to help Italians move into more desirable jobs as, for example, policemen, teachers and craftsmen. They also urged fellow-Italians to learn English and become American citizens. But, in grouping together as Italians, they also kept themselves apart from the American society as a whole, and that fact retarded a fuller acceptance of Italians in Oswego's wider community. This clannishness was a matter of concern to the local press. The *Daily Times* made its position clear in 1906 as Italian immigration began to mount in the city. Italian immigration is a cause for concern, said the editor. Italians do not spread out over the country; they congregate mostly in large cities where their labour is least needed; their colonies are alien to American institutions and language; they fail to assimilate with the American population and customs. Getting to the local scene, the tone changed.

> Oswego has a considerable Italian population which is being constantly augmented. As a class . . . [they have] proved well-behaved and amenable to law and order. There are individuals . . . lawless and unfit for responsibilities of American citizenship . . . [they are] few in number and can be coped with. . . .

In general, the problems of Italian immigration could be handled through wise legislation (not spelled out) and by inculcating American principles. The moderate approach set by the *Daily Times* might well have signalled the growing political value which the local Republican party saw in the Italians.[11]

The *Daily Palladium*, which usually backed the Democrats, spelled out its position on Italian immigration about five months later. It deplored the congregating in the East by the new immigrants. Erroneously assuming that Germans and Irish were willing to go anywhere, the paper described them as

> old stock . . . hardier and better stock. . . . All they wanted was a chance to work. The country is better and richer for their coming here. It is a matter of regret that we can't have more immigrants from Germany or Ireland and fewer from Southern Europe.[12]

In the face of such obvious prejudice, therefore, it was only natural that, initially, social life in Oswego for Italians revolved around their own group and on family happenings. Weddings and christenings provided the first large-scale functions. The baptism of Tony Gero brought out two hundred guests as did the wedding of Mike Mitchell, boot-black extraordinary, the "J. Pierrepont Morgan" of Oswego's Italian colony. Italians looked forward to such events. They fussed over such joyous occasions. They regarded them as opportunities to get out and socialize.

Sunday was an important day socially as well as religiously. If there were no formal events to attend, people would get together with guitars and mandolins, pull back the carpets if they had any, and dance the day away. "Big dinners, where the food you ate stuck to your ribs," was the order of the day. Depending on the occasion, the fare might range from home-made specialties such as macaroni, sausage, biscotti, filled cookies, pizza, pizza fritta and bread, to dandelions (in season), salads and legumes. During pre-Lenten, carnival time, Italians would dress up in homemade costumes, don masks and veils, and make the rounds of friends and relatives who would invite them in to share many of these special foods. Few had riches—witness the custom of buying old flour sacks, bleaching them, and cutting and sewing them into undergarments or even, on occasion, into dresses and blouses. But simple pleasures were abundant. *Bocce* was a favourite pastime. Italians usually played it for money and drinks, mostly for wine. *Casa cavallo*, similar to *bocce*, but using hard cheese, was another popular game. Card games, especially American casino and the Italian *tre sette* and *briscola*, helped Italians pass many a gloomy period in Oswego's long, hard winters. The tarantella and the Naples jig, described by one observer as "done with hand clappers and remindful of the Highland fling and ballet," were the main dances in the Oswego colony at the turn of the century.[13]

With the forming of the Societa di Mutuo Soccorso Cristoforo Colombo in 1903 Oswego's Italian community had its first organization by which it could formalize its social life. The following year a second club was established when, encouraged by local Republicans, over two hundred Italian men and boys attended the launching of the Italian Roosevelt Club. Existing for the primary purpose of helping candidates in the upcoming election, the club was short-lived, but it afforded the Italians the opportunity for a few nights out on the town with plenty of free beer and smokes to relieve the monotony of dreary back-breaking labour that most of them performed on Oswego's streets, railroads and waterway projects.[14] One of the most exciting socials in the early years was the benediction of the Italian and American flags at the club rooms of the Cristoforo Colombo Society. Dignitaries from the state appeared and a cablegram describing the events was sent to King Vittorio Emanuele. When the King acknowledged the cable, it was believed that this was the first time that a direct message from a king had been received in the city of Oswego. The Italians were deliriously happy.[15]

Religious feasts were also occasions for socialization. The first major feast to be noted in the local papers was that of San Antonio, 13 June 1906. Sponsored by the Principe Umberto Society, seventy men in uniform preceded by thirty-five girls in white led by Oswego's own Phillip's Band, paraded through the streets. After a seemingly endless round of speeches by politicians and officials of the society, refreshments and cigars were passed out and club members danced to the music of "Cavert's full orchestra."[16]

By 1908 both Italian and Polish societies became visible in American celebrations. They participated in the traditional Fourth of July gala which included the usual parade and fireworks. Italians and Poles still take part in Independence Day celebrations.

Columbus Day is another holiday which Italians have celebrated since 1908. Though legally speaking an American holiday, few Americans except those of Italian descent make much fuss over it. Italians used the occasion in 1908 to parade, listen to politicians from both major parties and wind up the day with an evening of dancing.

Tragedy in Italy often brought a swift response from Italians in America. When a devastating earthquake hit Sicily in December 1908, taking over 100,000 lives, Italians in Oswego had special cause for alarm, as the provinces of Messina and Catania were especially hard hit. Moving quickly, Italians set aside factional quarrels and started a fund drive to aid their destitute countrymen. Within a month the Italian community had raised over $500.

Benefits continued to furnish Italians with reasons to join together socially. Until 1912, when musicians were needed at such celebrations, the Italians had to go outside their community. In that year, the Cristoforo Colombo Society sponsored the first local band. Membership was open to all comers, and twenty-eight answered the call. They rehearsed on Sundays as they struggled to get ready for their first concert at Easter. Complaints from the neighbours about "noise" complicated matters, but did not deter them. When summer came the local band was able to perform at Italian picnics held at nearby beaches on Lake Ontario. Audiences ranged from four to five hundred people who enjoyed the festive air, the food, drink, field games and music. Socializing aside the ethnic group was virtually unheard of at this time, unless one went to fund-raisers or belonged to a union which held its own picnics and smokers.

In March of 1913 James Sereno announced the founding of the Italian-American Citizens Association. Citizenship or the filing of naturalization papers was a requirement for membership. An active Democrat at this time, Sereno offered, through the club, instruction in American history and civics twice a month. Realizing that only one-seventh of Oswego's two thousand Italians were citizens, he was anxious to encourage the Americanization of his fellow immigrants, politically as well as socially. By the end of the year the organization was in operation. The membership of this club and that of all other Italian societies provided the nucleus which created the modern Sons of Italy. By World War One it had emerged as an organization with two branches, one on each side of the river. It finally jelled as a single lodge located on the west side.

When Columbus Day rolled around in 1914 the Italians had a field day. All the societies and their bands participated: the Cristoforo Colombo Society, Principe Umberto, Isola Stromboli, the Italian-American Citizens Club and others. Led by the outstanding American band in the city, the Phillips Band, in which some Italian musicians served their apprenticeships, the Italians strutted their way around the city and removed to Richardson Hall where, after the customary political speeches, they ate, drank and danced the night away.

Most celebrations noted here have been connected with American or Italian national holidays. Also noteworthy were the many religious feast days celebrated by Italians. When St. Joseph's Church was organized in 1915 the San Bartolomeo Society was formed as an auxiliary group. Its membership was drawn from people from the Lipari Islands group, which included Lipari, Stromboli and Salina. San Bartolomeo is the patron saint of the Lipari Islands, and his feast day was an occasion for great rejoicing. Liparians got together on that day, hired a band, paraded with the traditional statue carried by those who had donated money to the church for the privilege, and topped the day with a bazaar in the basement of the church.[17]

The social life of the itinerant Italian workers provided a sharp contrast to the many intimate and, at times, elaborate, functions enjoyed by Oswego's Italian families. Having little chance to avail themselves of family celebrations or of organized activities, the migrants often entertained themselves around the job sites by singing and dancing with one another while one of their fellow-workers played the concertina.

Italians had come a long way socially by 1917, but they were not yet accepted fully in Oswego. One big event, World War One, brought them closer. Encouraged by President Woodrow Wilson, Italian immigrants in the United States prepared to celebrate Italy Day, 24 May 1918, as a means of commemorating the entrance of Italy into the war in 1915. A giant celebration took place locally. Thousands of citizens lined the curbs to watch a patriotic parade which included U.S. soldiers from Fort Ontario and a number of draftees who were waiting their call to military duty. Among the various speakers was the pastor of St. Joseph's Church who told his listeners in Italian to be loyal to America. This duality was given visible reinforcement when two Italians, one dressed as Uncle Sam, the other as Italia, highlighted a dramatization of Italian immigration to America. A roar of approval went up from the crowd when Mayor John Fitzgibbons ended the formal part of the ceremonies with an announcement that twelve young Italian-Americans would be joining a group of over fifty locals who would leave on the morrow for military service at Camp Dix. This salute to Italy proved to be an inspiration to Italian-Americans, and encouraged numerous Italians to give their all for the war effort. And it gave Oswegonians reason to pause and to reassess their judgments of these "foreigners" who had been there for barely a generation.

Yet old attitudes died hard. Even during World War One the *Daily Palladium* was still expressing apprehension over immigration. It noted that the requirement to register for army service revealed "an alarming proportion of aliens in our population." Recognizing that many of them would be an asset either in the U.S. Army or with allied forces, the paper expressed concern over the vast majority who "will be a drag on our civic and social life at a time when we particularly need unanimity of ideals and action." Though it was late, the editor went on, the situation could be saved through education and immigrant acceptance of the "gospel of Americanism."[18]

The war presented Italian immigrants with an unprecedented opportunity to expand their horizons in Oswego. First of all, it gave reasoning people a chance to see the fallacious distinctions between the old and new immigrants. No longer could the old automatically be preferred to the new. War with Germany gave many Americans reasons to doubt the desirability of German-Americans. Hyphenated Americans from Italy and other Southern and Eastern European countries, once thought as having little to contribute to America, were now viewed in a different and positive light.

Unlike their back-breaking labour and personal sacrifices which were largely taken for granted or ignored, immigrants' efforts in World War One were too significant to cast aside. Italians were mixed in with all the draftees whose names were published in the papers. They were conspicuous in the lists of soldiers going off to war. They were found among the wounded and the dead. And they had their share of heroes. No longer could they be isolated and relegated to a back page. They were an integral part of the war effort on both the home and the war fronts. Oswegonians had read for years of the Black Hand and the Mafia, of petty family squabbles, of murder and mayhem. Now they were reading of war. They were learning that when it came to fighting for the United States there was very little difference between natural-born citizens, naturalized citizens and aliens.

Italians and Italian-Americans served as combatants in three ways. When Italy first entered the war, a handful of Italians returned to serve in the Italian army. Newspapers in Oswego carried the names of ten such individuals. Undoubtedly there were more. About an equal number joined the New York National Guard, which was activated for the war. An additional eighty were drafted. Approximately 10 per cent of the land forces personnel that came out of Oswego were Italian. This is consistent with what one would expect from looking at the population figures for the city. No Italians appear to have joined the U.S. Navy though some were listed as having been drafted into that service.

Among the casualties were Sam Fabrizio, who died in France, and Sam Furnari, who contracted pneumonia and died in Oswego.[19]

Two Oswego soldiers received decorations for valour on the battlefield. One was J. Edward Campbell, from a well-known mercantile family in town, the other was an Italian, Dominic Spataro. Spataro, who later became a muck farmer despite losing one of his legs in the war, "broke up an enemy machine gun nest with hand grenades, and took four prisoners without assistance. He also volunteered as stretcher bearer for a period of twenty-six hours and performed valiant service until severely wounded." He was saved by Campbell. Both received the Distinguished Service Cross; Spataro was also decorated with the Croix de Guerre.

Such acts of heroism were not taken lightly. Until his death in 1959 Spataro's acts of heroism were a constant source of pride for the American-Italian community in Oswego. He and Campbell were frequently honoured side by side at veterans' affairs, a constant emotional and visual reminder of World War One and the closing of ranks between immigrant and native community which the war occasioned and facilitated.

The First World War marked the beginning of a new era for

Italian immigrants. They would not yet be accepted as Americans completely—that did not come for many of them until after World War Two. But no longer could they be considered by the majority of Oswegonians simply as "birds of passage," common day labourers, dangerous aliens to be shunted aside.

Politics

The Italians may not have been fully accepted into the community at the beginning of this century. But quite early on both Democrats and Republicans found it to their advantage to bid for their support. Rallies were held in which Italians were flattered and given beer, snacks and smokes in the hope that they would go out and vote the right way. The initial successes went to the Republicans who persuaded first Rosario D'Angelo and then John Lapetino to work for the party. Republicans were pleased with D'Angelo, especially in 1907 when they won the mayor's post and a majority on the city council (they also elected six of eight supervisors to the county board of supervisors). D'Angelo was made a notary public and, though he never got the post, his name was rumoured for fire marshall. After D'Angelo moved from the city, Lapetino became the unchallenged Italian Republican leader in the second and fourth wards on the east side. Though he never ran for public office, politics became a way of life for Lapetino. He served as a notary public, a commissioner of deeds and a deputy sheriff for most of his years in Oswego.[20]

On the Democratic side was Alfred E. D'Amico, the only Italian elected to office in the city before World War Two. D'Amico lived on the west side, in the Neapolitan area, which was in a predominantly Republican ward. After serving for two years as a supervisor, he twice lost re-election bids before settling for honorary posts such as water commissioner and whatever jobs of interpreting the Democrats could throw his way.[21]

In the early 1900s Republicans needed to build their strength in the second ward. It was the least populated in the city, and Italians were settling there by the hundreds. If Republicans could win their support, it could mean the difference between victory and defeat for many ward positions. Working through Lapetino, the GOP hoped to convince the Italians to "vote for the bird," the symbol of the party. The success Republicans had in the twenties and thirties in local contests in the second ward, while Democrats were sweeping the ward in state and national contests, indicates a great deal of ballot splitting went on. It also points to the probable success that Republicans had in attracting an increasing number of Italians to the party's cause. For Italian candidates, however, it did not ensure victory. As a matter of fact, second ward politics raised the question of what Italians were more attracted by—party politics or ethnicity.

The first Italian to run for office in a second ward election was F.

Signorile, standing for alderman in 1933 on the Republican ticket. He lost by 115 votes and only by 13 in his home district. It was the best showing by a Republican candidate for alderman since the GOP won that seat in 1927. In 1935 he cut the margin of defeat to only 36 votes. The same year another Italian candidate, B. Famularo, ran for county supervisor on the favoured Democrat Party ticket, but he lost by 124 votes. Voters in the second ward obviously split their tickets as Famularo got 46 fewer votes than Signorile's 367.

Whether or not the Italians stuck together for these two candidates, regardless of party, is difficult to determine. The most likely explanation is that while Italians voted their party affiliations, others in the ward were splitting their tickets as they elected the opponents of the Italians, one a Democrat, the other a sole Republican victor.

The third and fifth wards also had large numbers of Italians. The third ward usually voted Republican. Out of thirty-eight contests for aldermen and supervisors, only two were Democrats in the forty-year period. One of them, Alfred E. D'Amico, was an Italian immigrant who won in 1923. D'Amico's victory is noteworthy on three counts. First, he was the first local Italian to run for elected office in the city. Second, he was the only Democrat to win in the ward. Third, he was the first Democrat elected to the post of supervisor from the third ward since Civil War days. It is hard to determine whether D'Amico was prouder of that fact or that he was the first Italian to win at the pools. Obviously, citizens did not vote a straight ticket. D'Amico's victory came as a result of winning margins in the second and third districts where virtually all of the Italians in the ward were located. A Neapolitan, D'Amico apparently had the support of his fellow Neapolitans and Romans.

But D'Amico could not hold on to his victory. Throughout the 1920s Republicans had won the most powerful elected post in the city, that of the mayor. And word in the community had it that after D'Amico's victory local Republicans were putting enormous pressure on Italians to register and vote Republican. Fearing loss of patronage and the closing of their speakeasies, some Italian Democrats felt compelled, at least outwardly, to switch to the Republican side. Then, in 1925, the Republicans ran one of their strongest vote-getters against D'Amico and beat him 854 to 740.

The Italian vote can be put into some kind of perspective if one examines the enrolment books. How many Italians are we talking about? In 1916 there were 79 Italians, accounting for .017 per cent of the total enrolment. The figures rose to 366 and .038 per cent in 1929, when Italian Democrat enrolments surpassed Republican for the first time. During this period the second ward always had the most registered voters with Republicans easily outnumbering Democrats. The fifth and third wards came next. In both wards, Italians preferred to identify with the Democrats by far. The first ward was evenly split between the two major parties, and the fourth ward, contiguous to the second ward, favoured the Republicans. In these five wards the number of registered Italians goes from a low of 9 (first ward) to a high of 109 (second ward) in 1929. The totals are small. Yet some local elections were settled by as few as 5 votes. Moreover, there were only eight wards in the city. If one could control the Italian vote in those five wards, make it solidly Republican or Democrat, one could rule the city council (each ward had one alderman) and even elect a mayor. Elections, of course, are not won simply by enrolments. But, as the figures show, the Republicans had a good start by using the likes of D'Angelo and Lapetino to line up Italians in the second and fourth wards. Democrats enjoyed a similar advantage under D'Amico's initial leadership in the third and fifth wards. Overall, Republicans had a slight advantage in the early years, but by 1929 the Democrats had won the enrolment battle citywide.

The one Italian-American to become mayor in Oswego was Vincent Corsall, an out-of-towner who came to the city to teach science in the high school. When he was elected as an independent with support from labour, the local politicos believed that he had solid backing from fellow Italian-Americans. Corsall lasted only long enough for the major parties to regroup their battered forces—one term. When Corsall declared as a third-party candidate in the 1963 mayoral campaign, a poll revealed that Corsall had little support in the traditional Italian areas. Indeed, his opponent, Shapiro, the incumbent mayor, won easily, and Corsall wound up a weak third.

As the sons and daughters of immigrants move out of the wards and out of the city, the old patterns started to break down. Political observers question whether there is any Italian vote left now in the second ward. They may be right. Others question whether there is any Italian vote in the city. When Bart Gentile, former Democrat alderman and city clerk from the third ward, ran for mayor in 1973, he was beaten by a newcomer to politics, a Polish businessman who had extraordinary support from his Polish home ward, the seventh. Some said that it was time for a change; the Democrats had been in the mayor's post since 1961. Gentile's inability to garner the Italian vote cost him the election. There are those who question whether Italian-American officials have done much for the Italian-American community at large. That is matter for another occasion. But it could be that Gentile, having been in office for a number of years, proved no different from other politicians when it came to a question of producing for the local Italian-Americans.

The Italian Community Today

An examination of the Italians' political history in Oswego reveals something less than a monolithic community. It gives one cause to wonder if the Italian-American community is a creation more of non-Italians than of the Italian-Americans themselves. To be sure, there is such a group. But its size and cohesiveness are not what non-Italians believe it to be. Outsiders continue to have an old, stereotypical image of Italian-Americans: they still view it as a large group of citizens who are in the main close-knit, clannish, family-oriented, "Mafioso," male-dominated, and so on. In other words, the Italians are a body apart from the mainstream in Oswego today.

In actuality, the descendants of Italian immigrants are more American than they are Italian. They see disunity and complain of lack of support from their own kind. They are plagued with petty jealousies. Marriage to non-Italians is running as high as 80 per cent. Italian women are as liberated as any others in the city. Like other youngsters, the American-Italian children have problems with drugs, sex, parents, school, and so on. What is most telling, both the number who qualify as Italian-Americans and the number of those who are willing to identify as such are dwindling.

In essence, the reservoir from which is drawn the supply of members for the Italian-American society is slowly but surely drying up. The ethnic revival in America is just delaying the inevitable, the ever-shrinking world of the Italian-American. When those who care read the handwriting on the wall, they will cherish their way of life more than ever and strive to maintain their traditions. Perhaps, then, the unity, supportiveness, and self-esteem which have eluded Italian-Americans for so long will be theirs.

Notes

1. The development of Oswego is treated in Charles M. Snyder, *Oswego: From Buckskin to Bustles* (Port Washington, 1968), *passim*. See also Luciano J. Iorizzo, "The History of Italians in Oswego, Part 1," *Twenty-ninth Publication of the Oswego County Historical Society* (1967-68), pp. 88-112.

2. The families traced were taken mainly from the membership of St. Joseph's Roman Catholic Church. The remainder came from newspapers articles, obituaries, etc. Identification of family names with Italian place names was made essentially through church records, personal interviews, and obituary notices in Oswego's dailies throughout the twentieth century. City directories and oral interviews made it possible to locate where the Italians settled in Oswego.

3. City directories and conversations with many members of the Italian-American community.

4. Over the years the location of so many Italian homes close to railroad tracks was visual proof of the importance of railroad employment to Italian immigrants in Oswego.

5. Numerous conversations (from 1962 to the present) with Albert Canale, one of the last survivors of the Italians' mass migration to Oswego in the first decade of this century. Interviews with others confirm Canadle's assessment of Sereno. See, for example, notes in the author's possession of occasional chats with Charles Caroccio, Sam Gero, Charles Loschiavo, Ferdinand Tremiti, Virginia Sereno Wahrendorf, and other from 1962 on.

6. New York State Census, "Manuscript Books of the County and City of Oswego," 1905.

7. *Daily Palladium*, 25 January 1913.

8. A good friend and lodge brother of the writer, Canale was one of the most knowledgeable persons on the Italian-American experience in Oswego. He came to the city in 1903 and died, at the age of ninety-two, on 29 June 1979.

9. *Daily Palladium*, 16 November 1916.

10. *Daily Times*, 16 October 1917. The dangers that Culkin had in mind were the padrone system and crime: "The influence of the padrone should be destroyed by teaching him that there is nothing unusual and mysterious about the American system and that pull has no proper place in our scheme of things. He should be made to understand that the law is superior to the gang, and vigorous punishment should follow the commission of all crime." Culkin's comment on "pull" strikes some Oswegonians as somewhat less than candid since he was a master politician who went on to become an active and well-regarded U.S. Congressman.

11. *Daily Times*, 18 December 1906.

12. *Daily Palladium*, 18 May 1907.

13. *Daily Palladium*, 4 March 1902, and *Sunday Herald* (Syracuse), 27 January 1889, p. 6; memoranda of interviews on many occasions with Alfred E. "Allie" D'Amico and Josephine "Josie" Morabito Scaglione, especially 28 November 1966 and 10 April 1979 respectively.

14. *Daily Times*, 26 November 1903, and memoranda of numerous conversations with Albert Canale from 1963 to the present, especially 14 April 1963.

15. *Daily Palladium*, 28 and 29 May 1906.

16. Ibid., 14 June 1906.

17. Memorandum of interview with Lawrence "Allie" Familio, a "Liparian," 22 May 1979; *St. Joseph's Church Dedication Book*, 27 April 1958. Most likely the San Bartolomeo Society was an outgrowth of the Stromboli Society which disappeared after the former was organized. When the Reverend Francis J. Furfaro became pastor in 1949 he was anxious to Americanize the members of his parish. One of the things he did along that line was to replace statues with regional or provincial significance (e.g., San Bartolomeo and San Rocco) with those of broader attraction (e.g., St. Joseph and the Blessed Virgin Mary). Though the Italian parishioners generally admire Furfaro, some old timers have never gotten over what they considered unwarranted callous treatment of their patron saints. In earlier years the banished statues were kept in basements to be taken out only on the appropriate feast day.

18. *Daily Palladium*, 15 June 1917.

19. See records of Local Draft Board #1, Beecher Aston, Chief Clerk, an unpublished manuscript on Oswego in World War One, located at the headquarters house of the Oswego County Historical Society. See also various records therein as well as newspapers clippings for the period.

20. Iorizzo, "History of Italians in Oswego." Election results for 1907 are printed in the local newspapers. For more on D'Angelo and Lapetino, see Luciano J. Iorizzo and Salvatore Mondello, *The Italian Americans* (New York, 1971).

21. Election results in the local press, especially 1923, 1925, 1927; Luciano J. Iorizzo, "The Italians in North America," an annotated reading list published by the Balch Institute (Philadelphia, 1975), contains a brief sketch on D'Amico. See also Iorizzo and Mondello, *Italian Americans*.

Canadian Industrialization versus the Italian Contadini in a Decade of Brutality, 1902-1912

Antonio Pucci

Though the documentation of Italian-Canadian history is still in its infant stage, at least one basic view has stuck in our popular historical consciousness: that Italian immigrants passively submitted to the harshest conditions of a burgeoning North American industrial capitalism. The aim of this essay is to demonstrate that this generalization is not applicable to the experience of the *contadini* who settled in the twin Canadian cities of Fort William and Port Arthur (present-day Thunder Bay), Ontario. It will be seen that Italian workers in these two cities, by their militancy, played a key role in the shaping of industrial relations during the decade from 1902 to 1912.

The first Italians began to arrive in the area in the 1880s and many of the original settlers came via the United States. It was railway construction and later freight and coal handling that attracted them to settle there. The two major employers of Italians and other "foreigners" were the Canadian Pacific Railway and the Canadian Northern Railway; it was natural, therefore, that two "Little Italies" should emerge around the railway yards early in the twentieth century.

First Lessons in Industrial Struggle, 1902-1903

In the years between 1900 and 1913 Canadian and American industrial relations were marked by a high frequency of labour unrest and vio-

THE TWIN CITIES 1914

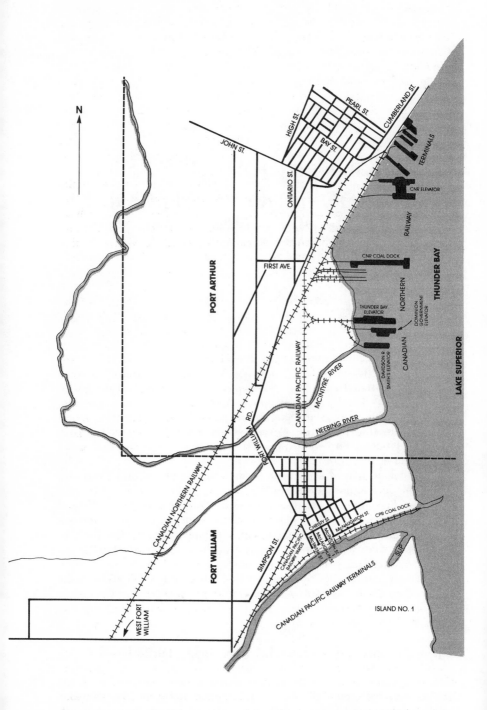

N

PEARL ST.

CUMBERLAND ST.

HIGH ST.

BAY ST.

JOHN ST.

ONTARIO ST.

TERMINALS

CNR ELEVATOR

RAILWAY

PORT ARTHUR

FIRST AVE.

CNR COAL DOCK

NORTHERN

THUNDER BAY

THUNDER BAY
ELEVATOR

DOMINION
GOVERNMENT
ELEVATOR

CANADIAN PACIFIC RAILWAY

McINTYRE RIVER

CANADIAN

DAVIDSON &
SMITH'S ELEVATOR

LAKE SUPERIOR

FORT WILLIAM RD.

NEEBING RIVER

CANADIAN NORTHERN RAILWAY

FORT WILLIAM

SIMPSON ST.

CHRISTY ST.

McLAREN ST.

McINTOSH ST.

MCNAUGHTON ST.

MCNAUGHTON ST.

CPR COAL DOCK

CANADIAN PACIFIC
RAILWAY YARDS

SLIP

WEST FORT
WILLIAM

CANADIAN PACIFIC RAILWAY TERMINALS

ISLAND NO. 1

lence. Underlying factors which gave rise to this unrest included the concentration of wealth by ruthless industrialists, and widespread poverty among the workers. Social disorganization also stemmed from the large-scale immigration.[1] This also was the time when two distinctive Italian colonies were emerging in Fort William and Port Arthur. The *contadini* immigrants to the Twin Cities came from a semi-feudal society and pre-industrial cultural background and had little experience with industrial relations. An examination of the role of Italian workers in a number of strikes which occurred in these two centres will show that when provoked by unbearable conditions they engaged in fierce struggles. An analysis of Italian workers' participation in strike situations will also shed light on the process of Canadian industrialization and its impact on community relationships.

During this period Fort William and Port Arthur enjoyed rapid industrial development. For the *contadini*-turned-proletarians and for the "foreigners" in general who had come to do the heavy work such as freight and coal handling there was no similar economic gain. Rather, life for the Italian communities was marked by constant conflict as the *contadini* struggled to squeeze periodic wage increases from their employers and to safeguard themselves against virtual exclusion from their place of work.

Although details about early strikes are sparse, it seems that the Italian immigrants had begun to play a role in the industrial relations of Fort William and Port Arthur by 1902. On 2 July of that year, a number of Italian and Finnish workers employed in the freight sheds and in the yards of the CNR in Port Arthur approached management for an increase of their wage to 25 cents an hour. The company responded by immediately dismissing the workers and the next day they had all been replaced.[2] This uncompromising attitude came at a time when the CNR was facing a strike in its Winnipeg operations, which had commenced at the end of June. Following the firing of the Italians and Finns, local workers started a full-scale strike at the Port Arthur operations on 5 July 1902.

Two days later the CNR responded by importing strikebreakers and armed men. A "gang of Italians" numbering forty men was brought from Montreal and replaced the strikers at the docks. At the same time the company swore in ten men as "special" policemen to prevent the strikers from interfering with the strikebreakers or the company's facilities at the docks. Presented with this quick and formidable action the strikers offered no counterchallenge and the strike collapsed.

A year later at the opening of the 1903 navigation season once again Italian freight handlers employed by the Canadian Northern were the chief protagonists in attempting to improve working conditions at the dock. This time the *contadini* were primarily interested in bringing an end to the practice of hiring casual labour at the dock. Company policy was to hire men on a daily basis for specific tasks such as moving cargoes from ships. Between the arrival of vessels, the dock workers were expected to remain idle and of course, without pay. When on 20 May the workers protested, the local authorities read the Riot Act and arrested their leader. The exact nature of the workers' protest is not outlined by the newspaper account; it merely states that "The workers became quite ugly this morning..."[3] Apparently a crowd of Italian workers had to be dispersed from the docks by the police. Then they were given their pay and were immediately replaced by other workers and the one-day strike was declared over.

From these two short-lived unsuccessful strikes the Italian workers realized how easily they could be replaced and prevented from prolonging their strike by "special" private policemen and the local authorities. Nevertheless, within the next nine years the *contadini* longshoremen would come to challenge their employers three more times—in 1906, 1909 and 1912.

"Contadini," Violence and Reprisal, 1906-1907

By 1905 the economic developments that had taken place in Fort William and Port Arthur led the immigrant agent, R. A. Burris, to conclude in his annual report that the two localities constituted a "great commercial centre" where great prosperity prevailed.[4] For the workers employed at the waterfront, this assessment was ironic; little of the prosperity had yet reached them. In an attempt to improve their plight two major strikes were staged in 1906, one against the Canadian Pacific and the other against the Canadian Northern railways.

On 29 September ten Italian freight handlers employed at the CPR freight sheds on the outskirts of Fort William's Little Italy worked out without warning, demanding an increase in pay. The next day they were joined by the rest of the workers, who included Greeks and Hungarians. Their current hourly rate was 17½ cents an hour for day work and 20 cents for night work. They were also entitled to a bonus of 2½ cents an hour provided they remained until the end of the navigation season. Throughout this period the bonus system was a source of serious irritation for the Italian workers. Since the employers hired their workers on a day-to-day basis depending on a fluctuating need, the system served to maintain an abundance of labour throughout the season. When work was scarce at the waterfront, freight or coal handlers were reluctant to accept work elsewhere since in doing so they would have to forfeit their bonus money which represented a significant percentage of their wages. The employers thus had complete control over the labour market.

While the *contadini* struck primarily over wages, there may have been an even more important underlying reason for their action. "Railways Plan to Shut Out Italians?" was how the *Daily News* broke the story in a front-page headline on 2 October 1906. The *News* had learned from an informant that the current strike had come about as a result of the Italians having heard that the CPR, the CNR and the Grand Trunk Pacific were in the future going to do away with Italian labour altogether.

The informant conceded to the *News* that the current strike would not prevent the companies from carrying out their plans. He was certain that the CPR had been considering this strategy for several months. In place of the Italians for the 1907 season the railroads were apparently counting on an influx of "thousands of brawny English-speaking men and youths" from the "Old Country." These arrivals would allow the companies to give up their dependency on Italian labourers, although, he added, the Italians themselves "know their services are accepted for no other reason than that none else has been available." The informant went on to say that the companies would continue to hire other "foreigners" of "sturdy races," mainly Finns, Swedes and Scandinavians since they were thought to be order-loving and permanent settlers and thus would make "the best of British citizens." The *News* suggested to the informant that his story may have been an orchestrated attempt in conjunction with CPR officials to intimidate the Italian strikers into ending the strike. His reply was:

> It could, but my information demonstrates that the determined attitude of the strikers is the result of their having received wind of the contemplated action of the railroads and they are now making a last stand.

Events at the CPR freight sheds did not go unnoticed by the CNR freight handlers at the Port Arthur docks where at the opening of the navigation season a two-day strike had ended in defeat for the workers.[5] On 30 September, the day following the start of the strike in Fort William, the Canadian Northern handlers walked out in sympathy when they learned that part of the cargo that they were unloading from a vessel belonged to the CPR. They wasted no time in appointing a six-man committee to press for increased wages. They demanded an additional 5 cents and 7½ cents an hour for day and night work respectively and 7 cents an hour on Sundays. In addition, they wanted the company's retention of the 2½ cent an hour bonus until the end of the navigation season discontinued.[6]

Determined to win, the strikers attempted to bring pressure to bear upon the CPR by widening the conflict to a general strike. On the morning of 2 October the strikers instituted a blockade of Little Italy and prevented the *contadini* from going to work. Consequently, in the two cities about one thousand men, all "foreigners," were on strike, of whom about six hundred were freight handlers and the rest employed in the construction of public works such as sidewalks and the excavation of sewers.

Developments on the strike site moved rapidly, culminating in a confrontation at one o'clock, when CPR superintendent G. Bury arrived from Winnipeg with a carload of men who were to have replaced the strikers. Approximately one hundred strikers armed with guns, clubs and revolvers converged at the freight sheds after they had learned of the arrival of the men from Winnipeg. The strikers had Bury in his private railroad car and the men who were in another car surrounded when Constable Taylor, chief of the CPR police, ordered the "dissatisfied foreigners" to go away. The latter opened fire and before the shooting came to a halt at least two strikers were injured and Taylor had been grazed by a bullet. Throughout the violent clash Bury and the men remained out of sight in their car and suffered no injuries.[7]

Following the rioting the strikers (or the "mob" as the press called them) gathered on McTavish Street while a delegation of two Italians who were fluent in English conferred with Superintendent Bury. Nothing came of this meeting as Bury's attitude was that the company would only consider their demands if they returned to work. At the announcement of this proposal by the two Italian negotiators, the strikers rejected it with loud jeers and repeated that they wanted 25 cents and 30 cents an hour for day and night work respectively. Meanwhile, as the negotiations had been taking place, the CPR freight sheds were transformed into an armed camp as additional armed men were hired hy the railway to patrol the installations.

In spite of these reinforcements, there was much anxiety in the community. Many believed that the situation warranted the intervention of the local militia or regular troops from Winnipeg. The threat of further violence was once again heightened when later in the day the CPR brought an additional four carloads of men from Winnipeg to replace the strikers Accompanied by heavily-armed constables, Bury successfully led the new men to the freight sheds to commence work. In reaction the Italians demonstrated their determination to keep on fighting by shooting into the air.

An agreement to settle the strike came unexpectedly that evening through the mediation of Mayor Rutledge, Councillor Morton and a young Italian interpreter, Bosco Dominico. Under the terms of the compromise settlement, the CPR agreed to give the men a retroactive increase to the beginning of the shipping season of 2½ cents an hour for both day and night work. Very grudgingly the strikers accepted this compromise, thus ending one of the most serious labour disputes that had occurred up to that time in Fort William.

In Port Arthur the strike was resolved less violently. While a committee of two Italians and three English workers directed the strike, as in Fort William it was the Italians who were the most militant. Their aim was also to widen the area of conflict to a limited general strike.

On 1 October, the day following the start of the strike, a "mob" of strikers of various nationalities made its way to the Port Arthur CPR station where, across from it, Italian and other workers were engaged in the town's excavation and blasting operations. Once the strikers reached the site, "in picturesque Italian the men were called upon to leave their work." Eventually a few of the Italian workers left their work, and after repeated appeals and jeers "the remaining Italians joined their howling countrymen." The non-Italians remained at their work. It is difficult to determine whether the Italian excavation workers joined the CNR strikers in a display of class or ethnic solidarity or whether their action was occasioned by fear. The *News*, which adopted an anti-Italian stand, credits fear as having been the determining factor. The strikers did not leave until a police officer had scuffled with one striker and threatened to use a gun if the strikers did not disperse.[8]

The CNR strategy in combatting the strikers was similar to that of the Canadian Pacific. Despite a commitment not to introduce outside men to break the strike, on 2 October sixty-four men arrived on the CPR train from Winnipeg. At the station the new men, who were unaware of the strike, were met by the strikers, who informed them of the conflict. These strikebreakers were of different nationalities; but after learning of the strike from their respective countrymen, they decided not to commence work at the docks. Instead they took their packsacks and started walking up town while the strikers loudly cheered them. Many of these men who found themselves destitute were taken care of by Italians who made sure that none of them went hungry.

The solidarity of the imported strikebreakers with the local men was a major blow to the company. At the same time in Fort William the CPR had settled its dispute. These two factors prompted the CNR to offer its striking freight handlers a compromise similiar to the CPR formula.

The resolution of the Port Arthur strike without resort to the type of violence which was used in the Canadian Pacific freight sheds has been credited in part to the moderation of the British workers. Having come from an industrialized milieu, they favoured an orderly and legalistic approach to the protest.[9] For instance, on the day that the strike began in the Port Arthur sheds of the CNR, "the Englishmen especially tried their best to impress their associates with the advisability of committing no violence."[10] On the other hand, since the imported strikebreakers never did reach the work sheds of the CNR, there was no need for an armed confrontation.

The militancy of the *contadini* in the 1906 strikes aroused considerable adverse reaction in the Anglo-Canadian community. An editorial in the *News* on 1 October focused on the Italian workers. The "foreigners" and in particular the Italians were not criticized for having made unreasonable demands but rather for having introduced tactics in their dispute which were contrary to the British mode of behaviour. The major concern, the editorial argued,

> is the circumstance that among the strikers are a majority of foreigners, chiefly Italians, who are reported to have prepared to meet opposition to their demands at the point of the knife, the national weapon of the "dago." ... To strike for more pay is the legitimate prerogative of any man or body of men. But for a community of British citizens to have to submit to the obloquy of insult and armed defiance from a disorganized horde of ignorant and low-down mongrel swash bucklers and peanut vendors is making a demand upon national pride which has no excuse.

All this was the result, the editor argued, of a lenient policy which the community had adopted in its dealings with Italians of a "baser sort." The editor predicted that the Italians were likely to turn the strike into a "guerilla war" and introduce stabbing and shooting men in the back as a regular feature in industrial bargaining processes.[11]

Editorial opinion on 2 October was no less critical of the Italian strikers. Reminding his readers that Canada was a nation under the British flag, the editor charged that the Italians were violating British law in defiantly assembling in "riotous" congregations:

> It is only incidental that bodies of Italians, ranging in number from fifty to one hundred, may without fear, congregate in public places and openly assume an attitude of defiance to British law.... Self-preservation being the first law of nature it would be not advisable to offhand attempt by a peremptory command to compel a congregation of striking Italians to disperse. The nature of the Italian demands that he be not driven unless he is outnumbered.

Had the Italian workers a better understanding of British Law, argued the editorial, they would have returned to work once the company had agreed to review their demands. Under the circumstances the editor stated that the CNR was perfectly justified in following the CPR strategy of importing constables and strikebreakers to its works. Finally, the editorial concluded that the Italian strikers were doomed to fail since "the Italian makes the mistake of not realizing that the British method of conquest is not intelligent. It's a waiting game, and the Italian cannot or will not wait."[12]

This hostile attitude toward the *contadini* could only serve to incite Anglo-Canadians against the Italians and make the issues involved in the strike insignificant. At the same time this type of opinion served to justify to the citizenry the employers' position of refusing to bargain and importing constables and strikebreakers.

The 1907 shipping season commenced with a determination by both railway companies to shatter the gains that their freight handlers had won as a result of the strikes of the previous October. First came the news that, as had been rumoured during the strike, Canadian Pacific was going to exclude Italians and Greeks from working at the freight sheds. Work for them would be limited to the track lines and construction camps. This action was being taken because of their militancy in the strike. Their places were to be filled by two hundred or two hundred and fifty Britishers who were being boarded at the rear of the sheds and "should trouble arise it is expected that the Briton will be more than a match for the Greek."[13] Along with British workers, Hungarians, Poles and Finns were included among the eight hundred men hired. Next the Canadian Northern announced that for the 1907 season the rate of pay for its freight handlers would be 19 cents and 22½ cents an hour for day and night work respectively, thus reneging on the agreed rate of 22½ cents and 25 cents which had ended the strike the previous year.[14]

In response to the CNR wage cutback, the British workers at the sheds proceeded to organize a longshoremen's union. Before the union had consolidated its position, however, about three hundred men of various nationalities spontaneously went on strike on 8 June. This action may have been provoked by the company's firing the day before of L. Torrey, a British freight handler who had been canvassing the men with the goal of establishing a union. Demands brought forward by the strikers included the reinstatement of Torrey, more regular work, and wages of 25 cents and 30 cents an hour for day and night work respectively.

On 12 June the CNR brought one hundred and fifty men consisting of Italians, German and a few British from Winnipeg. When these men heard of the strike on their arrival about one hundred of them joined the strikers even though many of them were "practically destitute." On 14 June the strikers, realizing that they were not going to win, surrendered their demands in return for the mere promise that management would not discriminate against the men who had been active in the strike.

At the Canadian Pacific sheds the "Britishers" and the "foreigners" who had replaced the Italians and the Greeks did not remain indifferent to the longshoremen's strike at Port Arthur. On 10 June the British workers started a walk out and were joined by the rest of the "foreigners," making wage demands similar to the Port Arthur strikers. On the evening of 11 June at a strikers' meeting, about four hundred handlers joined the recently established union of the Port Arthur workers. This action was rather late as earlier in the morning the CPR had already hired new men to replace the strikers. "Greeks and Italians Seem to Have Broken the Freight Handlers Strike" was the startling newspaper report of 11 June. It was even more ironic since the strikebreakers were the same Italians and Greeks who had led the strike the previous fall and who had consequently not been hired at the beginning of the 1907 season.[15]

In spite of information reaching the police, the Italians and Greeks who had been refused employment in the spring had not resorted to violence. They had accepted their plight and sought alternative employment. But they harboured a great deal of resentment against the British workers who had replaced them. It is not surprising, then, that attempts to get these men to join the strike failed. "The Englishmen, the Italian and Greek strikebreakers claim, had no scruples about going to work when they were shut out and they certainly do not intend to turn around and help them out when they are shut out."[16]

The 1906 and 1907 industrial disputes of Fort William and Port Arthur clearly demonstrate that a heterogeneous workforce greatly enhanced the employers' power of manipulation of the workers. For their part the Italians were both at the forefront of labour militancy and were also manipulated to act as strikebreakers.

Troops Intervene in Little Italy's Affairs, 1909

The defeat of the freight handlers in the 1905 and 1907 strikes had only added to their discontent and after a short two-year peiod, the longshoremen were once again on strike. In 1909 a strike at the CPR freight sheds (adjacent to Fort William's Little Italy) surpassed in scope any of the previous ones that had occurred in the city. While the strike lasted only six days, from 9 to 15 August, before it was over the conflict took on the character of a miniature civil war between the residents of the "foreign quarter" on the one hand, and the CPR special constables, the local police, the local militia and some regular troops who arrived from Winnipeg. Once again, as had been the case in 1906 and 1907, the Southern Europeans, and in particular the Italians and the Greeks, were perceived as the instigators and the ones who directed the course of the conflict.

On 9 August, without warning, six hundred freight handlers, most of them "foreigners," walked out.[17] This action was in violation of the Industrial Disputes Investigation Act of 1907. The terms of the Act stipulated that in the transportation industry differences between employers and employees had to be referred for conciliation or arbitration to a Board of Conciliation and Investigation appointed by the Minister of Labour.[18] It is doubtful that the strikers, who were "very generally foreigners, and with perhaps few exceptions without more than the rudiments of education," were aware of this legislation. Leaders of the strike later advanced this position in defence of their action.[19]

The strikers demanded an increase from 17½ cents plus 1 cent bonus an hour for day work to 22½ cents, and an additional 4 cents an hour for night work which currently stood at 21 cents an hour. The 1909 wage scale was lower than it had been in 1906, which must have caused considerable economic hardship for the handlers. During this period across Canada wages lagged behind prices in spite of the rapid expansion in the economy. In part, this economic imbalance was caused by the large labour supply which was the result of the persistent influx of immigrants. Besides wages, the strikers were seeking the abolition of the bonus system and were demanding better treatment from their foremen.

The foremen were only one of the aspects of the ordeal of working at the CPR docks. Every day it involved a virtual fight to get hired. The sad human drama began at the dock before daybreak when the hundreds of men showed up, hoping to be in front of the long line in order to get a "check" (a number) and be put to work.[20] In the long line both the weak and the strong would struggle or even fight to be among the lucky ones to receive a check. On 16 August a Greek striker, Macineo Diligines, spoke to a *News* reporter on the working conditions at the sheds and made the following remarks:

> But we should not have to fight to get the little checks. That is where I gotta my ribs break. In the crush. I was much strong when I come seven years ago but each season this fight for the little check it get harder. We should not have to fitta for a chance to work so hard.

Even more frustrating, according to Diligines, was the preferential treatment accorded to Northern Italians over the rightful place of Greeks and possibly over the Southern Italians:

I strike because we not all get treated alike. They hold out checks at another window while I fight to get at the regular place! I finda them handing out checks to them they like at another window. Then we say it is not fair and the man he say go to hell. Then we strike. There is not work for all. I fight to window and they tell me there are no more wanted but I see them hand out the little checks at another window to big Italian man big and strong he from the north. So we say again it is not right. I was so strong seven years ago that I always git in first but it is not so now.

When the clerk would have hired the number of men he thought to be adequate, the rest of the men would sadly go home or wait for other boats to arrive. In the evening a second struggle to get a check might be repeated and this was a way of life that required the acceptance of perpetual daily abasement.[21]

It was in an effort to deal with such conditions that the workers also wanted the CPR to recognize a longshoreman's union, which was in the process of being formed. Their strategy was to attempt to form the union and to resist the importation of strikebreakers. On 10 August, the morning following the start of the strike, the strikers began to patrol Little Italy armed with sticks and stopping anyone who gave the appearance of being a potential strikebreaker.[22] Signs of the company's determination not to give in to the strikers' demands came swiftly. When the strikers saw that a number of freight cars were placed on the siding at the junction of the freight sheds and McTavish Street, thus creating a barrier between the strikers and the freight sheds, they surmised that the cars were to provide cover for armed officers protecting strikebreakers to be imported from Montreal.

While Fort William's mayor, L. L. Peltier, was attempting to negotiate a peaceful settlement between the strikers and the company, violence broke out. The immediate catalyst was the moving of thirty CPR special constables who had been brought from Winnipeg to the sheds. On the morning of 12 August, when the constables moved to the company's boardinghouse near the sheds, they were soon surrounded by angry strikers who believed that the new men were strikebreakers and not constables. A gun battle ensued.

The armed confrontation lasted about half an hour. The CPR men were driven back to the bunkhouse. As the strikers were preparing to storm the house, they were dissuaded by the appeals of the local police who had just arrived on the scene. For a while, however, the strikers continued intermittent fire regardless of the presence of the police, who were urging them to disperse in the name of the King. While no fatalities occurred, at least fourteen men received serious injuries.

On learning of the shooting the mayor went to the scene of the clash where he read the Riot Act and called out the militia. One hundred and fifty men of the Ninety-Sixth Regiment took up positions at the outskirts of Little Italy and order was restored.

A wartime atmosphere took hold of Little Italy. Groups of soldiers patrolled the area with orders to shoot to kill if necessary. Finding themselves surrounded by troops, with all exit points of the area blocked, the strikers had no choice but to submit to a personal search. The police found a number of revolvers. Following this systematic search of the strikers themselves, a second search of the houses of Little Italy was mounted. "The chief of police and four squads of five soldiers ransacked the residences and outbuildings for weapons and ammunition." The search unearthed only about thirty revolvers and rifles.[23]

On 13 August the CPR brought in French-Canadian workers to replace the strikers. At this point the mood of the Italians was one of rage:

> All yesterday afternoon while the strikebreakers were being taken into the yards the Greeks and Hungarians and Italians stood around the lines of military with anger reflected on every face and muttering threats against the soldiers and those who had gone to the sheds to work. Many of these men own their own homes in Fort William and would find it inconvenient to leave so that the prospect of not being able to procure work again is none too pleasing.[24]

About fifty of the one hundred penniless French Canadians, having been made aware for the first time of the dispute, decided to comply with the strikers' wishes and walked away. In all, about two hundred men were working at the shed guarded by as many soldiers, and the unloading of cargo was proceeding on a limited basis.

Faced with such company determination backed with military protection, the strikers of various nationalities managed to hold a "conference of all nations" in Little Italy to assess the situation. Italian, Finnish and other workers agreed that they would not return to work unless the CPR rehired all the men who had gone on strike. Meanwhile, company officials had successfully managed to shift the focus of attention from the men's demands to the question of who had instigated the strike. They charged that the strike had been caused by Greek workers, but this assertion was quickly denied by Greek spokesmen who claimed that workers from all the nationalities, including British workers, had initiated the strike.[25] Canadian Pacific officials made it clear to the press that they would not agree to any settlement of the strike which would require their employing Greeks in any capacity. They also declared that they were not going to employ any longer the Italians and Hungarians who had been at the forefront of the strike.

Commenting on the strike situation, General Agent R. Armstrong inferred that there might be some exception made for the "white Italians," that is, Northern Italians:

> The Greeks I blame mostly for the disorder. The big Italians from the north of Italy are our best men. They are called the white Italians. The little fellows from the southern peninsular are willing but weak. I have on our books plenty of these men.[26]

In the parlance of the time the concept of "white" was considered synonymous with Northern European and with being "Canadian."

In their attempt to improve the harsh conditions at the freights sheds the "foreigners," and particularly the Southern Europeans, became the object of prejudicial commentaries. In a letter to the editor of the *News* a local labourer stated that Canadians had little in common with "hot-blooded foreigners." He justified the CPR's low wage scale arguing that if they earned more, they would have simply sent more to their families in Europe and Canadians would be so much poorer. The letter concluded by inferring that the strikers were anarchists: "Here's wishing Canadians and white men always get top wages and confusion to secessionists and anarchists."[27]

The strike had also brought reporters covering it face to face with the poor living conditions within Little Italy. Crowded dwellings and unsanitary conditions existing both within houses and on the streets were attributed to the imported habits of the "Latin races of Southern Europe." This front-page article also asserted that the sleeping quarters of the "foreign quarter" were worse than their equivalent in the slums of Rome or Athens and that "baths are practically an unknown quantity with the Latin residents of the district."[28]

On Sunday, 15 August, at a mass meeting at the corner of McTavish and McIntyre streets, the strikers listened to Mayor Peltier announce that he had an agreement in writing that the CPR was prepared to accept all the striking employees, including the Greeks, with the exception of any individuals the courts might find guilty of having committed violence. On the wage question, the CPR was prepared to accept the decision of a board appointed under the Industrial Disputes Investigation Act. Nearly all the men present promised the mayor that they would accept this formula and would return to work. Erroneously convinced that the CPR had agreed to comply with their demand for 5 cents an hour increase, the freight handlers returned to work the morning of 16 August. Only after a newspaper reporter explained to them precisely what the mayor had said did they realize that they had returned to work at the old pay scale. Even an Italian worker who had been born in the United States and was fluent in English had understood the mayor to say that the company had agreed to grant the strikers their wage demands.

On 15 August the Minister of Labour, Mackenzie King, commissioned F. A. Acland, Deputy Minister of Labour, to settle the dispute under the provisions of the Industrial Disputes Investigation Act. Acland arrived on 17 August, the day after the men had returned to work, and proceeded to appoint a board.

In its unanimous report, released on 26 August, the Board recommended an increase of 3 cents an hour, making the wages 20½ cents and 23½ cents an hour for day and night work respectively and the abolition of the bonus system. Bosco Dominico, the spokesman of the strike committee, told the press that all the longshoremen were dissatisfied with the new wage scale but that they had little choice but accept it.

As for the brutal conditions which existed at the freight sheds, they remained undisturbed by the entire affair. The Board's inquiry had not even substantiated one of the strikers' grievances about alleged harsh treatment by some of the company's foremen.[29] Aside from a small raise in pay, the strike brought little gain to the Italians.

At the outset of the 1910 shipping season, much to their disappointment, the Italians found that their activism of the previous year was going to cost them even more. Repeating its 1907 strategy, a statement on 8 April from the CPR flatly announced that Italians and Greeks would no longer be given employment in the freight sheds. A press report the following day suggested that the "white Italians" were not included in the lock-out but that only about "300 Greeks and natives of South Italy" would be affected. Some confusion, however, persisted on this point, as on 14 April Superintendent R. Armstrong told a reporter that all Italians were included in the lock-out.

The Canadian Pacific policy of exclusion came as a surprise, and many thought that this threat would not be implemented.

> Although there are many who thought that the railway officials would, when the navigation season approached, rescind their mandate not to re-engage the Greeks and "Black" Italians who were implicated in last year's rioting, there seems to be little foundation for such an opinion.[30]

A sign of the company's determination to implement its discriminatory policy was the arrival of C. H. Andrews, their chief secret service agent. When Andrews arrived in Fort William on 13 April he told a reporter that he was aware that the company's edict of exclusion and the presence of three hundred and fifty imported men to replace the Italian and Greek handlers might provoke a riot. He further assured the reporter that the company was now in a position to thwart any disturbances as it was well armed.

> Yes, I know all about that trouble, but you can bet your life that they won't make as much headway as they did last fall. The police department of the C.P.R. is organized this year, and just now enough constables could be mustered to compete with a company of soldiers, let alone a bunch of foreigners who would not stop running if they saw a red coat walking down the coal docks streets. We don't anticipate any trouble, but should the Greeks and Italians start a riot we will be on hand.[31]

Intervention on behalf of the Italians and Greeks failed to get the Canadian Pacific to change its announced policy. The local Trades and Labor Council engaged H. Sanderson, their eastern agent, to discuss the matter with General Manager G. J. Bury, who steadfastly refused to entertain any thought of conciliation. Bury claimed that the company's lock-out of the Italians and Greeks was going to be for the benefit of the CPR and for Fort William as well.

Besides having to counter the railway's special constables in 1909 in order to prevent strikebreakers from taking their livelihoods the strikers had also to bear the brunt of the Canadian military. With such an ally, the CPR had little trouble in bringing the strikers to submission. Finally, the *contadini* were made to suffer for the second time the humiliation of being refused employment at the sheds. While citizens blamed the Italians for ignoring British law in their struggle, no British article of law made any provision to guarantee their livelihood against the threat of strikebreakers.

The Deprenzo Case, 1912

The last major industrial conflict prior to the Great War in which the *contadini* commanded the focus of attention occurred in the summer of 1912. While the setting of the drama was in Port Arthur, many of the participants were from Fort William's Little Italy who commuted there daily to work for the Canadian Northern Coal and Ore Dock Company. At noon on 29 July members of the Coal Handlers' Union, Local 319, went on strike. In the evening Italian strikers were involved in a violent encounter with a squad of city policemen, which left a number of men seriously injured and ended with the Riot Act's being read. While the violence involved lasted only two or three minutes, its ramifications for the Italians were longstanding. For the Deprenzo brothers, in addition to receiving numerous bullet wounds, it meant a ten-year prison sentence.

Since its inception in March 1911, Union Local 319 had been influenced by *contadini* both at the leadership and at the rank-and-file level. At its organizing meeting two of the officers elected by the nearly fifty men present were Italians; Mike Pento was elected president, and Nicolo Ciacco treasurer.[32] Mike Pento was in many ways a typical Italian immigrant. Born in 1878 in San Angelo, Avellino, he left his home town at the age of 15 and went to the United States. Following job opportunities on railway construction, he made his way to British Columbia in 1904 and from there he came to Fort William and in 1905 moved to Port Arthur. Like many of his fellow-countrymen, he had received no formal education.[33] Being a veteran immigrant who had acquired a working knowledge of the English language, he was in a position to play a leadership role among his fellows who had little or no knowledge of English.[34]

Some evidence that many of the original rank-and-file members were also *contadini* is apparent in the minutes of the second official meeting of the union. On this occasion, following remarks made to the men by the president of the Port Arthur Trades and Labor Council, the president of the local, Mike Pento, "Luterjoerated [reiterated] them [the] same in Italian. . . . " Of course, the official minutes do not record the names of the rank and file in order to avoid reprisals from the company.[35]

From its inception the relationship of the union with the employer had been one of hostility prompted primarily by repeated attempts by management to undermine the union's structure. When the union presented its first set of demands in May 1911, the company responded by dismissing both Mike Pento and the union's secretary, George Ross, and a few other men.[36]

In response, the union contacted the federal Department of Labour to apply the Industrial Disputes Investigation Act. The Department complied and by 19 June a Board of Conciliation and Investigation submitted a unanimous report outlining a one-year agreement that would expire 30 April 1912. On the question of wages, the men were granted part of what they had demanded. The company also agreed to reinstate the five men that it had dismissed in May and the men received an assurance that the company would not discriminate against union members in the future.[37]

A year later in the spring of 1912, during the course of negotiating another agreement for that year, Superintendent Jorpland sent a letter of dismissal once again to both Pento and Ross and stated that the company would no longer negotiate a contract with these union officers. Jorpland's action apparently was in retaliation for one-hour strikes on two occasions during the 1911 work season which the company suspected had been incited by Pento and Ross and Nicolo Ciacco, the treasurer of the union, who was also discharged.[38] When eighty rank-and-file union members were read Jorpland's letter at a meeting, they gave their officers a vote of confidence and resolved t~ "ask the Government to afford another Concilation [*sic*] Board."[39]

On 19 July a three-man board which the Minister of Labour had appointed on 23 May rendered its verdict on the two basic questions in contention, the matter of wages and of the company's dismissal of union officials. This time the Conciliation Board, not having reached a unanimous stand, produced a majority and a minority report.[40] The majority report, which expressed the findings of the company representative and the chairman, Judge McKay, was short and upheld the Coal Company's stand that the men be paid according to the 1911 pay scale, arguing that the men's monthly wages were one-tenth higher than what their counterparts were being paid by the CPR. The only exception to the 1911 agreement was that the company would pay 25 cents an hour for dock work all year round.[41] On the matter of the dismissal of the union officers the report admitted that the Board had been unable to find any evidence that the two one-hour strikes in 1911 had been induced by the union's president, secretary or treasurer. Nevertheless, the report made no recommendations to have the officers reinstated but only stated the company's attitude:

> The Company insists on exercising their alleged right to engage such employees as they may deem proper during the year 1912, and the three employees in question appeared to have secured employment elsewhere, one of them at least at equally satisfactory employment.[42]

The minority report submitted by Frederick Urry,[43] a Port Arthur alderman, who was representing the interests of the coal handlers on the Board, differed totally from the majority report. Urry's report urged that the handlers be granted an increase and pointed out that the claim of the majority report that the men were earning one-tenth higher monthly wages than their CPR counterparts was strictly due to longer hours. As to the issue of the two one-hour walkouts which the handlers had undertaken in 1911, Urry found no reason to blame the union officers that the company had dismissed. The first walkout, he explained, was justifiable as it had occurred following a company announcement one evening that, starting the next morning, only three men would be performing the work that up to then had been done by four men on each car. This abrupt change of policy had come shortly after the company had accepted the agreement of the 1911 Board of Investigation and the men had viewed this change as an obvious violation of their agreement and wanted an explanation. The second walkout had taken place also spontaneously when a union member was dismissed while working, but neither Pento nor Ross had been present.[44]

Unhappy with the majority report, the coal handlers went on strike on 20 July. Their picket line was up at the corner of Second Avenue and Fort William Road, a strategic point which commanded the only entrance to the coal docks. This point was also adjacent to Port Arthur's Little Italy. Over fifty strikers, the majority of them Italian, were manning this point determined to prevent strikebreakers from going to work. In the evening when a couple of men were attempting to cross the picket line to go to work, they were seized by the strikers and were being discouraged from proceeding to the coal docks by an Italian who was "flourishing a revolver" when Constable Silliker of the local police arrived on the scene. When Silliker attempted to arrest the Italian, five or six other Italian strikers drew revolvers and pointed them at the constable. Disarmed, Silliker was allowed to depart.

On learning of the incident Chief of Police Angus McLellan, along with Silliker and three other officers, went to the scene where they found a "mob" armed with clubs. Constable Silliker identified the striker that he had attempted to arrest but when two constables tried to arrest him the man ran into the bush. The two constables then placed under arrest the "ring leader," an Italian simply known as "Tony the Shoemaker." According to the account in the *Daily Times-Journal*, the other strikers, armed with clubs, sticks and revolvers, went to the rescue of the "shoemaker." In the ensuing struggle blows and bullets were exchanged. Police Chief McLellan suffered a slight fracture of the skull and other head injuries caused by blows from clubs and a cut in the scalp from a bullet. Three constables suffered slight club and bullet injuries, and an undetermined number of wounded strikers fled the scene and went into hiding. The Deprenzo brothers suffered the most extensive injuries. Dominic was hit by seven bullets, one of which had "pierced his heart," while Nicolo had five bullet wounds and both his hands had been "shot off."

The local press report of the violence attributed responsibility to Italian coal handlers only and to the Deprenzo brothers, who were perceived as "ring leaders":

Eye witnesses of the riot say that the Austrians, Hungarians and Finlanders did not take any part in the trouble. All the shooting and wielding of clubs was done by a gang of from 25 to 35 Italians who were urged on by the Denico [*sic*] brothers.

When Chief McLellan was clubbed to the ground unconscious with a stick larger than a baseball bat two Hungarians rushed to his aid and cried out, "Oh, our good chief is killed!" Denico got the first clout at the chief and when he was down the brother landed two more blows just as the Hungarians interfered. The ring leaders retreated but not before they were fairly perforated with bullets, which for a period of two or three minutes were flying in all directions.[45]

News of the confrontation at the entrance to the coal docks reached Mayor Ray of Port Arthur, who quickly summoned the Ninety-Sixth Regiment and made his way to the scene where he read the Riot Act. Ironically, sketchy news of the violence also reached the remainder of the strikers who were meeting elsewhere in the Finn Hall in preparation for a parade which proceeded through the principal streets of Port Arthur and was headed by an "Italian band."[46] The procession was composed of over one hundred and fifty socialists and labour men including a labour activist, Madison Hicks.[47] When the parade came to a halt, speeches were made and were translated into Italian "warning the men against using violence in striving for their rights." Needless to say, these remarks were too late. Hicks was charged on 2 August with having taken part in an unlawful assemblage and for having headed this parade. Even though the parade had been nowhere near the scene of the violence the magistrate upheld the interpretation of the prosecutor's witnesses (who included Mayor Ray, Colonel Little of the Ninety-Sixth Regiment and a police constable involved in the shooting), who testified that the assemblage had constituted a menace to law and order. Speaking in his defence, Hicks condemned the Italians for the violent incident, stating that he was against "mob rule." Furthermore, had he been at the scene at the time of the confrontation he would have sided with the police squad.[48] The *contadini* were thus abandoned by a socialist organizer and a former ally of their cause.

On the day following the riot "the police squad and soldiers ransacked the Italian houses in Port Arthur coal dock district ... to see if they could recognize any who took part in the riot."[49] The police were not successful in making additional arrests nor did they find any firearms. According to the *Times-Journal* it was likely that the Italians had anticipated the raid and hidden their weapons. Also part of the difficulty was that many of the strikers were residents of Fort William.

By 31 July the situation had calmed down and the troops were withdrawn. However, the strike was also effective as no one ventured to work at the docks even though protection was offered. Although the troops were withdrawn, the company's property was not left undefended. "A special squad of policemen armed with Winchester rifles with sufficient ammunition to blow the inhabitants of Port Arthur's

'Little Old Italy' into eternity" were soon patrolling the property of the Canadian Northern Coal and Ore Dock Company.[50]

On 3 August, five days after the strike had commenced, the company acceded to most of the demands of the coal handlers and the strike came to an end. The company agreed to reinstate the union officers, although it reserved the right to hire men regardless of whether or not they might belong to the union. On the matter of wages, the company agreed to a general 2 cents an hour increase, as well as agreeing to pay the men time and a half for overtime and double time for Sundays and holidays.

Two factors seem to account for the company's abrupt conciliatory attitude. First, the militancy attributed to the Italians had effectively discouraged local workers from acting as strikebreakers even when offered police protection. The company had also failed to recruit strikebreakers in Winnipeg as a result of the general knowledge that violence had occurred.[51] Furthermore, in 1912 locally unemployed labourers were scarce and nationally the situation was much the same. For instance, the CPR was faced with a shortage of two thousand labourers in its system.

The coal handlers had accomplished at least a partial victory, but the strike had proven tragic for the Deprenzo brothers, who had been arrested after their bodies had been riddled with police bullets. On 8 October 1912 they were brought to trial before Judge Middleton and a jury.[52] Dominic Deprenzo was charged with attempting to murder Police Chief McLellan and Nicolo was charged with assaulting Constable Peterson. Peterson gave the court evidence that when he saw Sergeant Burleigh, his colleague, on the verge of being attacked by Nicolo with a club, he went to prevent the attack. In the scuffle, after having fired five bullets into Nicolo, the injured man managed to land a club blow on his head that caused Peterson to pass out. Burleigh then stated that when Peterson was on the ground Nicolo was intending to hit Peterson again when he fired another shot into Nicolo's hand and subdued him. The crown prosecutor also rested its case on the testimony of Burleigh who claimed that Dominic had struck Chief McLellan.

The testimony given by Nicolo differed considerably from the police version. According to Nicolo, his brother Dominic was lying on the ground shot and was calling for help when a policeman actually raised him up, the better to administer another shot. In appealing to the jury the defence attorney reminded them to be cautious that the testimony of the crown prosecutor's witnesses might have an advantage since they presented it in fluent English and might sound more convincing, whereas the defendants had difficulty in speaking English and therefore were likely to be less convincing. He also pleaded to the jury that his two clients, in addition to their language handicap, did not know the laws and customs of Canada and went on to dwell upon the humble virtues of the *contadini* and the important role they were playing in the industrial process:

He said they were mostly coarse, rough, uneducated peasants

from southern Italy, their only advantage being their strong frames and tough sinews that made them an invaluable acquisition to Canada, for performing the rough, dirty work such as handling coal. They were, he said, the hewers of wood and drawers of water. They were thrifty and saving. Most of them had dependants away back in Italy and as each pay day came along they sent home their savings to support their loved ones at home.

The defence attorney suggested to the jury to keep in mind the overall circumstances of the Italian immigrants in their deliberation.

In his address to the jury, Judge Middleton discredited the defence attorney's appeal in no uncertain terms. He stressed that the law had to protect police officers, who represented the welfare of the entire community, in executing their duties. The judge told the jury that Dominic must have been guilty, drawing his conclusion from the following evidence:

> He [Judge Middleton] drew attention to the fact that there must have been very good reason for the suspicion that pointed at Durenzo [*sic*] as the man who struck down the chief, as he was evidently the target of the police after the riot began and had received, according to reports, not less than seven bullet wounds. It was strange, he said, that where there were more than 150 people, this man should be singled out as the one object of attack.

It was no consolation for the Deprenzo brothers, but it was common knowledge in the Italian community that in fact "Tony the Shoemaker" was the man who had struck the Chief over the head with a pick handle, and having fled the riot scene he burrowed his way deep into a hay barn and successfully avoided a police probe into the hay with steel rods. Eventually the "Black Handers" (a group of new Italian Port Arthur merchants who were involved in prostitution, gambling and bootlegging) smuggled "Tony the Shoemaker" into the United States.[53]

Judge Middleton saw the trial of the Deprenzo brothers as an opportunity to teach the "foreigners" and particularly the Italians a lesson:

> The point that he emphasized was that those foreigners must not be led to believe that they can take the law in their own hands, throwing aside the measures provided by civilized society for the punishment of crime. If this condition was once allowed civilization would descend to barbarism and anybody having a grievance would be inclined to take the law in his own hands and resort to violence and outrage to avenge his wrongs. The law would be overthrown and the courts of Justice would be a hollow mockery. The point that must be brought home to these people was that violence in any form will not be tolerated in this country, regardless of

any custom or usages prevailing in Russia, Finland, Italy or whatever country the foreign element comes from.

After weighing the various arguments the jury took one and a half hours to return with a verdict for Dominic. They found him guilty of unlawfully wounding and resisting arrest, but recommended that the charge of attempted murder be dropped. After twenty minutes of deliberation in the case of his brother Nicolo, the jury returned also with a verdict of guilty on the charge of assaulting a constable. Judge Middleton sentenced both brothers to a prison term of ten years at Stoney Mountain Penitentiary.[54] The fate of the Deprenzo brothers caused grief among those who had benefited from the strike and they viewed the judge's stiff prison sentence as a case of "vindictive justice."

Even though in 1912 the *contadini* coal handlers had the advantage of striking within the framework of a union, nonetheless, violence marked this strike just as on the previous occasions when they struck without the benefit of being organized. It appears that the *contadini's* application of violence in the dispute came as a last resort and in order to safeguard the effectiveness of the picket line against would-be strikebreakers. Their confrontation with the police force was to protect their leaders who, in the process of enforcing the picket line, were facing arrest and in this sense their violence in the 1912 strike had been both selective and limited.[55] In this case the *contadini's* preparedness to risk their lives against armed policemen had been an essential factor to the partially successful outcome of the strike. It was because the news of the shooting spread to traditional hiring centres of labourers that the company was unable to recruit replacements, and had eventually to compromise on the workers' demands.

Conclusion

It is apparent that the violence employed by the *contadini* in these strikes was prompted by their employers' conduct in the bargaining process.[56] Management's first step in response to a strike was almost instinctively to turn to local or imported recruits to break the strike. The only effective means that the *contadini* had to maintain alive the possibility of winning concessions was to introduce physical force to prevent others from taking their jobs. Without this resolve to risk their lives against the introduction of strikebreakers, the strike would in many cases have been a lost cause from the moment that it started.

During this turbulentt decade of Canadian history, the *contadini* of Fort William and Port Arthur, who came from Italy with no previous experience in industrial conflict, faced with determination the employers' strikebreaking schemes. Paradoxically, they too, for a short time, became a tool of strikebreaking in 1907 after the British and other "foreign workers" had allowed the CPR's policy of excluding Italian labour without a challenge. It should be apparent, however, that the *contadini* made their greatest impact in the Twin Cities as effective strikers and not as strikebreakers.

The high degree of militancy that the *contadini* displayed in their new proletariat roles in the Twin Cities was not a trait that originated in the new industrial milieu. Rather, their militant actions were an application of the "revoltist traditions" which were deeply rooted in their agrarian background.[57] The militancy and violence of the Italian immigrants was a response to harsh working conditions and was aimed at resolving immediate problems: low wages, the notorious bonus system, long and irregular work hours and the threat of strikebreakers. In the process the Italian workers were perceived by Anglo-Canadians of the Twin Cities as people of a "baser type" and of being a threat to the British ideals of law and order. Inevitably, this initial impact of the *contadini* upon the communities of the Twin Cities meant that Fort William's Little Italy was left with the task of coping with this stigma.

Notes

1. Stuart Jamieson, *Times of Trouble: Labour Unrest and and Industrial Conflict in Canada, 1900-66*, The Task Force on Labour Relations, Study No. 22 (Ottawa: Privy Council Office, 1968), pp. 63-67.

2. *Daily Times-Journal* (Fort William), 3 July 1902. The newspaper account does not state the current hourly pay rate. Both the newspapers at the Lakehead, the *Daily Times-Journal* and the *Daily News*, contain detailed reports of industrial disputes during the decade under study, and the author has made full use of their files in his research for this essay.

3. *Daily Times-Journal*, 20 May 1903.

4. *Sessional Papers*, 1906, No. 25. Report of R. A. Burris to the Superintendent of Immigration, Port Arthur, 13 July 1905.

5. A committee of six handlers, which included one Italian, one Russian and four Englishmen representing workers of their respective national groups, was able to obtain only one small concession. On the issue of the retention of the bonus, the company would still hold it back until the end of the season, but if a man wanted to leave he would be able to receive it provided that management received ten days' notice. *Daily News*, 5 and 8 May 1906.

6. *Daily Times-Journal*, 1 October 1906.

7. Ibid., 2 October 1906. An estimated one hundred and fifty bullets were fired in the short encounter.

8. *Daily News*, 1 October 1906.

9. Jean F. Morrison, "Community and Conflict: A Study of the Working Class and Its Relationships at the Canadian Lakehead, 1903-1913," M.A. dissertation (Lakehead University, 1974), p. 70.

10. *Daily News*, 1 October 1906.

11. Ibid.

12. Ibid., 2 October 1906.

13. Ibid., 30 April 1907.

14. It seems that the CNR, in lowering its wages, was attempting to follow the CPR wage scale since the latter, during the strike of the previous fall, had been able to end the strike with a smaller wage compromise of 19 cents and 21½ cents for day and night work respectively. *Daily Times-Journal*, 11 June 1907.

15. *Daily Times-Journal*, 11 June 1907. According to the *News* there were also some Finns who had taken the place of the striking Britishers. *Daily News*, 11 June 1907.

16. *Daily Times-Journal*, 12 June 1907.

17. Ibid., 9 August 1909. The report of the Deputy Minister of Labour, F. A. Acland, states that seven hundred freight handlers were involved in the strike. *The Labour Gazette* Ottawa, X (September 1909), p. 341.

18. The Industrial Disputes Investigation Act prohibited strikes and lockouts in certain key industries, such as coal mining, transportation and communication, before the grievances involved in a dispute were submitted to a three-man board. Neither party was necessarily bound by the board's recommendations. H. A. Logan, *Trades Union in Canada* (Toronto: Macmillan of Canada, 1948), p. 450.

19. *The Labour Gazette*, X (September 1909), p. 343.

20. Taped interview with Giuseppe Zuliani (born in Fiume, Veneto, 1888), 4 June 1974.

21. *Daily News*, 16 August 1909.

22. A police search of the strikers in the evening of the start of the strike resulted in the seizure of one gun and the owner was arrested. *Daily Times-Journal*, 10 August 1909.

23. Ibid., 13 August 1909.

24. *Daily News*, 14 August 1909.

25. There were two hundred Greeks out of five hundred handlers employed by the CPR.

26. *Daily News*, 16 August 1909.

27. Ibid., 23 August 1909.

28. *Daily Times-Journal*, 21 August 1909.

29. *The Labour Gazette*, X (September 1909), pp. 341-48.

30. *Daily News*, 13 April 1910. "Black" Italians refers to Southern Italians.

31. *Daily Times-Journal*, 13 April 1910; the new imported men were French Canadians who had been hired at Montreal.

32. Thunder Bay Historical Museum Society Archives, Port Arthur Coal Handlers Union, Local No. 319, Minute Book, 18 March 1911. The name Pento appears spelled in different ways, such as Paanto and Pionto.

33. Interview with Mike Pento's son Anthony, 30 July 1976. Pento's leadership of the union came to an end on 7 December 1912, when two new Italian workers were elected as officers: Frank Colosimo and J. Tiboni were appointed president and secretary respectively. Then on 6 April 1913 the minutes of the union record that Pento was dismissed: "Mike Pento cast off the Union." (Port Arthur Coal Handlers Union, Minutes, 7 December 1912; 6 April 1913.) According to his son, Mike Pento had been induced by the company to accept a promotion to general foreman. This step was taken since Pento had too much influence over his fellow Italians. The company

hoped that as general foreman he would divert his influence toward the interest of management rather than the interest of the union.

34. The writer has not been able to locate relatives or persons able to provide information as to the background of Nicolo Ciacco.

35. At their first union meeting, in order to keep the membership as secret as possible, the men were given a "pass word."

36. *Daily News*, 11 May 1911. Pento had worked for the Canadian Northern Coal and Ore Dock Company for four years.

37. "Report of Board in Dispute Between The Canadian Northern Coal and Ore Company, of Port Arthur, Ont., And Certain Employes, Members of Coal Handlers' Union, No. 319," *The Labour Gazette*, XII (July 1911), pp. 47-49. The men had wanted 32½ cents and 27½ cents an hour for boat work and dock work respectively. They also wanted time and a half for work after six o'clock and double time for Sunday and for work between midnight and six in the morning. (Port Arthur Coal Handlers' Union, Minutes, 25 April 1911.) The Board of Conciliation and Investigation granted the handlers 25 cents an hour for dock work and 30 cents an hour for boat work and a lower rate of 22½ cents an hour when the navigation season closed. Time and a half was also granted for work performed on Sunday and for overtime between seven in the evening and six in the morning. *The Labour Gazette*, XII (July 1911), p. 49.

38. "Report of Board in Dispute Between the Canadian Northern Coal and Ore Dock Company and Employees," *The Labour Gazette*, XIII (August 1912), p. 132.

39. Port Arthur Coal Handlers' Union, Minutes, 1 April 1912.

40. *The Labour Gazette*, XIII (August 1912), pp. 130-38.

41. Ibid., p. 133. The handlers had demanded 32½ cents and 27½ cents an hour for boat and dock work and 25 cents an hour for winter work (ibid., p. 132).

42. Ibid., p. 133.

43. Urry had come to Port Arthur in 1906 from Birmingham, England. He had been a member of the Independent Labour Party before coming to Canada. Even though he was an architect by profession, he joined the United Brotherhood of Carpenters and Joiners and actively promoted the cause of labour. Among other things, he held the posts of labour columnist for the Port Arthur *Chronicle* and local correspondent for *The Labour Gazette* (Morrison, "Community and Conflict," p. 98).

44. *The Labour Gazette*, XIII (August 1912), pp. 133-37.

45. *Daily News*, 30 July 1912.

46. I have not been able to find any additional information regarding the existence of an Italian band in Port Arthur at that time. It is likely, however, that the band was organized by Ralph Colosimo, who emigrated to Fort William in 1907 and who later conducted an Italian band in Fort William's East End.

47. The *Daily Times-Journal* on 2 August provided an interesting profile of Hicks. Before coming to Fort William he had spent a few months in Brantford and Hamilton, Ontario, in 1911. There he had claimed to be a minister of the Gospel and expounded "socialistic and semi-religious" political ideas. *Daily Times-Journal*, 2 August 1912.

48. On 10 October he was found guilty as charged and was released on a suspended sentence under a $500. bond. *Daily News*, 10 October 1912.

49. *Daily Times-Journal*, 31 July 1912.

50. Ibid., 1 August 1912. The force consisted of twenty constables hired from various secret service agencies in Winnipeg and ten local men.

51. According to a newspaper article the company had offered good money to labourers in Winnipeg "but when they heard that there had been shooting they backed down, notwithstanding the fact that fancy wages were offered with the guarantee of steady work the year round". *Daily Times-Journal*, 30 July 1912.

52. The following account of the trial is based on the *News's* account of the proceedings.

53. Interview with Anthony Pento. Constable Peterson had said in his testimony that "We went to arrest Tony Shumacke [*sic*], and I saw the chief walk up to him and put his hand on his shoulder." At this point Peterson and Constable Thurlow left McLellan and went after another striker. *Daily News*, 9 October 1912.

54. After serving their sentence the two brothers returned home to Reggio, Calabria, in southern Italy. Interview with Anthony Pento.

55. Even the *Daily News*, whose editorials during the previous strikes had been very critical of the conduct of the *contadini*, commented in its report of the "riot" of 29 July that: "One of the remarkable things about the attack of the mob upon the police is that when they had most of the officers down and out they suddenly gave it up and retreated. A few more blows with the murderous clubs or a few more shots would have meant the annihilation of the small force." *Daily News*, 30 July 1912.

56. In her study of "Ethnicity and Violence," Morrison concluded that a relationship did exist between Italian workers and violence. However, she is also of the opinion that the violence stemmed from the nature of industrial relations of the railways with immigrant labour. (Morrison, "Ethnicity and Violence: The Lakehead Freight Handlers before World War I," in *Essays in Canadian Working Class History*, ed. Gregory S. Kealey, Peter Warrian [Toronto: McClelland and Stewart, 1976], pp. 143-60.) Also by the same author see "Ethnicity and Class Consciousness: British, Finnish and South European Workers at the Canadian Lakehead before World War I," *Lakehead University Review*, 9, no. 1 (Spring 1976), 41-54.

57. Horowitz points out that in many pre-industrial societies protest against oppressive conditions is usually unorganized, giving rise to "revoltist traditions." In rural Italy, both in the south and the north central, "revoltist traditions" were particularly entrenched. Daniel L. Horowitz, *The Italian Labour Movement* (Cambridge, Mass.: Harvard University Press, 1963), pp. 23, 327.

Contributors

Michele Del Balzo completed his graduate studies at McGill University and l'Université du Québec à Montréal. He is presently teaching sociology and ethnic studies at Dawson College, Montreal.

Robert F. Harney is Professor of History at the University of Toronto. He is academic director of the Multicultural History Society of Ontario, and president of the Canadian Italian Historical Association. He has written extensively on Italian immigration and is co-author of *Immigrants: A Portrait of the Urban Experience, 1890-1930.*

Luciano Iorizzo is Professor of History at the State University College at Oswego, New York. He has authored numerous studies on Italian immigration to America and is co-author of *The Italian-Americans.* He is currently completing a research project on the identification of organized crime figures by race and ethnicity.

Richard N. Juliani is Associate Professor of Sociology at Villanova University, Villanova, Pennsylvania. He has published several articles on the role of settlement houses, the church and labour unions in the life of Philadelphia's Italians.

Gary Mormino is Assistant Professor of History at the University of South Florida. He is associate editor of *Tampa Bay History,* and director of the South Florida Oral History Program.

Anthony P. Pizzo graduated from Stetson University, Florida. He has taught a course on Tampa's Latin roots at the University of South Florida and has published *Tampa Town 1824-1886: "The Cracker Village with a Latin Accent."* He is a well-recognized scholar of Tampa's early history.

George E. Pozzetta is Associate Professor of History at the University of Florida, Gainesville. His extensive research and writing have focused on the history of Italian immigration to America and he has edited *Pane e Lavoro: The Italian American Working Class.*

Antonio Pucci completed his graduate studies at Lakehead University, Thunder Bay. He is the author of several articles on the Italian community of Thunder Bay. He is currently employed as a teacher with the Lakehead Board of Education.

Bruno Ramirez is Assistant Professor of History at the University of Montreal. He has written several articles on Italian and U.S. labour history and has published *When Workers Fight: the Politics of Industrial Relations in the Progressive Era.*

J. Vincenza Scarpaci is Associate Professor of History at Towson State University, Baltimore. She has published articles dealing with Italians in the South and the Italian American woman. She is currently working on a study of the Italian community of Baltimore.

292-4 44